Chŏng Yagyong

To Tom

下学而上達

"STUDY THE MUNDANE,
ATTAIN THE SUBLIME."

Affectionately,

Mark

SUNY Series in Korean Studies

Sung Bae Park, Editor

Chŏng Yagyong

Korea's Challenge to Orthodox Neo-Confucianism

Mark Setton

State University of New York Press

Frontispiece: "View From Tea Mountain," by Sung-sook Hong Setton

Published by
State University of New York Press, Albany

Printed in the United States of America

For information, address the State University of New York Press,
State University Plaza, Albany, NY 12246

Production by M. R. Mulholland
Marketing by Fran Keneston

Library of Congress Cataloging-in-Publication Data
Setton, Mark.
Chŏng Yagyong : Korea's challenge to orthodox neo-Confucianism / Mark Setton.
p. cm. — (SUNY series in Korean studies)
Includes bibliographical references and index.
ISBN 0-7914-3173-8 (alk. paper). — ISBN 0-7914-3174-6 (pbk. : alk. paper)
1. Chŏng, Yag-yong, 1762–1836. 2. Neo-Confucianism. I. Title. II. Series.
B5254.C564S48 1997
181'.119—dc20

96–3772
CIP

10 9 8 7 6 5 4 3 2 1

Contents

Figures

Foreword

It may not be wholly appropriate to begin comments on the nature and value of the present volume with a thought that is more in character with the Taoist thinker Chuang Tzu. But if what I have to say is at all accurate, perhaps I may be granted this indulgence. The thought is that in order to understand, we often have to unlearn what we already "know." This notion captures the tenor of much of Tasan's (Chŏng Yagyong) work. He challenged and often successfully refuted the common knowledge of his own age and in so doing opened the way to a more accurate understanding of the Confucian tradition.

This volume offers a lucid and lively account of Tasan's critique and criticism of the Ch'eng-Chu orthodoxy. These descriptive and critical writings are highly original, thorough, and insightful, and are balanced with a genuine appreciation for the accomplishments of these Sung dynasty giants. Moreover, Tasan's views are more carefully and extensively developed than the similar and equally trenchant insights one can find in certain works by his contemporary, the remarkable Ch'ing dynasty scholar Tai Chen.

The writings of both these thinkers should be studied not only by those who specialize in eighteenth-century Confucianism in Korea and China but by all those with an interest in the tradition. For their work concerns not only particular thinkers and periods but also the general character and history of the Confucian tradition. Moreover, Tasan and Tai Chen were right: the Confucianism of the Sung, Yüan, and Ming dynasties, as fascinating and inspiring as it is, constitutes a new and distinctive form of the ancient tradition. It should not be read back into our understanding of the pre-Ch'in founders. While Tasan and Tai's motivation for arguing this point, that is, exposing Taoist and Buddhist influences in the later Confucian tradition in order to facilitate a return to the pure form of its original vision, is not shared by most contemporary scholars, their basic point is nevertheless of great importance. It is a lesson that needs to be learned by many historians and philosophers throughout East Asia and the West even today. And it is one that must begin by unlearning much of what is today's accepted orthodoxy.

This insight into the later tradition and its relationship to its early predecessors helps us to see and appreciate the rich diversity and dynamic quality of Confucianism. It is no exaggeration to say that there is not just one Confucianism but a remarkable variety of Confucianisms. What is more, this state of affairs has existed both diachronically and synchronically not only within China, but within and across a number of distinctive East Asian civilizations. Here is another case in which the richness of Tasan's thought is reflected in the character and form of the present work. For this study not only provides a sophisticated account of Tasan's unique interpretation of the tradition, while locating it within the contemporary landscape and past history of Korean thought, like Tasan's own work, it also shows the connections and points of divergence between his views and those of the Chinese and Japanese thinkers who most influenced him.

Thus *Chŏng Yagyong: Korea's Challenge to Orthodox Neo-Confucianism* can be seen as providing a precedent and new paradigm for the modern study of the complex and fascinating phenomenon of Confucianism across different East Asian cultures. This too may be of more than historical interest. For again like Tasan's own philosophy, it may be understood as offering a model for a contemporary intercultural dialogue about the present state and future character of the tradition.

Philip J. Ivanhoe
Stanford University

Acknowledgments

Where do I start? Over the nine years of research that it took to write this book many kind colleagues and friends have made more of a contribution to this work than they realize.

I am very grateful to the Korea Research Foundation, whose generous grant supported my research during its important initial stages at Oxford, as well as the Korea Foundation, who provided me with a visiting scholarship toward my research at the Academy of Korean Studies in 1992–93. I am also indebted to many of my colleagues in the Oriental Institute at Oxford, the Academy of Korean Studies, and the State University of New York at Stony Brook, who in various ways contributed to my training, or went out of their way to assist me in my research.

A key contribution to my research was provided by my supervisor at Oxford, James McMullen. In view of the small mountains of attendant tasks that blanket his desk, his attention to detail was impressive. He gently coaxed me into taking a more historical, rather than purely philosophical, approach, which, when applied to Korean critiques of orthodox Neo-Confucianism, turned out to be quite productive.

I am deeply indebted to another perfectionist, P. J. Ivanhoe, who went through my work several times with a fine-tooth comb and provided invaluable advice and moral support.

Sung Bae Park also provided thoughtful advice and encouragement to the detriment of other pressing issues awaiting his attention at the fast-moving Korean Studies Program in Stony Brook.

Martina Deuchler and my brother Robin Setton were patient enough to read through the whole work and provide detailed comments and criticism.

As this book neared completion the cheerful cooperation of Mr. Choongnam Yoon and his colleagues at the Harvard Yenching Library proved invaluable.

I am also especially indebted to William Boot, David Faure, Keum Chang-t'ae, Lew Seung-kook, Ian McMorran, Tim Read, and Yang Mu, for the very varied forms of support and encouragement they offered. I also want to thank my parents for taking a great interest in my work despite my unsociableness during the most intensive periods of research.

These acknowledgments would not be complete without a heartfelt thank-you to my wife Sung-sook and my children, Emily and Jeremy, whose encouragement and ebullience tided me through when the going was rough.

Explanatory Note

Names of persons and titles of works which are Korean, as well as the Korean pronunciation of terms, are romanized according to the modified McCune-Reischauer system described in the *Guide to the Romanization of Korean* (London: British Standards Institution, 1982). Names of persons, titles of works, and terms which are Chinese or Japanese are romanized following the Wade-Giles system, and the system used in Kenkyusha's New English-Japanese Dictionary, respectively. When both Chinese and Korean renderings are given, the Chinese form precedes the Korean, and the two are separated by a slash.

English translations of all Chinese, Japanese and Korean terms and titles of works mentioned in the text are given for their first appearance. English translations of titles cited in the notes are given in the list of works cited. English translations of Korean government offices and posts are based on those listed in appendix A of Edward W. Wagner, *The Literati Purges: Political Conflict in Early Yi Korea* (Cambridge, East Asian Research Center, Harvard University, 1974).

Many of the translations of passages in the Confucian Classics have been inspired by the renderings of Wing-tsit Chan, *A Source Book in Chinese Philosophy* (Princeton: Princeton University Press, 1963); Daniel K. Gardner, *Chu Hsi and the Ta Hsueh: Neo-Confucian Reflection on the Confucian Canon* (Cambridge, MA: Harvard University Press, 1986); D. C. Lau, *Mencius* (Hong Kong: Chinese University Press, 1984); and James Legge, *The Chinese Classics* (Hong Kong: Hong Kong University Press, 1960). Unless otherwise indicated, all translations of Chong Yagyong's (Tasan) work are my own.

Chinese characters for all names of persons, book titles and terms appearing in the text are included in the glossary.

In bibliographic notations, volume and page number are separated by a colon.

Classical (pre-Ch'in) works commonly quoted have been translated into English as follows:

Chou-li:	*Rites of Chou*
Chung-yung:	*The Mean*
Hsiao-ching:	*Classic of Filial Piety*
I-li:	*Book of Etiquette and Ritual*
Li-chi:	*Record of Rites*
Lun-yü:	*Analects*
Meng-tzu:	*Mencius*
Shang-shu (Shu-ching):	*Classic of Documents*
Shih-ching:	*Classic of Odes*
Ta-hsüeh:	*Great Learning*
I-ching:	*Classic of Changes*

Abbreviations

CYC	*Chŭngbo Yŏyudang chŏnsŏ* (by Chŏng Yagyong). Seoul: Kyŏngin munhwasa, 1970.
DKJ	*Dai kanwa jiten*, ed. Morohashi Tetsuji. Tokyo: Daishukan shoten, 1960.
HYISIS	Harvard-Yenching Institute Sinological Index Series. Peiping: Yenching University, 1935–50.
NRI	*Nihon rinri ihen*, ed. Inoue Tetsujiro and Kanie Yoshimaru. Kyoto: Rinsen Shoten, 1970.
SPPY	*Ssu-pu pei-yao*. Shanghai: Chung-hua shu-chü, 1927–35.
SSCCS	*Shih-san ching chu-shu*, ed. Jüan Yuan. Kyoto: Chu-wa, 1974. Photolithographic reprint of 1815 edition.
SSY	*Saam sŏnsaeng yŏnbo*, ed. Chŏng Kyuyŏng. Seoul: Chŏngmunsa, 1984.

Introduction

During the last two decades interest in the Korean thinker Chŏng Yagyong (Tasan, 1762–1836) has been growing exponentially. The rate of publication of articles and books on Tasan has jumped in proportion to a growing preoccupation with the "discovery" of the cultural roots of Korea's economic and political modernization. This is particularly understandable in view of Tasan's reputation as a critically-minded, creative thinker, who wrote an enormous amount of prose and poetry vividly detailing the social problems and political injustices of his time, as well as formulating exhaustive proposals for their solution.

Until recently, it was commonly assumed that this enthusiasm for Tasan's writings was a purely modern phenomenon, and that the views of even the most well-known late Chosŏn critics of the traditional order and ruling ideology had little effect on immediately successive generations of thinkers.[1] In an article on "The Relationship between the "Sirhak" Movement and 'Enlightenment' (Kaehwa) Thought" Kim Yŏng-ho, among others, has shown that this is far from the case.[2]

More than a century before the recent boom in studies of his political and economic thought, Tasan's works were consulted by influential figures at the pinnacle of the ruling elite. His major works on administrational reform, such as the *Mongmin sinsŏ* (Reflections on Fostering the People), and *Hŭm hŭm sinsŏ* (New treatise on the legal system), were treated as authoritative texts by government officials and at least one head of state.[3] Unlike many of his modern admirers, who have tried to single out particular themes in his work with a view to giving him recognition as a figurehead in the quest for the indigenous roots of modernization, his nineteenth-century audience was more interested in the specifics of implementing his proposals for reform.

In view of the recent eagerness to associate Tasan's thought with modern intellectual trends, a key question posed by this book is, to what extent did Tasan's philosophy reflect the ideology of the Neo-Confucian state he once served, and to what extent, and in what ways, if any, did his work transcend the boundaries of Neo-Confucian and Confucian ways of thinking? Rather than dealing with it on a purely synchronic level as an independent set of ideas, it will examine Tasan's worldview from the viewpoint of intellectual history. Specifically we try to pinpoint Tasan's contributions to Korean and indeed East Asian thought by tracing certain themes that emerged among his Chinese, Japanese, and Korean intellectual predecessors and discussing how he built on them.

This study of Tasan's views focuses on his interpretation of five books which constitute the philosophical core of the Confucian classics, the Four Books (*Ssu-shu/Sasŏ*),[4] and the *Classic of Changes*, as well as essays on related topics and relevant pieces of personal correspondence and poetry.[5] The study shows how Tasan's interpretations contrast with those of Chu Hsi and the Ch'eng brothers, the "Neo-Confucian" giants of the Sung dynasty whose interpretation of the classical teachings, which came to be known as "Ch'eng-Chu learning," had become orthodoxy throughout East Asia. In particular we focus on three issues close to the heart of Neo-Confucians and central to their worldview, human nature (*ren-hsing*), self-cultivation (*hsiu-chi*) and the "ordering of society" (*chih-jen*).

Much has already been written on criticisms levelled at the attitudes of the *Yangban*, the powerful Neo-Confucian scholar-bureaucrats who governed the late Chosŏn. This is not surprising as many Korean writers and performing artists regularly profited from satirizing the attitudes and excesses of the *Yangban* class, being fully aware of the glee this aroused among their audiences. Hong Taeyong's *Dialogue on Iwulü Mountain* (*Ŭisan mundap*) and Pak Chiwŏn's *Tale of a Yangban* (*Yangban chŏn*), both written in Tasan's time, are celebrated and influential examples of this genre.[6]

On the other hand, little systematic research has been done on challenges to the official ideology of the Yangban, as opposed to their attitudes and policies. One reason is that the task of distinguishing ad-hominem critiques of orthodox Neo-Confucian attitudes from critiques of the Neo-Confucian philosophy and worldview itself is complicated by the fact that few scholars were eager to be labelled as heretics and thus provide those in power with the best of excuses to be rid of their criticisms. The scholar-officials in government well knew that such a challenge to the ruling ideology, the symbol of their authority if not the substance, would raise questions about their political legitimacy. Consequently such challenges were often veiled in the time-honoured mode of commentaries on the classics, where shades of nuance in discussions on Chu Hsi's exposition of metaphysics, ethics, or ritual could imply decidedly novel approaches.[7]

An important distinction is drawn between "Neo-Confucian orthodoxy" on the one hand, and "orthodox Neo-Confucian thought" on the other. As Nathan Sivin points out in his foreword to Benjamin Elman's ground-breaking work on Ch'ing scholarship, "It is hard to think of any idea responsible for more fuzziness in writing about China than the notion that Confucianism is one thing."[8] In this book "Neo-Confucian orthodoxy," in both China and Korea, refers to the multitude of institutions that were affected by the orthodox Neo-Confucian worldview, including state and family rituals, the structure and ethos of officialdom, whose upper ranks were populated by Neo-Confucian scholar-bureaucrats, the state educational system geared toward the civil service examinations, and "orthodox Neo-Confucian thought" itself, which informed all of these areas. Although this study focuses on Tasan's critique of "orthodox Neo-Confucian thought," it also examines attitudes toward "Neo-Confucian orthodoxy" prior to Tasan, because, as indicated in chapter 2, the growing dissatisfaction with the various manifestations of orthodoxy led to disenchantment with the ideology that had spawned them.

The intention of this book is not simply to clarify the nature of Tasan's critique of orthodox Neo-Confucian thought, but also to fathom his positive contributions to Confucian thought in general. For his dissatisfaction with, and critique of, the Neo-Confucian worldview served as a springboard for the formulation of alternative views, which he based, or at least claimed to have based, on a reassessment of the Confucian classics themselves. Furthermore we attempt to show that these views, and particularly Tasan's concepts of human nature and self-cultivation, represent a major development in Korean, and indeed East Asian, philosophy, that deserve as much recognition as his work on institutional reform.

In an article on Ch'ing dynasty Evidential Learning (*k'ao-cheng hsüeh*), Benjamin Elman has pointed out that the general view of the nature of Confucianism from the Sung dynasty onwards is that it was a synchronic set of philosophical concepts and interpretations, and that the philosophy of the Ch'ing period did not mark a distinctive break away from the perimeters set by the leading Neo-Confucian schools of Chu Hsi and Wang Yang-ming.[9]

Indeed, the historian Fung Yu-lan was, for some reason, so intent on showing that Ch'ing Confucianism was a continuation of themes developed in the Sung that in his popular *History of Chinese Philosophy* he entitled the chapter on the philosophy of the period "The Ch'ing Continuation of Neo-Confucianism." "Even in this school", argues Fung,

> the topics that were discussed, ... and the classical texts that were used, ... remained the same as those of the Sung and Ming Neo-Confucianists. From this point of view, therefore, the Han Learning of the Ch'ing was a continuation of Sung and Ming Neo-Confucianism, the major contribution of which lay in its new answers and interpretations to the latter's traditional problems and texts. This new approach, moreover, had already been foreshadowed by certain tendencies taking place within Neo-Confucianism itself during the latter decades of the Ming and early part of the Ch'ing. Hence those adherents of the Han Learning who concentrated on philosophy should, despite their outward opposition to Neo-Confucianism, properly regarded as its perpetuators and developers, rather than as the founders of a completely new school."[10]

According to de Bary,

> We cannot fail to observe that its [the Ch'ing dynasty "School of Han Learning"] achievements were largely critical and negative in character, rather than productive of new philosophical speculations.[11]

Elman has argued that the "evidential learning" philosophers Tai Chen (1724–1777), Juan Yuan (1764–1849), and Chiao Hsun (1763–1820) were doing more than simply attacking Neo-Confucian philosophy, in the respect that they were "deconstructing" the imperial ideology, and that this represented a preliminary contribution to its rejection in the late nineteenth and early twentieth centuries.[12] But at least several unanswered questions vis-à-vis the work of this group of scholars await more detailed research. Did they contribute to the unravelling of Confucian thought per se as well as its Neo-Confucian variants? And if they did not, what were the positive contributions these thinkers may have made to the development of new strains of thought, in terms of reconstructing Confucian philosophy and employing new frames of reference independent of the Sung dynasty Neo-Confucian cosmology?

This book, focusing as it does on an outstanding thinker of the late Chosŏn, does not answer these questions directly. But it does indicate that, at least in Korea, Confucian thought did not simply stagnate within the Sung dynasty framework until the twentieth century. Far from it. As described in chapter 1, the eighteenth-century saw a new burst of philosophical creativity that paralleled the vigour of the sixteenth-century Neo-Confucian golden age, when Yi Hwang (T'oegye, 1501–70) and Yi I (Yulgok, 1536–84) took Chu Hsi's ideas on human nature to new heights. A key figure in this reinvigoration is Tasan, although it is only recently that his philosophical contributions have begun to be seriously evaluated. What is remarkable is that one of Tasan's most innovative and systematic bursts of creativity also revolves around the question of human nature. This topic fascinated Korean Confucians, and it could be said that it is particularly in this area that Korean philosophy came into its own.

As discussed in this book, one of the stimuli that prompted the invigoration of Korean Confucianism in the eighteenth century was the absorption of new modes of critical scholarship from the Ch'ing. Tasan employed the new analytical methods of Ch'ing Evidential Learning to reevaluate the language and concepts of the original Confucian teachings. On that basis he challenged Chu Hsi's "Neo-Confucian" interpretation of the classics, and particularly its metaphysical frame of reference. But Tasan was not content to simply criticize and "unravel" Neo-Confucian philosophy. He used his analysis of the classical texts to reexamine the very issues that the Neo-Confucians were interested in, and particularly questions regarding human nature and self-cultivation. As he did so, an alternative system emerged that rivalled that of his Neo-Confucian predecessors in terms of internal consistency and breadth of scope.

Chapter 1, on "Tasan's Intellectual Heritage," explores the relationship between political developments and the emergence of critical attitudes toward Neo-Confucian orthodoxy in Korea during the seventeenth and eighteenth centuries.[13] In the course of the background research necessary for this chapter it became apparent that Tasan was particularly indebted to members of his faction, the Southerners (Namin), for a number of themes central to his philosophy, as well as methodological approaches, and special attention is paid to the relationship between ideological trends and factional alignment. Consequently, we begin by discussing the inadequacy of popular conceptions of intellectual trends in the late Chosŏn which do not take factionalism into account, and particularly the much talked about concept of a *Sirhakp'a* or "School of Practical Learning," of which Tasan is considered to be a leading member. This is followed by a discussion of critical attitudes toward Neo-Confucian orthodoxy prior to Tasan, and the impact of factional politics on developments in this area.

Chapter 2 outlines Tasan's life and major works. It begins with a description of such formative factors as his family background, his intellectually vibrant circle of friends who introduced him to the encyclopedic scholarship of Yi Ik, and "Western Learning," which was filtering into the Korean peninsula through China. Then we examine Tasan's brief but turbulent period in government service, which saw continuing hostilities between his faction, the Southerners, and the more powerful and ideologically conservative Old Doctrine (Noron) faction. The last portion of the chapter describes the highly productive period of Tasan's exile, when he devoted himself to scholarship.

Chapter 3 deals with Tasan's critique of orthodox Neo-Confucian thought, or Ch'eng-Chu Learning, the bulk of which is formulated in his commentaries on the Four Books. This is entitled "Tasan's `Classical Learning'," in view of the fact that Tasan based his critique of Ch'eng-Chu Learning on a reinterpretation of the Confucian classics themselves. The opening section discusses his dynamic view of human nature, on the basis of which he criticized Chu Hsi's application of the so-called *li-ch'i* cosmology to the influential theory of "original nature" (*pen-jan chih hsing*) and "physical nature" (*ch'i-chih chih hsing*). Tasan's interpretation of human nature as appetites or tendencies seeking fulfillment through moral action, in turn provided the psychological foundation for a thoroughly outward-looking theory of self-cultivation. This "moral activism" was also formulated on the premise that virtue could only exist as a result of moral conduct. The final section deals with the political implications of Tasan's philosophy, and particularly his theory of government through moral example with its concomitant, anti-legalistic emphasis on the moral autonomy of the individual.

Chapter 4 discusses the relationship between Tasan's thought and two principal currents of reaction to Chu Hsi's Neo-Confucianism, the Evidential Scholarship of the Ch'ing "Han Learning" movement, and the so-called "Ancient Learning" (*Kogaku*) of Tokugawa Japan. The opening section examines Tasan's attitude toward Ch'ing scholarship and compares his work with that of Ch'ing scholars such as Tai Chen, known as a strident opponent of Chu Hsi's views, and Juan Yuan. Tasan was one of the rare Korean scholars who not only read Japanese scholarship but admitted to his admiration for some of it, namely, the work of the three giants of "Ancient Learning," Itō Jinsai, (1627–1705), Ogyū Sorai, and Dazai Shundai (1680–1747). The concluding part of this chapter draws attention to some intriguing similarities—particularly with regard to the concepts of Heaven (*T'ien*), human nature and virtue (*te*)—as well as sharp differences between Tasan and these three contrasting figures.

Drawing out the implications of the preceding chapters on Tasan's philosophy, chapter 5 attempts to answer a key question posed in this introduction, that is, the extent to which Tasan's work represents a departure from the confines of the Neo-Confucianism of Chu Hsi, which had hitherto exerted such a powerful grip on the Korean literati, as well as a departure from the classical Confucian teachings themselves.

1

Tasan's Intellectual Heritage

No discussion of Tasan's intellectual pedigree would be complete without a mention of the so-called *Sirhakp'a* (lit., "School of Genuine Learning" or "School of Practical Learning") of which he is widely considered to be a leading member. Many historians have eulogized Tasan as being the *chiptaesŏngga* or "synthesizer" of this school, claiming that he weaved together various strands of thought within "Practical Learning" to form his own extensive system.[1]

Consequently this chapter begins with an overview of the most widely accepted theories on Korean "Practical Learning" followed by a discussion of the significant weaknesses inherent in them. Then we provide an alternative framework for the historical context of Tasan's thought, including an overview of Korean Neo-Confucianism prior to Tasan, the emergence of critical attitudes toward Neo-Confucian orthodoxy, and the impact of factional politics, including the influential Rites Disputes of 1659 and 1674, on developments in this area.

It is widely recognized that factionalism had a profound impact on the politics of the late Chosŏn. Furthermore, nearly all the outstanding thinkers of this period belonged to factions representing the political opposition. In spite of this, very little work has been done on the relationship between intellectual trends and factional associations. Many contemporary Korean students and scholars express distaste or even embarrassment at the influential role of factionalism in their history. It is generally maintained that Japanese scholarship underscored the pervasiveness of Chosŏn factionalism to illustrate the inability of the Koreans to govern themselves, thereby lending a hint of legitimacy to the Japanese colonial rule of Korea. This focus on factionalism is generally regarded by Korean scholars as an essential theme in the "colonial view of (Korean) history."[2] This may explain why the most widely acclaimed Korean treatments of intellectual developments during the period in question, including Tasan's thought, avoid any detailed treatment of the impact of factionalism.[3]

It is, of course, regrettable that factionalism was used to legitimize the colonial rule of Korea, but it would also be regrettable to leave factionalism out of the picture in any historical discussion of Korean Confucianism. A large portion of the Confucian teachings is devoted to political ethics, as Confucius himself spent most of his time grooming conscientious young people for morally enlightened political leadership. Seeing that Confucianism became enormously influential as a political ideology, it is only natural that there should be close links between the Korean political order, which during the late Chosŏn was largely influenced by factional considerations, and the development of Korean Confucian thought. This was a two-way street, with the Confucian teachings providing the ideological framework for the political order while they were simultaneously adapted to suit the needs of the same order.

Consequently, this chapter begins with a discussion of the inadequacy of popular categorizations of late Chosŏn dynasty intellectual trends which do not take factionalism into account.

The Sirhakp'a: Myth or Reality?

During the last several decades few papers or books have been written on the history of the Chosŏn period without mention of the *Sirhakp'a* (School of Practical Learning) and its various subschools.[4] This term generally refers to a very diverse group of late-Chosŏn dynasty scholars who nonetheless were considered to have shared a dissatisfaction with the general political inertia or apathy of the ruling elite, and to have made concrete proposals for political, economic, or social reform.

In recognition of the broad spectrum of interests and ideological inclinations shown by the Sirhak or Practical Learning proponents, continual efforts have been made to classify their diverse approaches into subcategories. One of the most popular analyses, made by Lee Woosung, subdivided Sirhak thought into three schools: The School of Administration and Practical Usage (*kyŏngse ch'iyongp'a*), which was founded by Yi Ik (1681–1763), concentrated on institutional reform with particular emphasis on government administration and the land system; the School of Profitable Usage and Popular Benefit (*iyong husaengp'a*) centering on Pak Chiwŏn (1737–1805), which focused on technological reform, advocated the expansion of commercial activities and improvement of the means of production; and the School of Verification Based on Actual Facts (*silsa kusip'a*), which became a fully-fledged movement through the influence of Kim Chŏnghŭi's (1786–1856) scholarship, used Ch'ing evidential methodology in epigraphy and the study of the classics.[5]

A principle flaw of the above schema is that the first two categories are based on fields of study, whereas the third is based on a methodology, and it is precisely this philological methodology, derived from the *k'ao-cheng hsüeh* or Evidential Learning movement of Ch'ing-dynasty China, that thinkers in all three categories relied upon to varying extents in their studies. The weakness of this categorization becomes evident when we apply it to the case of Tasan, who was strongly influenced both by Yi Ik's work on institutional reform and the critical approach of Ch'ing Evidential Learning.

A number of attempts have been made at classification of Sirhak scholars on the basis of historical periods. Among the earliest and most influential of these has been Ch'ŏn Kwanu's analysis of Sirhak development into three periods: The Preparation Period, which began in the mid-sixteenth century and lasted for one century, saw the introduction of Western Learning from China by the scholar-official and encyclopedist Yi Sugwang (1563–1627) as well as Kim Yuk's (1580–1658) ideas in the fields of administrative reform and technology. The Development Period which began in the mid-seventeenth century and lasted for the following century, was characterized by the evidential learning of Yu Hyŏngwŏn (1622–73) and later Yi Ik, who adopted the same methodology and combined it with the systematic study of Western Learning. Other outstanding figures of this period included Pak Sedang (1629–1703) and An Chŏngbok (1712–91), a close disciple of Yi Ik. The Flourishing Period, which extended from the mid-eighteenth to mid-nineteenth century, according to Chŏn, marks the final stage in the maturation of Sirhak. It was in this period that the study of the Chinese and Korean classics,

"Northern Learning" or Ch'ing scholarship, as well as the natural sciences, reached a new peak in the writings of such representative figures as Pak Chiwŏn, Hong Taeyong (1731–83), Pak Chega (1750– ?), Chŏng Yagyong, and Kim Chŏnghŭi. It was also in this period that Catholicism became influential and fueled politically revolutionary ideas. At the end of this period Sirhak was finally replaced as a main intellectual current by the modern thought of the *kaehwa* movement introduced from Europe.[6]

One problem with this analysis is the difficulty of determining in what way the diverse scholarship of the "Flourishing Period" represented a maturation of the scholarship in the "Development Period." Pak Sedang, for example, used methods akin to those of Ch'ing scholarship to analyze the language of the Chinese classics well before the Northern Learning of the "Flourishing Period." Furthermore, it is now broadly recognized that figures who played a major role in laying the intellectual foundation of the *kaehwa* or "enlightenment" movement, including Pak Kyusu (1807–76) and O Kyŏngsŏk (1831–79), built on the ideas of previous thinkers such as Pak Chiwŏn and Chŏng Yagyong rather than simply replacing them with European concepts.[7]

The usage of the concept "Sirhakp'a" itself presents considerable problems. Recently, scholars in Korea and the United States have pointed out that the character *p'a* (school) appearing in the term "Sirhakp'a" is a misnomer, since the so-called Sirhak proponents did not share a particular doctrine or comprise a single lineage of scholars bound by master-disciple relationships. None of them referred to themselves as members of a "Sirhak" school. Indeed, it was only in the 1930s that these late-Chosŏn would-be reformers were grouped together under the rubric "Sirhakp'a," to indicate a common concern they were perceived to have had in the down-to-earth problems faced by late-Chosŏn society, as opposed to the preoccupation shown by orthodox Neo-Confucians in metaphysical questions.

Even if one loosely defines "school" as a body of scholars adhering to similar doctrines and involved in some form of regular academic exchange, there were, at the most, only two schools within the Sirhakp'a. As discussed at the end of the chapter, these can be referred to as the School of Yi Ik and the School of Northern Learning (*Pukhakp'a*), although even within these "schools" there was a great deal of diversity. Members of the School of Yi Ik, or in Yi Usŏng's terminology, the School of Administration and Practical Usage, were indeed very interested in institutional reform, about which they had gleaned many ideas from the work of Ch'ing as well as Korean scholars such as Yu Hyŏng-wŏn and Yi Yulgok. On the other hand, the School of Northern Learning was so named because all of its proponents had personally visited the Ch'ing, and had consequently written a great deal about the various facets of Ch'ing culture that had so impressed them. The title "School of Profitable Usage and Popular Benefit" conferred on them by Yi Usŏng is somewhat misleading as their interests in economic and technological development were shared by members of the School of Yi Ik.

Regardless of whether it is referred to as a school or not, there are other problems presented by the usage of the term *Sirhak* or "practical learning" itself.

The main problem is that the same expression was used long before—in a more philosophical, ethical sense—by Chu Hsi and other orthodox Neo-Confucians, referring to the relevancy of their teachings for the task of self-cultivation (*hsiu-shen*).[8] Chu Hsi and generations of his Confucian predecessors, following the lead of Confucius himself, took pride in their emphasis on practical ethics, comparing themselves with the Buddhists whom they considered to be flouting a cardinal principle: the attainment of self-realization through proper conduct in human relationships. It has since been demonstrated that the so-called Sirhak scholar Yun Chŭng (1629–1714), who used the term *Sirhak* more often than most, saw the relevancy of his teachings in these terms rather than in an overtly political or practical sense.[9] In addition to their keen interest in the concrete business of improving the people's livelihood, many other Sirhak thinkers, particularly Pak Sedang and Chŏng Yagyong, were intent on reviving the spirit of ethical practicality which they regarded to be the essence of Confucian thought, and which they considered to have been obscured by the introspective approach of their Neo- Confucian contemporaries. In effect, they were accusing these Neo-Confucians of the same weaknesses the Neo-Confucians had once accused the Buddhists of.

Most Sirhak thinkers could indeed be referred to as "practical" in both the ethical and more concrete senses of the term. In spite of this, many popular writers and even historians, misled by the modern, more material connotations of the term "Sirhak," have conveyed the impression that its proponents were utilitarians or even pragmatists who had little time for ethics and other branches of philosophy in their quest to improve the conditions of their society. There is no question that most of the "Sirhak" thinkers were very practically minded individuals, but none of them went as far as rejecting the Confucian assumption that moral renewal was an essential ingredient of social harmony.

The distinction between Sirhak thinkers and their predecessors is further obscured by the fact that the Neo-Confucian reformers of the late Koryŏ and early Chosŏn were also galvanized by dynastic decline and the need for a new order to involve themselves in "practical affairs," including the cultivation of the ruler's virtue as well as proposals for concrete institutional reform. Indeed, the sought-after status of a "scholar of the Sirhakp'a" has understandably been claimed for Korean Neo-Confucians as early as Yi Yulgok, who was practically minded in both senses.

Furthermore, the reform-minded "Sirhak" proponents lived over a span of almost three centuries, and were inspired by a variety of contrasting if not incompatible worldviews, from the orthodox cosmology of the Ch'eng brothers and Chu Hsi to the moral activism of Wang Yang-ming and the Evidential Learning of the Ch'ing.

Recognising the inadequacies inherent in treatments of the Sirhakp'a as a particular school of thought, including the diversity of the thinkers it has traditionally included, Ch'ŏn nonetheless has made an attempt to define three tendencies characteristic of the Sirhak spirit.

The first is the spirit of criticism, particularly directed at the excessive dependence of the literati on the nearly absolute authority of the Ch'eng-Chu school. The members of the School of Northern Learning, referred to as the "School of Profitable Usage and Popular Benefit" by Yi Usŏng, criticized the tendency to adulate the Ming, and advocated the study of Ch'ing culture and scholarship. Not a few intellectuals attacked political attitudes and institutions, and among these many surreptitiously turned to the forbidden study of Yang-ming's philosophy and Catholicism. Another phenomenon issuing from critical attitudes toward established authority was the advocacy of Confucian political humanism or *minbonjuŭi*, which gave primacy to the welfare of the people and national consciousness, both of which formed the backbone of the increasingly popular National Studies (*kukhak*).

Secondly, the spirit of verification, symbolized by the expression *silsa kusi*, "the pursuit of truth based on actual fact."[10] This was the approach of the evidential research movement of the Ch'ing, and it was vigorously applied by Sirhak scholars not only in the examination of the classics but also in such fields as history, geography, and linguistics, as well as proposals for political and economic reform.

A third characteristic of Sirhak, Ch'ŏn maintains, is the spirit of practicality. This constituted a reaction to the idealism of Chosŏn Neo-Confucian learning, which treated administrative concerns as "the province of petty officials" and productive technique as "artfulness." Sirhak thinkers rejected this traditional disdain for practical affairs and instead highlighted the importance of scholarship for the sake of the people and technology for productivity.[11]

It should be pointed out that the "practicality" singled out by Ch'ŏn took the contrasting forms previously discussed. The great majority of "Sirhak" figures did indeed pay unprecedented attention to such concrete issues as administrative reform and technological development, areas that had been neglected by their fellow scholar-bureaucrats. On the other hand, many of them also called for a return to the practical ethics of Confucius and Mencius in reaction to what they saw as the excessive involvement of their contemporaries in metaphysical issues. Although Tasan has become a household name in Korea on account of his detailed work on administrative reform, it is in this other branch of practicality, particularly his development of an innovative worldview based on the practical ethics of classical Confucianism, that his work merits much greater attention. It is this contribution of Tasan's to the development of Confucian philosophy that is a primary focus of this book.

The spirit of criticism which Ch'ŏn refers to also has a particularly important bearing on the subject matter of this book. It is clear that many reform-minded thinkers of the late Chosŏn criticized the ruling scholar bureaucrats and their policies, including the various aspects of Neo-Confucian orthodoxy that symbolized their authority.[12]

Consequently there is a widespread tendency to depict Sirhak thinkers as a breed apart from orthodox Neo-Confucians who represented literally "ex-Chu Hsi learning," or were generally "anti–

Chu Hsi learning," (*p'an chujahak*). These misconceptions are often associated with, or result from, the depiction of "Sirhak" as a discrete new stage in Korean thought following the supposed decline of Neo-Confucianism.

This depiction is misleading for two reasons.

To begin with, attitudes toward Neo-Confucian orthodoxy shown by the would-be reformers of the late Chosŏn showed great diversity. An Chŏngbok, a follower of Yi Ik who is associated with the Sirhak movement, was a vigorous defender of Chu Hsi's doctrines. On the other hand, many criticized what they saw as dogmatic attitudes toward orthodox Neo-Confucian teachings. For example, the outstanding proponents of institutional reform including Yu Hyŏngwŏn, Yi Ik, and Tasan, as well as the scholars of Northern Learning, frowned on the narrow-minded attitudes of literati who sought to discourage alternative interpretations of the classics, or who became excessively involved in the more metaphysical side of Neo-Confucianism to the neglect of practical affairs.

A much smaller group of scholars criticized certain aspects of the orthodox Neo-Confucian teachings themselves. For example, Pak Sedang and Yun Hyu challenged the validity of Chu Hsi's edition of the so-called Four Books, the philosophical core of the Confucian classics, and particularly his suggested amendments to the order and content of certain passages. Criticisms were also made of certain key philosophical concepts developed by Chu Hsi. At the same time most critics, in varying degrees, continued to use the metaphysical framework and terminology introduced by Ch'eng I and Chu Hsi to discuss philosophical issues. A prominent exception is Tasan, who, inspired by previous critiques as well as new schools of thought imported from abroad, directly assailed the foundations of Chu Hsi's cosmology.

The second reason why it would be misleading to label all members of the so-called Sirhak movement as "anti–Chu Hsi," or as being disillusioned with Chu Hsi, is that the expressions of orthodox Neo-Confucianism itself were very broad, a measure of the enormous impact Neo-Confucian values had on Chinese and Korean culture. As implied in the introduction, a great deal of confusion has resulted from a failure to distinguish between the various manifestations of Neo-Confucianism that late Chosŏn figures were reacting against, including Sung Neo-Confucian philosophy per se, the multitude of ways this philosophy was reflected, and indeed refracted, in the political ideology of the ruling scholar bureaucrats, the educational system and curricula tailored toward success in the civil service examinations, and the philosophies of the literati who were out of power.

Consequently, before taking a closer look at critical attitudes toward Neo-Confucian orthodoxy, we should begin by briefly exploring the origins of Neo-Confucianism and various facets of its impact on Korea.

Neo-Confucian Orthodoxy in Korea

Without exception all the figures traditionally associated with the so-called Sirhak movement, including Tasan, were descended from the families of scholar-bureaucrats. From an early age they were immersed in the traditional Neo-Confucian teachings, being rigorously groomed for government service by means of a thorough indoctrination in the Confucian canon, that is, the Four Books and Five Classics, presented almost entirely through the eyes of the Sung dynasty Neo-Confucians Chu Hsi and his predecessors the Ch'eng brothers. Even prior to their study of the Confucian classics the sons of the aristocracy were exposed to Chu Hsi's view of the world at an early age, through such essential primers as the *Hsiao-hsüeh* or "Lesser Learning," a collection of passages on ethics drawn from the classics by Chu Hsi's student Liu Tzu-ch'eng.

The extent of this immersion in the Neo-Confucian teachings is not surprising seeing that the Chosŏn had become the most orthodox Neo-Confucian dynasty in the history of East Asia. In the early years of the new dynasty the architects of the Chosŏn, including Chŏng Tojŏn (1337–98), the close confidant of the dynastic founder, made good use of recently imported Neo-Confucian critiques of Buddhism to chip away at the legitimacy of the Buddhist establishment, which presented a formidable challenge to the power of the new dynastic order.

Politics was not the only reason why Chu Hsi's Neo-Confucianism came to exert such a powerful grip on the Korean intelligentsia of the late Koryŏ and early Chosŏn periods. Unlike Buddhism, classical

Confucianism, for reasons which will appear more evident in chapter 3, lacked a sophisticated metaphysics that systematically dealt with the relationship between human beings and the rest of the cosmos. Furthermore, although Confucius and Mencius strongly emphasized the cultivation of virtue, their recorded teachings did not provide a clear program of self-cultivation that could compete with the Buddhist promise of enlightenment that had enticed so many to the temples. It was only in the Sung dynasty that Chu Hsi, building on the work of such pioneering metaphysicians as Chou Tun-I (1017–73), Chang Tsai (1020–77) and the Ch'eng brothers (Ch'eng Hao, 1032–85; Ch'eng I, 1033–1107), synthesized a new philosophical system that addressed both of these areas. Using two metaphysical concepts, *li* or "principle" and *ch'i* or "material force," Chu Hsi formulated a new explanation of human nature that integrated it within a sophisticated cosmological framework.[13] Furthermore, he drew attention to the *Great Learning*, a chapter of the *Record of Rites* that provided a clear program of self-cultivation, and enlarged on it in terms of his unique cosmology, placing unprecedented emphasis on the accessibility of sagehood through profound reflection and moral effort.

These two developments strongly appealed to succeeding generations of literati. By the Yüan dynasty Chu Hsi's edition of the Four Books, which included his voluminous commentaries on them, became core subject matter of the civil service examinations.

Although Chu Hsi's philosophy reigned supreme in official circles, a strong critic of his approach, Wang Yang-ming (1472–1529), became extremely influential during the Ming dynasty. Yang-ming, who was inspired by the work of a similarly iconoclastic philosopher Lu Hsiang-shan (1139–93), sharply criticized what he considered to be Chu Hsi's bookish attitude and strongly exhorted his followers to rely on their "innate knowledge" as their true guide on the path to sagehood, warning against passive dependence on the prescriptions of the classics. Yang-ming's moral activism spoke directly to the consciences of many literati who felt that the Ch'eng-Chu school had become bogged down in introspection and intellectual triviality. As a result, the two contrasting schools of Neo-Confucianism, the Ch'eng-Chu school and the Lu-Wang school, competed for attention from the Ming dynasty onwards.

Although the teachings of Chu Hsi retained their great influence in government circles as the officially recognized interpretations of the Confucian classics in the curricula of the civil service examinations, in both Ming China and late Tokugawa Japan the teachings of the Lu-Wang school continued to be widely, and openly, studied and respected.

On the other hand, the intellectual climate of the Chosŏn dynasty left little room for the spread and development of alternative schools.

As this chapter indicates, not only did the Chosŏn scholar-bureaucrats adopt the teachings of the Ch'eng-Chu school as their ruling ideology, but they vigorously championed it to the exclusion of rival Confucian schools. The dynasty had founded its legitimacy on the orthodoxy of the Ch'eng-Chu teachings, which had been used as a spearhead in the successful attempt to challenge and weaken the authority of Buddhism. Consequently the scholar-bureaucrats saw it as their *raison d'être* to ensure that Ch'eng-Chu Neo-Confucianism remained supreme. Once the "external" threat from Buddhism had been removed, or at least subdued, they showed even more sensitivity toward challenges from within, that is, challenges from rival schools within the Confucian camp.

Why was the new orthodoxy promoted even more aggressively in Korea than in China? The vigorous adoption and defense of a Chinese orthodoxy by Korea may well have been an expression of a "survival instinct" to transform itself, in the eyes of its powerful neighbor China, from a potentially threatening "barbarian" border state to a "younger brother" in the extended family of the Chinese cultural sphere. The success of this transformation became reflected in the special tributary status it had gained in its relations with China.[14]

Thus the vigilance against ideological "infiltration" continued, and by the sixteenth century such eminent Korean scholars as T'oegye were warning against the insidious attractions of heterodox teachings, and particularly those of Yang-ming, whose writings had recently been introduced to Korea. Naturally a focus of criticism was the supposed affinity of these doctrines with Buddhism.

Throughout the dynasty, philosophical development and dialogue largely revolved within the basic framework set out by Chu Hsi and the Ch'eng brothers. This is particularly understandable given the pride which such influential scholars as T'oegye, and later, Song Siyŏl (1607–89), took in their identity as defenders of the "orthodox" Confucian way. As discussed in this chapter, the boundaries of orthodoxy became even more clearly defined following severe ideological conflict between Chosŏn dynasty factions during the seventeenth century, especially in the wake of the momentous "Rites Disputes" of 1659 and 1674.

This is far from saying that the creativity of the Korean literati was stifled. For example, the two most well-known debates in the history of Korean philosophy, the so-called "Four-Seven" and "Horak" debates, which focused on Chu Hsi's interpretation of human nature, drew out its implications, and fathomed its ambiguities, with unprecedented detail and ingenuity.[15] Furthermore, many scholars continued to surreptitiously study "heterodox doctrines," and a small number of these—inspired by these alternative worldviews, and dissatisfied with dogmatic, unquestioning attitudes toward Chu Hsi's teachings—began to voice their doubts.

There were political as well as philosophical reasons for the growing dissatisfaction with the prevailing worldview. The behavior and policies of the Neo-Confucian ruling elite came under question during a period of social and economic upheaval following the Japanese (1592, 1597) and Manchu (1636) invasions, when the need for political and social reform was keenly felt. Many of the would-be reformers in the political opposition pointed to the unproductive nature of the speculative discussions on metaphysics indulged in by the Neo-Confucian bureaucrats. They felt the balance between the two great poles of Confucian learning, "self-cultivation" (*hsiu-chi*) and the "ordering of society" (*chih-jen*, which referred to ideal government), as defined by Chu Hsi, had been lost.[16]

At the same time, most of them did not overtly challenge the relevancy or orthodoxy of Chu Hsi's learning itself, still less question its conceptual foundations. But we shall focus our attention on a more limited group of late-Chosŏn Confucian thinkers particularly Yun Hyu (1617–80), Pak Sedang, and of course, the reform-minded Tasan, who criticized Chu Hsi's worldview itself based on their reevaluations of the spirit and letter of the classics.

The Challenge to Orthodox Neo-Confucianism

The Impact of Factionalism

The concern of the "Sirhak" proponents for the soundness of the national economy and the plight of the peasantry has been given prominence—and often exclusively so—in treatments of their intellectual orientations.[17] But one would be hard put to explain the work of these scholars, and especially critical attitudes toward Ch'eng-Chu orthodoxy exhibited by many of them, solely in these terms. One can hardly overlook the fact that the majority of them belonged to factions that formed the political opposition in their respective ages, and particularly to the Southerners (Namin), who through most of their history had been excluded from government on account of the maneuvering of the powerful Old Doctrine (Noron) faction. Not surprisingly their opposition was aimed mainly at members of the Old Doctrine faction, who, after ousting them in 1694, succeeded in playing most of the leading roles on the political stage by controlling the civil service examination system and appointments process.[18]

In an article on the intellectual genealogy of the "Southerners school" Hong Isŏp has stressed the fact that the majority of Sirhak thinkers were from the Southerners faction.[19] Although this claim is debatable, it can certainly be said that they were almost all members of the political opposition in their respective ages. Indeed, any characterizations of the approaches of these scholars and of the formative socioeconomic factors at work during this period must take into account factional alignments, or else run the risk of becoming exercises in abstraction. This is because, since the late sixteenth century, a number of factors such as the weakening of monarchical power and the scramble for a limited number of government posts led to the outbreak of factional strife that exerted increasing influence not only on the political life of the country but also on intellectual orientations.[20] Factional schisms originated primarily in disagreements over issues related to the delegation of political power, such as the appointment of officials to key positions, the designation of heirs to

FIGURE 1.1

Factional Affiliation of Critics of Neo-Confucian Orthodoxy in the Late Chosŏn Period

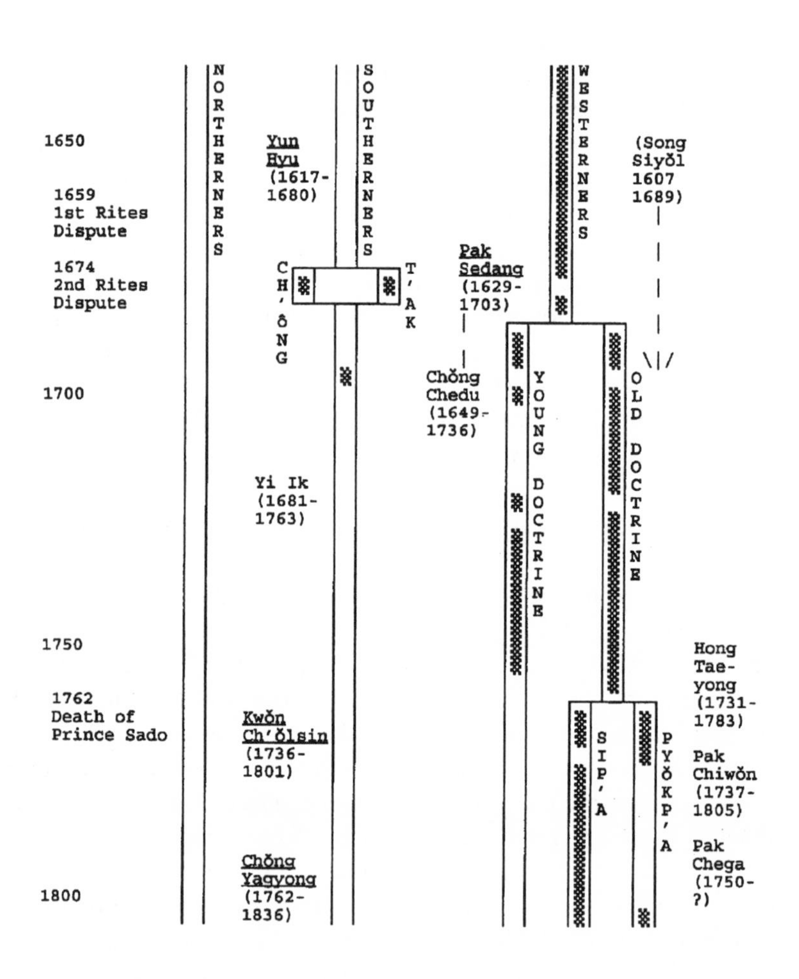

(Critics of orthodox Neo-Confucian thought underlined)
(Politically dominant factions shaded)

the throne, and the related problem of mourning rites. For a brief period after such schisms, when the controversies that had spawned them revolved around contemporary issues, allegiance to the nascent factions was to a certain extent changeable and subject to personal opinions and values. With the passage of time, however, current controversies became historical *faits accomplis*. As the factions took on a multi-generational dimension and the views to defend became those expressed by factional predecessors, the forces of such powerful norms as filial piety and loyalty came into play. Marriage as well as intellectual and social ties became increasingly endogamous, resulting in the association of certain lineages with particular factions. Factional associations became further ossified through accumulated hostilities that resurfaced during successive struggles for power, particularly after the Rites Disputes of 1659 and 1674. In consequence, by the end of the seventeenth century, changes of factional affiliation by dissenting individuals, and marriage between members of opposing factions, especially the Southerner and Old Doctrine factions, were much rarer.[21]

These trends resulted in the emergence of sharply distinct "factional cultures," as vividly depicted by Yi Ik in the early eighteenth century:

> These [factional divisions] were passed on from generation to generation. Their distant descendants remain enemies and slaughter one another. There are those who, serving in the same court and living in the same village, do not associate with each other to the end of their days.
>
> Therefore, when fortune or misfortune bring them together, they whisper in secret. When there is a case of intermarriage, they gang together and drive the offenders away. So different are their language, demeanor, and dress, that one can tell them apart on the street. They come from different regions and have different customs. The extent [of these differences] is so remarkable that they can be traced and identified.[22]

Since teacher-student relationships were also largely forged along factional lines, limitations were also set on ideological affiliations. Vindication of the positions of factional predecessors took on an important role in the diachronically oriented Confucian psyche, where the self-image of individuals was intimately bound to the public image not only of self but also of lineage, factional as well as ancestral.[23] These two kinds of lineage were closely linked due to the prevalence of intermarriage among the families of literati within particular factions.

Factional Alignment and Philosophical Orientations

From the time they were traditionally regarded to have been formed in 1575, the two rival factions of literati, the Westerners (Sŏin) and Easterners (Tongin), were loosely affiliated with the two main schools of Ch'eng-Chu Neo-Confucianism championed by Yulgok and T'oegye respectively.[24]

As time went by, factional, and with them geographical, associations with schools of thought further polarized. The followers of Yulgok came to be known as the *Kiho* (Kyŏnggi and Ch'ungch'ŏng provinces) school, as leading figures of the Westerners such as Kim Changsaeng (1548–1631) Song Siyŏl and Kwŏn Sangha (1641–1721) came from that area, and the followers of T'oegye came to be known as the *Yŏngnam* (Kyŏngsang province) school, as influential figures of the Southerners, a subfaction of the Easterners, such as Yi Hyŏnil (1627–1704) and Yi Sangjŏng (1710–81), were all from the Kyŏngsang region. Nonetheless, certain members of the Westerners did incline toward the views of T'oegye, and there were also exceptions among the Southerners. In the tradition of T'oegye the Yŏngnam school insisted on the primacy of principle (*li/i*) whereas their opponents from the Kiho school tended to emphasize the interdependence between principle and material force (*ch'i/ki*).[25] It was not only in the realm of metaphysics that the factions displayed distinct ideological trends, for, as we shall see, in consequent periods they also aligned themselves with distinct schools in ritual studies, literary styles, and research methods.

The Southerners

This is not to say, as some prominent historians have implied, that factional considerations stifled intellectual development and inhibited potentially creative individuals from transcending the frames of reference set by the orthodox Neo-Confucian teachings, within which the Yŏngnam-Kiho debate revolved. On the contrary, as this study suggests, critical attitudes toward Neo-Confucian dogmatism, and doctrines, that developed within the Southerners faction during the seventeenth and eighteenth centuries, particularly in the work of Yi Ik and his followers Kwŏn Ch'ŏlsin (1736–1801) and Tasan, were catalyzed, if not prompted by, factional tensions rather than appearing in spite of them. These critiques were double-edged, since they represented not only an attack on the perceived ideological roots of socioeconomic problems, but also an attack on the legitimating ideology of the faction in power, the Old Doctrine faction, a subfaction of the Westerners. Furthermore, these critiques are of philosophical as well as political significance, for dissatisfaction with the accepted orthodoxy led to curiosity about other worldviews, and provided a springboard for the development of alternative ideas. These "unorthodox" tendencies came to philosophical fruition in the work of Tasan, who not only challenged Chu Hsi's metaphysics, but went on to develop an alternative philosophical system that rivalled it in terms of internal consistency and breadth of scope.

It is no coincidence that Yun Hyu, one of the earliest critics of Neo-Confucian dogmatism, became associated with the Southerners faction, an opposition group through most of its history. One and a half centuries after Yun Hyu, Tasan, who gave critiques of Chu Hsi's learning their most systematic expression, rose to prominence from among the ranks of the Southerners, and drew a great deal of his inspiration from its members. In order to gain even a superficial understanding of the formative influences on Tasan's thought it is essential to understand the history of the Southerners and particularly the current of reaction to orthodox Neo-Confucianism with which it became closely associated. In addition, we should also explore the thought of the highly controversial Young Doctrine thinker Pak Sedang, who it seems, was more of a formative influence on Tasan than he was ready to openly admit.

The Southerners, together with the Northerners (Pugin) came into being in 1591 as a result of a split within their parent faction, the Tongin (Easterners) over the issue of succession to the throne of Sŏnjo (1567–1608). King Sŏnjo had no legitimate son, and Chŏng Ch'ŏl, a leading member of the Westerners, proposed that a son by one of

Sŏnjo's concubines succeed to the throne. The rival faction of the Westerners, the Easterners, consequently split into two subfactions, the Northerners, who urged the king to strongly denounce the proposal and deal harshly with its supporters, and the Southerners, who took a conciliatory position. It was the Pugin who had their way, and they succeeded in replacing the Westerners as the dominant faction when Kwanghaegun (1608–23), whom they had supported, took the throne. But after Kwanghaegun, they were ousted by the Westerners, who dominated the political scene most of the time thereafter. Through the Rites Disputes of 1569 and 1674, which we will discuss in more detail later, the Southerners managed to wrest power from the Old Doctrine faction for two brief periods during the reign of Sukchong (1674–1720). But for the following two centuries, from 1694 till 1863, the Southerners generally remained in opposition with little or no representation in government.[26] During this time the Old Doctrine faction assumed a tight grip on political power, especially by means of manipulating the appointments process and the civil service examination system.[27] This created particular difficulties for the Southerners. The literati in general were dependent for their livelihood on employment as government officials, but the Southerners more so than others. When high officials from the three southern provinces were excluded from government, they were nonetheless able to maintain themselves through income generated by land that their families owned. On the other hand, most members of the Southerners were from the vicinity of the capital and Kyŏnggi Province, where the quality of land was relatively poor and the population dense. Although some members of the Southerners had benefited from the wealth accrued by their ancestors' service in government, they were nonetheless exposed to the hardships of rural life in a region which was particularly exploited by the capital.[28]

Yun Hyu's Critique of Chu Hsi

Yun Hyu, a Confucian philosopher who rose to prominence on account of his markedly independent thinking, became directly involved in the factional turmoil revolving around the Southerners' second brief ascendancy to power during the reign of Sukchong. He is most well known for his role in the mourning rites controversies of this period, when he openly expressed disagreement with the views of the influential leader of the Westerners, Song Siyŏl. He also stands out sharply as the first to openly question the absolute authority of Chu Hsi's interpretations of the classics, and particularly for the outspoken manner in which he did so.

Yun Hyu was born during the reign of Kwanghaegun, just two decades after Hideyoshi's second invasion of Korea. His father, who was serving as a local official in Kyŏngju at the time, had studied the classics under Min Sŭpchŏng. Min was in turn a disciple of Sŏ Kyŏngdŏk, the great Neo-Confucian metaphysician known for his cosmological theories based on Chang Tsai's monism of material force. In his youth, Yun Hyu himself had been taught for a time by Yi Min'gu (1589–1670), a son of Yi Sugwang (1563–1628), whose encyclopedic scholarship is widely regarded as a precursor to Sirhak.[29] Yi Sugwang was one of the first to explore literature dealing with "Western Learning" introduced to Korea by Chosŏn emissaries returning from the Ming, and in his work we find the first references to Matteo Ricci's writings on Catholicism, in which he took a great interest.

In 1636, when Yun was twenty-one, the Manchus invaded Korea for the second time, took the royal family hostage in its refuge at Kanghwa Island, and forced King Injo to capitulate. Although the destruction wrought was on a scale far smaller than that incurred by Hideyoshi's troops, the blow to national pride was considerable. Yun met the prominent Neo-Confucian Song Siyŏl, who was serving as the king's tutor, and other scholars in the mountain retreat of Songnisan, and together they lamented over the tragedy and shame of King Injo's subjugation at Namhansan fortress. From this time on he resolved not to take the civil service examinations, and to concentrate on study in seclusion. Before long he was well known for his thorough grasp of the classics and histories, and became regularly involved in friendly and scholarly exchange with the outstanding Neo-Confucian scholars of his day.[30] Such was his standing that Min Chŏngjung and Kim Kŭkhyŏng, both leading members of the Westerners, affectionately called him "Yulgok," after the great Neo-Confucian scholar whom their faction in particular regarded with unquestioning respect. Yun became involved in such frequent exchanges with Song and other leaders of the Westerners faction, that he came to be regarded as one of them.[31]

From 1656, the seventh year of King Hyojong (r. 1649–59), Yun was repeatedly requested to serve in a number of important government positions which he consistently declined. This prompted Song Siyŏl to exclaim, "How fortunate it is that a man of such lofty ideals should treat secular affairs with the respect due to a worm," a mild but thinly-veiled jibe at Yun's notoriously high self-esteem.[32] Nevertheless, it was such idealism as well as scholarship that won him the respect and patronage of Song Siyŏl himself, who, in 1658, recommended him to yet another high government office which he again declined.[33]

But the cordial relations between Yun and Song had already started to sour on account of sharp differences in their approach to Chu Hsi's commentaries and learning in general. Yun Hyu was not timid about expressing his distinctive philosophical views, even when they clearly departed from Chu Hsi's interpretations.

Yun Hyu attempted to improve on Chu Hsi's commentary on the *Mean*, in two works entitled *Chungyong changgu ch'aje* (*Order of The Mean, in Chapters and Verses*) and *Chungyong Chuja changgu porok* (*Supplement to Master Chu's The Mean, in Chapters and Verses*). Song, in a letter to a colleague, accused him of being a *samun nanjŏk*, "a traitor of the Confucian Way," and of implying that his interpretations were more authoritative than those of Chu Hsi himself.[34]

We do not know what it was about these works specifically that Song may have taken issue with. The title *Supplement to Master Chu's The Mean, in Chapters and Verses* alone indicates that Yun considered Chu Hsi's interpretation of the *Mean* to be incomplete, and that, at least, he intended that his own interpretations should be considered together with Chu Hsi's. As its title indicates, in the *Order of The Mean, in Chapters and Verses* he had made emendations to the layout of the *Mean* as it had been published in Chu Hsi's commentary on the same work, *Chung-yung chang-chü* (*The Mean, in Chapters and Verses*), by rearranging the chapter divisions.

Furthermore Yun's perception of Heaven (*Ch'ŏn*), a concept which referred to the metaphysical foundation of existence in Confucianism, was very different from Chu Hsi's. This difference was thrown into focus in his exposition of the *Mean*. According to his chronological biography,

> Yun considered the teaching of the *Classic of Filial Piety* to be no different from that of the *Mean*. In his words, The *Classic of Filial Piety* describes the way of serving parents, and the *Inner Rules* [*Nei-ts'e*, a chapter of the *Record of Rites*] delineates the principles [of this way]. The *Mean* discourses on the way of serving Heaven, and the *Great Learning* defines the main points [of this way].[35]

As Miura Kunio points out, Yun frequently referred to Heaven in his works, and particularly, as indicated by the above passage, the centrality of "serving Heaven" (*sach'ŏn*). Instead of equating Heaven with principle, he regarded it as a supreme power directing all things including principle, and as a transcendent being which observed human affairs and reacted favorably or unfavorably to the conduct of the ruler. These views stood in stark contrast to the Ch'eng-Chu rationalistic portrayal of Heaven as principle (*li*). Nonetheless there was nothing particularly innovative about them. Yun Hyu appealed to a much earlier authority than the Sung Confucians for his depiction of Heaven, pointing out the ancients' constant mindfulness of *Shang T'i*, the personal deity mentioned in the writings of the early Chou to which the sacrificial rituals and even daily activities of the royal house were dedicated.[36]

Yun also showed his dissatisfaction with Chu Hsi's edition of the *Great Learning* by basing his commentaries on the old version of the classic as it had appeared in the *Record of Rites*.[37] As we shall see in chapter 3, Yun Hyu set a precedent that was reflected in the work of Tasan by disagreeing with Chu Hsi's interpretation of key concepts in the classic, such as the "comprehension of things" (*ko-wu*) and "sincerity of the will" (*ch'eng-i*).[38] He based these critiques on an examination of the concepts as they had appeared in the "old text" of the *Great Learning*, an approach that reflected the beginnings of the Evidential Learning movement that gained momentum in the late Ming, which put emphasis on the philological study of the "Six Classics." Nonetheless, Yun Hyu did not take the implications of the new Evidential Learning to the extent of challenging Chu Hsi's cosmology based on the concepts of principle and material force. He was very interested in the speculative debate on the relationship between the "Four Beginnings" (*ssu-tuan/sadan*) and the "Seven

Emotions" (*ch'i-ch'ing/ch'iljŏng*) pursued by the followers of T'oegye and Yulgok. As Chu Hsi had done, he associated the "Four Beginnings," introduced by Mencius, with principle, and the "Seven Emotions" mentioned in the *Mean* with material force, although his work on the debate showed differences of interpretation with both of the main Korean schools of thought on the subject.[39]

Aside from this departure into Ch'eng-Chu metaphysics, Yun Hyu tended to dwell on the words of the classics themselves, and he took the ideal institutions described in them as a model to be emulated in his own time. In reflecting on the *Rites of Chou*, a book which he considered had not received the attention it merited, Yun wrote,

> The ancient sages wrote the classics and revealed them to the world. There can be no imperfection in them. The principles of all-under-Heaven and the grandeur of kingly rule find complete expression in the classics.[40]

Yun vigorously defended his right to express his own opinions based on the study of the ancient texts themselves, as opposed to writing commentaries on commentaries, even though such opinions might contradict the views of acknowledged authorities.

Consequently, although he obviously respected Chu Hsi, Yun did not hesitate to question the prevailing reliance on Chu's exposition of the Confucian classics championed by Song.[41] It is clear that Yun did not consider Chu Hsi's commentaries to be the gateway to the classics through which all must pass. After the Southerners, with Yun in their forefront, had seized power through the second Rites Dispute, he caused a great stir by remarking that Chu Hsi's commentaries on the *Analects* should not be compulsory reading at the Royal Lectures.[42]

Furthermore Yun was quite ready to differ with Chu Hsi on the basis of his own careful analysis of the texts:

> When I read the works of Chu Hsi, and particularly his commentaries, I would write and then edit, edit and again write. Sometimes, if I had an insight, and at other times, on the strength of the arguments of friends and students, I would make changes.[43]

At the same time Yun insisted that he did not want to be different just for the sake of being different, but rather that he was simply enlarging on implications that he perceived in the classics themselves.[44] He considered a critical attitude to be a natural attribute of an inquiring mind:

> My purpose in writing is not to put forward views contrary to the interpretations of Chu Hsi, but simply to note down problems. If I had been born in Chu Hsi's time and were one of his followers, I wouldn't have just followed him blindly without seeking to satisfy my curiosity, and be content to sit down and heap praises on him. I would certainly have questioned him repeatedly, and thought things over time and again in order to come to a clear understanding.[45]

This perspective sharply contrasted with the well-nigh unquestioning reverence shown for Chu Hsi's doctrines by the mainstream literati of his day, and particularly Song Siyŏl, who firmly believed that all of Chu Hsi's teachings were just as applicable to his age as they were in the Sung. Song held that "The man of whom it could be said that all his words are correct, and all of his conduct proper, is Master Chu."[46] Such veneration of Chu Hsi was fed by a consciousness that he shared with fellow members of the Westerners—if not the general populace—that the Chosŏn dynasty was the custodian of Neo-Confucian learning and even civilization itself, after the Ming dynasty had been replaced by the rule of barbarian Manchus in 1644. Even prior to the Ch'ing, the Chosŏn literati had taken pride in their perceived identity as the most faithful adherents of the Ch'eng-Chu school and opponents of Yang Ming's heterodox doctrines, in contrast to the Ming bureaucracy, which had permitted the canonization of Wang Yang-ming in the Confucian temple.[47] This consciousness is apparent in the following frontal attack on Yun Hyu's untraditional approach, launched by a leading member of the Old Doctrine faction, Kim Manjung:

> One cannot do away with Chu Hsi's commentary on the *Analects*. In China the Lu-Wang school exists as a separate field of study.

> It does not adopt Chu Hsi's commentaries. But the whole of our country, starting with the king, follows Chu Hsi's commentaries, and has used them at the Royal Lectures for hundreds of years, so how can they be dispensed with now?[48]

In view of their whole-hearted espousal of Chu Hsi's teachings as a mainstay of national identity, it is no wonder that many members of the Westerners looked askance at Yun Hyu's critical attitude. Consequently, in the latter years of Hyojong's reign, Song's continuing patronage of Yun came under question. Even though Song himself considered Yun to be a "traitor of the Confucian Way," he seemed reluctant to sever ties with an old acquaintance and fellow scholar he still clearly respected.[49]

Yun Hyu and the Rites Disputes

But when King Hyojong died, Song and Yun, and their respective factions, became irreconcilable enemies through a bitter conflict, the Rites Dispute of 1659 (*kihae yesong*), which revolved around the period of mourning to be observed for the king by his stepmother, Queen Dowager Cho.

This debate had serious political and ideological consequences. On the surface, it appears to be a storm brewed in a teacup; however, rites (*li/ye*), and particularly mourning rites, assumed a great significance in the mind of Chosŏn Neo-Confucians.[50]

Among the Four Rites, which included capping, marriage, mourning, and ancestral offering, those associated with mourning took on added significance since they were regarded as a direct expression of filial piety, the North Star in the constellation of Confucian moral imperatives.[51] And since, in the words of the influential early Neo-Confucian Chou Tun-I (1017–73), the government of the empire took the family—and particularly the family of the ruler—as its model, the mourning rites observed by the royal family were endowed with a political dimension that made them a focus of concern for the Neo-Confucian bureaucrats.[52] It was they who, according to the stipulations of the *Five Rites of the Dynasty* (*Kukcho oryeŭi*) or the more detailed procedures recorded in such classics as the *Book of Etiquette and Ritual*, recommended the appropriate mourning attire to be worn in respect for deceased members of royalty.[53]

As JaHyun Kim Haboush has indicated, during the latter half of the Chosŏn period there existed a very delicate balance of power between the monarchy and the bureaucracy, a balance which was increasingly threatened by the consolidation of political power among certain factions, especially Song's faction, the Westerners, which later produced an even more powerful group of his supporters, the Old Doctrine faction.[54] In view of this delicate balance, or rather imbalance, of power, and also in view of the symbolic significance of the rites discussed above, particularly in relation to the status of members of the monarchy, it is not surprising that differences of interpretation over mourning attire triggered off severe controversy among the factions. In particular, the Rites Disputes of 1659 and 1674, which revolved around such differences, are recognized to have had far-reaching political consequences.

The consequences were not only political. Their whole hearted espousal of orthodox Neo-Confucianism imbued the leadership of the ruling scholar-bureaucrats, and particularly the Old Doctrine faction, with added authority, and in consequence, as this chapter will indicate, factional attitudes toward orthodox Neo-Confucianism became a target during the Rites Controversies. Many outstanding thinkers in Tasan's faction, the Southerners, including himself, were influenced by these ideological repercussions, and consequently to adequately understand his intellectual heritage, we should first turn our attention to the Rites Disputes themselves.

It was the fact that Hyojong, as a second son, had been granted the kingship in preference to his elder brother Sohyŏn, the primogenitary successor, that led to disagreement about his ritual status. Claiming that the ancient rites did not clearly stipulate whether the three- or one-year mourning period should be observed by Queen Dowager Cho for her stepson Hyojong, the ministers of Hyŏnjong (1659–74), Hyojong's successor, including Chief State Councillor Chŏng Taehwa, decided that the one-year period seemed appropriate. Song Siyŏl, who was also an acknowledged authority on ritual, concurred with their decision.[55]

But the issue was far from over. Yun Hyu, whose scholarship and views also carried authority, was consulted, and he maintained that, according to the ritual classics, the three-year mourning attire should be worn for the heir.[56] Consequently, Song defended his position, going as far as to say that Hyojong was, in the terminology of the *Commentary on the Book of Etiquette and Ritual* (*I-li chu-shu*), "an immediate offspring, but not the legitimate heir." He interpreted this to mean that, as a second son, Hyojong could not qualify for the three-year period of mourning.[57] Song and Yun became involved in a progressively acrimonious debate which drew on a number of sources and precedents, and polarized the positions of their respective factions, the Westerners and the Southerners. Certain basic differences of outlook which influenced their opinions on the mourning period are apparent. Song put greater emphasis on family relationships, and consequently on the common ground of family ethics that existed between monarchic and general family ritual. Whereas Song introduced the question of a distinction between eldest and younger sons, Yun put emphasis on the royal line of descent and the differences between royal and general family ritual, differences that were defined in early ritual classics such as the *Record of Rites*.[58] Yun regarded Hyojong's status as a second son to be irrelevant, claiming that "in the case of the royal family, priority is placed on the line of descent."[59] As the dispute escalated, he implied that Song and his associates were degrading the monarchy by making distinctions in the line of succession.[60]

Consequently, Hŏ Mok (1595–1682), Yun Hyu's teacher and mentor, and a leading figure of the Southerners, vigorously defended Yun's position. Yun Sŏndo (1587–1671), another prominent Southerner who had served as Hyojong's tutor when he was crown prince, attacked Song along the same lines and further raised the political tension by claiming that both Song and his faction were endangering the sovereign and state. The Westerners, perceiving these criticisms to be an effort on the part of the Southerners to expel them from power, rallied behind Song. The dispute escalated and intensified and eventually Hyŏnjong, voicing his distaste for such animosity among literati and surprise over the lengths to which they went to besmirch each other, sided with Song. The Westerners consequently succeeded in having Yun Sŏndo exiled and Hŏ Mok demoted to the status of a provincial official.[61]

FIGURE 1.2

Hyojong's Family Tree (Simplified)

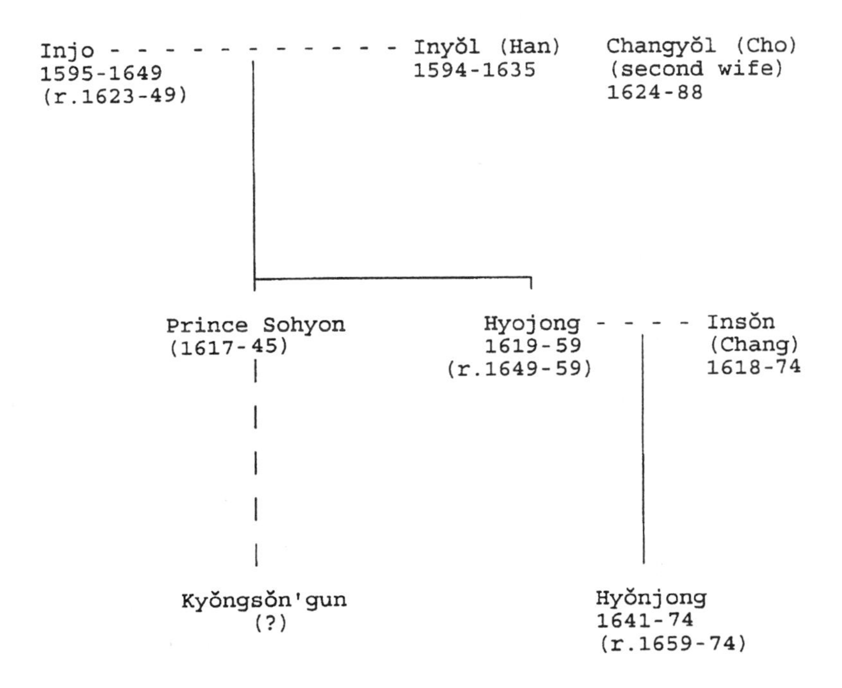

It was only after the mourning rites dispute of 1659 that Song and his factional associates publicly censured Yun for his unorthodox ideas, using them as a further pretext to defame him. On the strength of his unquestioning veneration and promotion of Chu Hsi's doctrines, Song had successfully established himself as the protector of orthodox Neo-Confucianism and, reinforcing the ruling elite's perception of the Chosŏn dynasty as the institutional embodiment of this civilized ideology in a barbaric world, fostered the idea that heterodoxy was unpatriotic. During and after the Rites Dispute of 1659 he was thus able to discredit Yun Hyu and strengthen his position by drawing attention to Yun's critical attitude toward Chu Hsi's views.[62]

In 1674 the issue of mourning rites surfaced again. Once more it was the attire of Queen Dowager Cho that became the focus of attention, this time to be worn in mourning for her recently deceased daughter-in-law, Hyojong's wife. This new dispute was based on the old argument made by the Westerners in the previous dispute that Hyojong should be treated as a second son irrespective of his succession to the throne. This time Hyŏnjong insisted that he be informed of the details of the arguments on both sides.[63] Unsympathetic with the kinship-oriented argument, he sided with the Southerners, promoting the leading Southerner figure Hŏ Chŏk to the position of chief state councillor, in effect handing over the reins of power to his faction.[64]

In response to the second Rites Dispute Yun Hyu presented a memorial to Hyŏnjong's successor, King Sukchong (r. 1674–1720), implying that the nine-month mourning period proposed by the Westerners for Queen Dowager Cho was suitable for a scholar-official rather than a member of royalty, and that Song's faction was blurring the distinction between the two classes.[65]

Through the disputes of 1659 and 1674 the issue of mourning rites took on a weighty symbolic significance, by means of which the opposing factions, particularly the Southerners and the Westerners, vicariously asserted their views on the status of the deceased monarch and even the status of the monarchy in general in relation to the class of scholar-bureaucrats. The distinctly political dimension of this bitter confrontation, and the scholarly repute of its two protagonists, ensured that it had an immediate, far-reaching impact, immediate in the respect that it sharpened and solidified the schism between the factions, and far-reaching in that it set a pattern for future interfactional struggle.

One trend which was set in this period was the advocacy of monarchical supremacy by leading Southerner figures, which served to drive a wedge between a monarchy apprehensive of the erosion of its authority on the one hand and the increasing power of the Old Doctrine faction on the other. The extremely sensitive question of the balance between monarchic and bureaucratic power had now been brought into the open through the challenge of the Southerners. In effect, they had accused the Westerners of making a concerted effort to systematically expand and consolidate their authority at the expense of the monarchy, by defining the ritual status of the king in ways that blurred the distinctions between royalty and the class of scholar-officials.

On the other hand, the Westerners claimed that the Southerners were politicizing the debate in order to alienate their rivals from the throne. Furthermore, and what is more significant for the purposes of this book, the Westerners also discredited the Southerners by accusing their champion, Yun Hyu, of ideological perversity.

An important consequence of this attack was that, through the Rites Disputes, ideological differences were thrown into relief. The more sharply Song and his successors defined the boundaries of orthodoxy, the easier it became to find heresy in the ideas of independently minded opponents. Conversely, by founding their legitimacy on their whole-hearted espousal of Chu Hsi's learning, they opened themselves to attack by later opposition thinkers who cast doubt on the relevancy of Neo-Confucian metaphysics, if not the orthodoxy of Chu Hsi's teachings themselves.

Shortly after the Rites Dispute of 1674, Hyŏnjong died and was succeeded by Sukchong, who facilitated the Southerner rise to dominance by consecutively granting high positions in government to such leading figures as Hŏ Mok as well as Yun Hyu, who was promoted to several positions in the powerful Board of Personnel. The king came under increasing pressure to make an example of Song, who was accused of distorting correct ritual procedure for having initially propagated the idea that second or younger sons who inherited the kingship could never be treated as eldest sons in terms of succession.[66]

Even after Song's consequent exile in 1675, a group of Southerners were still not satisfied that justice had been done, or on a more pragmatic level, that all possibility of Song's future return to power had been eliminated. The Southerners were split into two subfactions over Song's future, the hardline group (*ch'ŏngnam*) including Hŏ Mok, the Third State Councillor, and Yun Hyu on the one hand, maintaining that only death would be a fitting end to those who would denigrate the prestige of royalty, and the conciliatory group (*t'angnam*), including Hŏ Chŏk, the Chief State Councillor, on the other, who opposed such extreme measures.[67] The resulting rivalry and upheaval in the highest echelons of government incurred the wrath of Sukchong, who promoted the resurgence of the Westerners. In 1680, many leading Southerner figures including Yun Hyu were purged allegedly for their association with a plot against the crown instigated by Hŏ Kyŏn (? –1680), the son of Hŏ Chŏk, and Prince Poksŏn. Following this Yun was ordered by the king to put himself to death.[68]

The profound impact of the political and ideological conflict that arose between the persons and supporters of Yun Hyu and Song Siyŏl is indicated by the fact that it was a major factor in the formation of analogous splits within the Southerners into *T'angnam* (Turbid Southerner) and *Ch'ŏngnam* (Clear Southerner) on the one hand,[69] and the Westerners into Old Doctrine and Young Doctrine factions on the other. Differences of orientation between Old Doctrine faction and Young Doctrine were more fundamental than those between *T'angnam* and *Ch'ŏngnam*, which failed to divide the Southerners permanently. Although the reasons for the split within the Westerners were complex, the sharply contrasting attitudes of Song Siyŏl and Yun Sŏn'gŏ (1610–69), another influential member of the Westerners, toward the person and views of Yun Hyu, are widely regarded to be a decisive factor.[70]

Thus the reverberations of the mourning rites dispute engraved themselves in the basic factional alignment that lasted through Tasan's lifetime until the end of the dynasty, the so-called *sasaek* or "four colours," that is, the Southerners, Northerners, Old Doctrine, and Young Doctrine factions.

The respective attitudes toward Ch'eng-Chu learning of Song and Yun, as well as their positions vis-à-vis the monarchy, molded to a considerable extent the divergent ideological positions of the Southerners, the Westerners, and later its sub-faction the Old Doctrine, for the next one and a half centuries. Kang Chujin has pointed out that, whereas the families of Song Siyŏl, Yun Sŏn'gŏ, and Yun Hyu were linked through marriage ties as well as teacher-student relationships, after the Rites Disputes, sharp divisions between their respective factions are evidenced by the lack of such ties.[71] Thus the ideological schisms that appeared between them at this time were handed down and accentuated. Yun Hyu's individualistic attitude toward scholarship, characterized by his critical attitude toward Chu Hsi's learning and his emphasis on freedom of interpretation, set the pattern for his Southerner successors, particularly Yi Ik, the champion of institutional and administrative reform, and his students Kwŏn Ch'ŏlsin and Tasan. Although Yi Ik and most of his followers were understandably less ready to explicitly differ with Chu Hsi, they indirectly criticized the conservatively minded Old Doctrine faction by deploring narrow-minded attitudes and defending their right to make alternative interpretations. Significantly, it was Yi Ik's father who is recorded as giving his vigorous assent to Yun Hyu's proposition that Chu Hsi's commentaries not be compulsory reading in the Royal Lectures.[72]

Pak Sedang's Critique of Chu Hsi

Little more than a decade after Yun Hyu, a more systematic and direct critique of Ch'eng-Chu learning was launched by Pak Sedang in his exposition of the Four Books.

Pak was descended from a lineage of influential Westerner bureaucrats. The previous four generations of his ancestors had all served in relatively high government positions including the State Council and Board of Personnel.[73] He lost his father in childhood, and in those early years was taught by his elder brother and uncle.[74] After his marriage at sixteen he was supported by his relatively wealthier in-laws, and was educated for the civil service examinations by his wife's uncle Nam Isŏng (1625–83), and his brother-in-law Nam Kuman (1629–1711), whose factional affiliations with the Westerners, and later the Young Doctrine subfaction, he inherited.[75] Nam Kuman later became a leading adversary of Song Siyŏl after the split between the Old Doctrine and the Young Doctrine.

After passing the civil service examinations Pak successively served in a series of government posts, including positions in the National Confucian Academy (*Sŏnggyun'gwan*) and the Board of Rites. Like Yun Hyu, he was not one to mince words, and he soon made political enemies. At the age of thirty-four, while he was serving at the office of the censor-general under Hyŏnjong, he questioned the qualifications of Kim Chwamyŏng (1616–71) and Yi Unsang (1617–78), two high officials closely associated with Song Siyŏl.[76] Only two years later he incurred the disapproval of the conservative, pro-Ming, anti-Ch'ing Song faction in supporting the First Royal Secretary Sŏ P'irwŏn's conciliatory stance toward the Ch'ing envoy to the Korean court, arguing that Korea had already formally recognized the new dynasty.[77] As a result, Pak became known as one of the pro-Ch'ing "Five Villains." Nonetheless it appears that despite their antithetical views on external relations, Song Siyŏl still held him in some respect, and praised Pak for his painstaking and concise work on editing a commentary on the *Lesser Learning* (*Hsiao-hsüeh*) three years later.[78]

It was only at the age of fifty-two, in 1681, shortly after the Southerners were ousted by the Westerners and Yun Hyu died, that he started writing his commentaries on the classics entitled the *Sabyŏnnok* or *Thoughtful Elucidations*, and for which he was later to become stigmatized as an author of heterodox doctrines. At the time the work was first circulated, he received a warning from Yun Chŭng, the patriarch of his faction, the Young Doctrine, about his scholarship.[79] Yun Chŭng deeply respected Yun Hyu and was obviously concerned that Pak Sedang might run into the same kind of trouble with Song's faction. Intriguingly, no voices were raised at the time, and Pak's reputation continued to grow until he was seventy-three, as he successively turned down repeated requests to take up ministerial positions of the second rank. But a few comments he made for the inscription of Yi Kyŏngsŏk's (1595–1671) memorial tablet ended in his downfall. It was Yi Kyŏngsŏk who had first appointed Song Siyŏl to office, and who had earned renown as a staunch opponent of the Ch'ing when he served as chief state councillor under Hyojong. Yi and Song had parted ways over the Rites Dispute of 1659, and according to Pak, the resulting rift between them had been greatly aggravated by Song's vindictiveness, whose animosity and personal attacks on Yi contrasted with the latter's magnanimity and reluctance to become involved in mud-slinging. In view of this, Pak implied that Song had been disrespectful of an elder, and quoted the classics to underline how odious such an attitude was. These comments reflected the low regard Pak had harbored for Song Siyŏl's person since the beginning of Sukchong's reign.

This indictment incurred the wrath of Song's followers, and since they held the political reigns, the results were disastrous for Pak. Their attacks on him for criticizing Song in his composition of the memorial tablet in question were given further weight by the new accusation that Pak had derided Chu Hsi in his *Thoughtful Elucidations*, which led to his being accused of heterodoxy as a "traitor of the Confucian Way," the same stigma once given to Yun Hyu. One of Pak's antagonists, Kim Ch'anghŭp, maintained that this derision of Chu Hsi was a means of discrediting his teacher and champion, Song Siyŏl.[80] Pak's followers responded by arguing that the real reason for the attacks on Pak were those few lines in the memorial composition, and that Pak's philosophical views had long been known.[81] In 1703, after perusing both the memorial to Yi Kyŏngsŏk and the *Thoughtful Elucidations*, King Sukchong stripped Pak of government office and court rank and ordered the destruction of the two works. A decision to exile Pak to Chŏlla Province was not carried out on account of the petitions made to the king by two of his followers, who requested consideration of their teacher's ill-health as well as high integrity and distinction.[82] Pak Sedang succumbed to his poor state of health in the same year, no doubt aggravated by the storm of opposition he had recently faced.

It has been pointed out that although Pak wrote two commentaries on the Taoist classics *Lao Tzu* (*Tao-te ching*) and *Chuang Tzu*—commentaries which included sympathetic remarks as well as criticisms based on his essentially Confucian standpoint—he was accused of heterodoxy not on account of these but on his chapter-and-verse critique of Chu Hsi's interpretations in his *Thoughtful Elucidations*. The greater threat to the Old Doctrine faction was posed by his attack on Chu Hsi's orthodoxy, which made him a dangerous "rebel within" the Confucian ranks, rather than his relatively sympathetic exposition of totally heterodox teachings.[83]

An essential theme of Pak's critique of the Ch'eng-chu school was its estrangement from everyday affairs, the province of classical Confucianism. In his preface to the *Thoughtful Elucidations*, Pak cited a passage from the *Mean*, "when going a distance we must first traverse the space that is near", and expounded on it as the essence of the methodology of classical scholarship and self-cultivation.[84] The scholarship of his day sought to "skip the shallow and near and plunge into the deep and distant," and in so doing failed not only to grasp the more profound lessons of the classics but the plain and simple to boot.[85] For him the ultimate lessons of the Way lay in daily activities and nowhere else. Confucius' conception of "studying the mundane and consequently attaining the sublime"[86] not only formed the basis of Pak's criticisms of the Ch'eng-Chu school's cognitive and existential orientation but also of many of the alternative interpretations that he proposed in the *Thoughtful Elucidations*.[87]

Pak not only criticized Chu Hsi for his speculative philosophical standpoint and inconsistencies of argument, but also differed with him concerning the rearrangement of the order of certain classical texts. Like Yun Hyu, he maintained that Chu Hsi's amendments to the texts of the *Great Learning* and the *Mean* had still failed to restore the original form which had been lost during the Ch'in, and he advanced his own corrections.

Pak's distaste for metaphysical speculation reflects the characteristics of early Evidential Scholarship in the late Ming and early Ch'ing, and it is indeed probable that he obtained the works of contemporary Chinese scholars when he visited China as a member of the Korean embassy to the Ch'ing in 1668.[88]

It is worthy of note that the "heterodox" writings of both Yun Hyu and Pak Sedang were only publicly censured, and thus brought under the general scrutiny of the court and bureaucracy, after political confrontations with Song and his faction—in the first instance through the Rites Dispute of 1659, and in the second as a result of Pak's thinly veiled criticisms of Song in his draft for Yi Kyŏngsŏk's memorial tablet. Both of these events occurred during periods when the position of Song's faction was particularly insecure, poised either on the verge of being displaced from power, or attempting to consolidate it after a period of Southerner dominance. More research is thus warranted to explore the possibility that other critiques of Ch'eng-Chu interpretations were written during the same period or later by literati who did not propel themselves into center stage through the frank expression of their views and personal confrontations with Song's faction.

Whether or not such works existed, critically minded thinkers and opponents of the Old Doctrine faction would have been much less inclined to produce them after the treatment accorded to Yun and Pak, and even if they had, after 1694 the Old Doctrine faction were, for most of the time, in a secure enough position not to unduly concern themselves with attacks on their ideology, and thus expose such views to the light of history. In view of this, it is hardly surprising that more than a century elapsed before another detailed critique of Chu Hsi's views came to light, in the form of Tasan's exposition of the classics.

Factional Alignment and Attitudes toward Orthodox Neo-Confucianism

In the interim, criticisms were continually made of the institutional side of Ch'eng-Chu orthodoxy, if not the substance of its teachings, by a broad variety of thinkers associated with factions that had been displaced from power. Yu Hyŏngwŏn, one of the earlier reform-minded thinkers who, as a descendant of the powerless Northerner faction, stayed out of politics altogether, initiated a new trend with his major work *Pan'gye surok* (Writings of Yu Hyŏngwŏn). In this encyclopedic work he indicated dissatisfaction with the prevailing order by proposing systematic and often radical reforms in such areas as land ownership, the appointment and pay of officials, and government structure. On a philosophical level, as Chu Hsi had done, he equated the Great Ultimate, the cosmic source of change and transformation, with principle.[89] He also indulged in the traditional pastime of speculating about the relationship between principle and material force, but took a more monistic view than Chu Hsi and T'oegye, maintaining that, "Although one cannot point to material force and say that it is principle, outside of material force there is no principle. In short, principle is simply the principle of material force."[90]

Criticism of orthodox Neo-Confucianism in a broad sense was not limited to opponents of the Old Doctrine faction. More than a century later, Pak Chiwŏn, who was driven out of power by a rival clique within his own faction, the Old Doctrine, added weight and literary refinement to critiques of Neo-Confucian bureaucracy and its idiosyncracies. He accomplished this with his devastating attack on the class of scholar-bureaucrats in the satirical narratives *Tale of a Yangban* (*Yangban chŏn*), *Tale of Mr. Hŏ* (*Hŏsaeng chŏn*), and *Tiger's Rebuke* (*Hojil*). Pak Chiwŏn and his contemporaries Hong Taeyong, Yi Tŏngmu, and Pak Chega, were leading members of the "School of Northern Learning," so called because it reflected recent trends in Ch'ing thought and scholarship, particularly an emphasis on the growth of commerce and the use of technology for the benefit of the people, as well as new literary styles.[91]

On the other hand critiques of Ch'eng-Chu Learning itself as opposed to bureaucratic orthodoxy in general, and interest in unorthodox intellectual currents, took root and developed among the opponents of Song Siyŏl's faction. Chŏng Chedu (Hagok, 1649-1736), recognized as the outstanding proponent of the Chosŏn Wang Yang-ming school, took as his mentors Yun Chŭng and Pak Sech'ae (1631-95), both leading figures of the Young Doctrine whose opposition to Song's policies led to the decisive split in Old Doctrine–Young Doctrine relations.[92]

Other more direct confrontations with the Ch'eng-Chu school emerged among the Southerners, in the writings of Yi Ik and his school, after a period of respite following the tumultuous years of Yun Hyu's involvement in the Rites Disputes. Their dissatisfaction with the Ch'eng-Chu school was paralleled by a curiosity for, and involvement in, other intellectual currents such as Ch'ing scholarship and Western Learning, including Catholicism.

Although both schools of thought were essentially progressive in nature and pressed for reforms, the Old Doctrine–affiliated School of Northern Learning and the Southerner-affiliated school of Yi Ik showed clear differences in approach, not only in their critical stance toward the prevailing orthodoxy but also in the areas of reform they proposed. Leading Southerner thinkers such as Yi Ik and Tasan wrote a great deal on administrative reform, basing many of their proposals on the institutions outlined in the *Rites of Chou*, which depicts the structure and functions of Chou dynasty government.[93] Their critiques of Chosŏn government institutions and administrative methods, and proposals for their reform, would have certainly shed an unfavorable light on the accomplishments of the dominant subfaction of the Old Doctrine, with whom they were even more at odds than their counterparts in the school of Northern Learning.

Following the lead of Yun Hyu, Southerner thinkers such as Yi Ik, his student Kwŏn Ch'ŏlsin, and Tasan, rejected overdependence on Chu Hsi's exposition of the Confucian teachings. They were Confucian philosophers at heart, emphasizing the study of the Six Classics in addition, and sometimes in contrast to, the Four Books edited by Chu Hsi.[94] The expression "the study of the Six Classics" became a byword for the new tendency, inspired by the Han Learning movement of the Ch'ing, to revert to the whole of the Confucian canon rather than the Four Books which Chu Hsi had abstracted from it.[95] And as the Four Books had become the staple diet of candidates for the civil service examinations, the "Six Classics" symbolized the learning of the Way as opposed to the "vulgar learning" of those regarded to be pseudo-Confucian bureaucrats, or sometimes, as opposed to Ch'eng-Chu learning itself.[96]

The Evidential Learning of the Ch'ing greatly facilitated their attempts to uncover the classical meanings of concepts and phrases. The "Ancient Learning" to be found in the Six Classics through such methods was, particularly for Yi Ik, Kwŏn Ch'ŏlsin, and Tasan, the basis on which they questioned the authority of the Ch'eng-Chu worldview and tried to establish alternative perspectives. It was also the source of information on classical rites and institutions to which they ascribed great significance in the quest for humane government. The distinctively Confucian methodology of "familiarization with the old to understand the new"[97] might best summarize their approach. On the other hand, the Northern Learning scholars were a little more sceptical about the relevance of ancient teachings and institutions in general, and their comparative distaste for detailed metaphysical discourse and exegetical research reflected a characteristic impatience with abstractions and backward-looking orientations. They were interested in new literary forms rather than the classical exegesis of Evidential Learning which sought to uncover the past, using allegory for satirical purposes to assail Neo-Confucian attitudes rather than ideologies.

Tasan and the School of Yi Ik

Yi Ik is regarded as a major figure among late Chosŏn thinkers for his detailed work on the reform of political institutions, including central and regional political administration, the civil service examination system, and the management of the economy. Yi Ik also wrote extensively on the Confucian classics. He did not question the basic validity of the Ch'eng-Chu metaphysical system itself, and, in the tradition of Chu Hsi, associated human nature with principle.[98]

On the other hand Yi Ik did not appear to be happy with many of his contemporaries' blind dependence on Chu Hsi's scholarship, and their intolerance of other schools of thought. As Yun Hyu had done, Yi criticized excessive reliance on commentaries in general. In an essay on "Researching the Classics," he argued that it would be better to require students preparing for the civil service examinations to thoroughly grasp the content of one classic rather than achieve the required familiarization with a multitude of commentaries on the same. In the same essay he added that commentaries served simply as a guide in obtaining a personal appreciation of the meaning embedded in the classical texts.[99]

Although Yi appears to have had the greatest respect for Chu Hsi and his views as well as those of Chu's Korean counterpart T'oegye, he was at times, using the subtlest language, ready to differ. He went as far as implying that Chu Hsi's edition of the *Great Learning* was flawed, in the respect that his insertion of a new chapter of commentary on "investigating things" (*ko-wu*) was uncalled for, as well as expressing doubt about the content of the commentary itself.[100] Furthermore Yi derided scholars who venerated Chu Hsi's *Family Ritual*, a book which carried great authority in Korea, to the neglect of classical ritual, maintaining that it was an incomplete, sketchy work that Chu Hsi had written before his scholarship reached maturity.[101]

In the tradition of many of his Confucian predecessors, Yi also wrote an essay exclusively on the subject of "heterodoxy." What is remarkable is that, instead of launching an attack on the traditional enemies of the orthodox Neo-Confucian tradition such as Wang Yang-ming, he began by noting that Confucius had only warned about the dangers of *focusing* on heterodox teachings,[102] that this implied there was no harm in simply becoming acquainted with them, and even that there were things to be learnt from "lesser" teachings.[103]

Yi called his learning *Susahak* or "Classical Learning," referring to the rivers *Su* and *Sa*, (C: *Shu* and *Hsiu*) near the banks of which Confucius was said to have been born, and where he educated his followers. The usage of the term *Susahak* contrasted, perhaps intentionally, with the expression *Chŏngjuhak*, or Ch'eng-Chu learning.[104]

Two members of the school of Yi Ik, both of them prominent figures in the Southerners faction, became the most outspoken critics of Chu Hsi's views in the Late Chosŏn. One was a student of Yi Ik, Kwŏn Ch'ŏlsin, and the other was Tasan, an avid reader of Yi's writings.

Although Yi Ik was nearing the end of his days when Kwŏn became his student, he placed great value on his young follower, comparing his scholarship and behavior to that of Confucius' disciples Tzu-hsia and Tzu-kung, who were reputed to excel in these respective areas.[105]

Unfortunately, it appears that nothing except a few letters remains of Kwŏn's work, and so far the only accounts of his writings to be found that provide any detail at all are contained in the epitaph Tasan wrote for him,[106] as well as an outline,[107] also written by Tasan, of Kwŏn's interpretations of key concepts in the classics, particularly the *Great Learning*.[108] From these brief descriptions it is evident that some of Kwŏn's key ideas, including the concept of virtue (*te/tŏk*) and the role of "comprehending things and extending knowledge" (*ko-wu chih-chih/kyŏngmul ch'iji*) in self-cultivation, were taken up by Tasan. Yi Ik's ideas had a considerable influence on Tasan in the area of institutional reform, but it was the views of Kwŏn that were most closely reflected in Tasan's philosophical writings.

Even at the time Tasan wrote Kwŏn's epitaph, only two of Kwŏn's works, including two *chuan* or fascicles on the *Classic of Odes*, and one on the *Great Learning*, were still extant.[109] Nonetheless, having been well acquainted with Kwŏn, Tasan was able to provide a brief overview of his work on the classics. These scant details, and particularly their close correspondence to the views of Tasan, will be discussed in more detail in chapter 3. Here it will suffice to say that the particular philosophical views of Kwŏn mentioned in the epitaph, on the validity and content of the *Record of Rites* edition of the *Great*

Learning, and on the Mencian discussion of virtue and the "four beginnings" (*ssu-t'uan/sadan*), directly contradicted the views of Chu Hsi. Recognising the stark differences of viewpoint between the two, Tasan hastened to mention that "although some of these views differed from those of Chu Hsi, [*Kwŏn*] loved and respected Chu Hsi throughout his whole life" and that Kwŏn himself used to claim that "with all sincerity, nobody feels the same affection for Chu Hsi as I."[110]

According to Tasan, during an age when scholarship had become enmeshed in speculation and sophism that revolved around discussions of "principle and material force" or "feelings and nature," Kwŏn consistently placed emphasis on practical ethics, in his writings and in his life. This emphasis on the practical ethics of Confucius and Mencius, accompanied by a distaste for Chu Hsi's metaphysics, also permeated the work of Tasan and formed the backbone of his philosophy.[111] Most probably it was Kwŏn's rejection of Sung metaphysics and his reversion to earlier commentaries and classical sources that prompted Tasan to say that Kwŏn's "interpretations were based on ancient texts."[112]

At the turn of the eighteenth century, Tasan himself took Kwŏn's critical stance a step further by questioning both the relevance and the orthodoxy of the metaphysical framework that Chu Hsi had used to discuss human nature and ethics.

Like many of his fellow literati, Tasan's interests extended beyond philosophy. His encyclopedic scholarship included proposals on institutional and agricultural reform, technological development, and discourses on such varied subjects as history, geography, national defense, and medicine, as well as extensive and detailed research on the Confucian classics. His major works are listed in the appendix. His scholarship also evidenced the critical and practical spirit delineated by Ch'ŏn Kwanu as being a predominant characteristic of Sirhak thought.[113] Indeed, it is the detailed and concrete nature of his proposals on local administrative reform, spelt out in his *Mongmin simsŏ* (Reflections on fostering the people) that brought him recognition among nineteenth-century administrators, and recognition as a household name in present-day Korea. Nonetheless, as we shall see, it is in the realm of moral as well as material practicality, that Tasan brought a major theme of late Chosŏn scholarship to philosophical fruition.

Following the lead of Yi Ik, Tasan referred to his scholarship as "Classical Learning" (*susahak*).[114] In his attempt to reevaluate the teachings of Confucius and Mencius he found in the Evidential Learning of the Ch'ing, which emphasized proof and verification in analysis of the classics, an effective means of clarifying ancient terms and concepts. On that basis, he challenged certain key assumptions and teachings that formed the bedrock of Chu Hsi's Neo-Confucian worldview. He justified his views by appealing to a more ancient orthodoxy, claiming that the Han, Tang, and Sung interpretations of the classics had, far from providing clarification, thrown a veil over their original import.

Nonetheless, Tasan and for that matter, other Chosŏn critics of orthodox Neo-Confucian thought, were not as explicitly and diametrically opposed to the Ch'eng-Chu teachings as were many of their late Ming-Ch'ing counterparts, such as Mao Ch'i-ling (1623–1716), Yen Yüan (1635–1704), Li Kung (1659–1733), and Tai Chen (1724–77). One obvious reason for this tendency would be their reluctance to stir up the same animosities that had been provoked by the views of Yun Hyu, and that had had such disproportionate repercussions. At the same time, Tasan did not hesitate, time and again, to express his deep admiration for Chu Hsi, and as this book indicates, it is clear that such praise was not simply rhetorical artifice aimed at deflecting the disapproval of ideological conservatives. Tasan, in the tradition of his Southerner predecessors Yun Hyu and Yi Ik, was a defender of scholarly objectivity and freedom of expression. The appeal of Yun Hyu that he did not want to differ with Chu Hsi "simply for the sake of differing" could equally have been voiced by Tasan, who was ready to quote Chu Hsi's views when they corresponded with his own, as well as criticize them in detail when they conflicted.

Tasan was not only influenced by the scholarship of the Ch'ing, but also by the Tokugawa proponents of "Ancient Learning" (*kogaku*), and particularly by the work of Korean Southerner scholars such as Yun Hyu, Yi Ik, and his student Kwŏn Ch'ŏlsin.

Tasan had extensive family connections with Yi Ik, whose scholarship he greatly admired. Whereas Yi Ik's writings greatly influenced Tasan's outlook on political and economic reform as well as his approach to scholarship in general, it was Kwŏn's work, and through it the work of Yun Hyu, that made a clearly recognizable imprint on important facets of his philosophy. Yun, Kwŏn and Tasan were all monotheistically inclined, and their depiction of the Confucian Heaven as a personal being stood in stark contrast to Chu Hsi's interpretation of Heaven as principle. Kwŏn and Tasan in particular took an active interest in Catholicism, which, as one aspect of the recently imported "Western Learning," had only been an intellectual curiosity for Yi Ik. As will be implied in chapter 4, it is hard to say to what extent these interests in Western Learning affected their perceptions of the Confucian Heaven, as early Japanese *kogaku* figures, as well as Yun Hyu, seem to have been heading in a monotheistic direction before Western Learning had directly impacted the world of the East Asian literati.

It is hardly surprising that Tasan's attitude toward orthodox Neo-Confucianism was influenced by the example and work of Yun Hyu. Tasan's mother was a direct descendant of Yun Sŏndo, the Southerner patriarch who had defended Yun Hyu's position during the first mourning rites dispute and caused a furor by attacking the Old Doctrine faction for having degraded the status of the monarchy. Furthermore, Yi Hajin, the father of Tasan's indirect mentor, Yi Ik, had also been a principal supporter of Yun Hyu during the second rites dispute, and appeared to share Yun's critical attitude toward Chu Hsi's learning.[115]

The strong intellectual links between all of these Southerner figures are revealed by Kwŏn in the following remark, quoted by Tasan: "After T'oegye, the scholarship of Hahŏn (Yun Hyu) excelled, and after Hahŏn, the scholarship of Sŏngho (Yi Ik) passed on this inherited wisdom."[116] Pak Sŏngmu observes that, considering this was a time when the Old Doctrine faction were solidly entrenched in government, and few dared even mention the name of their historical enemy Yun Hyu, it must have been a considerable admiration for Yun's person that had prompted Kwŏn to use such language. And in turn, the fact that Tasan should quote such a comment indicates the importance that he placed on Yun's views.[117]

In conclusion, it appears that critical attitudes toward the Ch'eng-Chu teachings, accompanied by a call for a return to "classical learning," and a readiness to explore new currents of thought, germinated in the thought of Yun Hyu and flourished in the writings of Southerner scholars, and particularly Tasan. It was the Rites

Disputes that had propelled the "unconventional" views of Yun Hyu to center stage, and polarized, or at least set the pattern for, the divergent philosophical positions of the Southerner reformers and the Old Doctrine faction, based on the sharply contrasting worldviews of Yun Hyu and Song Siyŏl.[118]

This research does not imply that Tasan's extensive philosophy was essentially a by-product of factional dispute. Nonetheless, it does indicate that the conflicts between the factions, which in a Confucian world were often waged on a philosophical level, stimulated certain areas of inquiry, and particularly critiques of orthodox Neo-Confucian thought. In the case of Tasan, dissatisfaction with the ruling ideology served as a springboard for the development of a remarkably well-integrated, alternative view of the human condition.

2

The Road to Tea Mountain

Chŏng Yagyong, or Tasan, as he later came to be known,[1] was born in 1762, the 38th year of King Yŏngjo's reign. He was the fourth son of Chŏng Chaewŏn (1730–92), who had served a lengthy stint as magistrate of Chinju County, and his wife, Yun Sugin.[2] At the time of his birth, Tasan's family lived by the upper reaches of the Han River in Kwangju County, Kyŏnggi Province.[3] Earlier that year the country had been thrown into turmoil by the tragic death of Crown Prince Sado on the orders of his father, King Yŏngjo. Tasan's father, badly shaken by the event and its factional repercussions, had decided to leave politics. When he was born, Tasan was thus given the courtesy name "Kwinong" or "Returning to the land."[4]

At the end of the Koryŏ period, Tasan's ancestors on his father's side, the Chŏngs of Aphae, had lived in Paech'ŏn, Hwanghae Province, now part of North Korea. However at the foundation of the Chosŏn dynasty they moved to Hanyang, which is now Seoul. The first of the family to serve in government in the new capital was Chŏng Chagŭp (1423–87), who in 1460 took a position in the Office of Diplomatic Correspondence under King Sejo (1455–68) after passing the *munkwa*, the highest level of civil service examination. Including Chagŭp, nine consecutive generations of the Chŏng family served the kings of the Chosŏn in various government posts, including key positions in the influential State Council, the Office of Special Counsellors, and the War Board.[5]

In an age when social status was directly related to government office, Tasan was hardly exaggerating when he referred to his family as one of noble lineage.[6] Nonetheless he himself was not born into the higher echelons of the ruling elite. Chŏng Siyun (1646–1713), five generations prior to Tasan, and his second son Chŏng Tobok (1666–1720) were the last of the family line prior to Tasan's father to serve in public office, due to the exclusion of their faction, the Southerners, from senior positions in government after their fall from power in 1694.[7]

When Siyun left office in 1699 at the age of fifty-three, he moved to Mahyŏnri, by the banks of Lake Tu in Kyŏnggi Province, Tasan's eventual birthplace. His second son Tobok served in office in the capital, but his first son Tot'ae, Tasan's direct ancestor, remained in Ch'och'ŏn, near Mahyŏnri, where Siyun built a thatched cottage, and where Tasan spent his youth.[8]

Chŏng Siyun studied the Neo-Confucian teachings for three months under the scholar Chŏng Sihan (Udam, 1625–1707) of the Southerners faction. His second cousin, and two of his sons, Tot'ae, Tasan's direct ancestor, and Toje (1675–1729), were taught by Udam on a regular basis.[9] Furthermore, Chŏng Siyun was an intimate lifelong friend of Yi Chik, a second cousin of Yi Ik, and as a result a long-standing relationship was established between the two families. In his youth Yi Ik met Chŏng Siyun a number of times.[10]

Yi Ik had deep regard for Udam's scholarship and person, and consequently very much regretted not having studied under him, since Udam was still alive in his youth. According to Yi, Udam was the orthodox heir of the T'oegye school.[11] Tasan heaped even more praises on Udam for the same qualities, and frequently mentioned him in the context of his family background.[12]

Chŏng Toje inherited Udam's learning to the extent that he came next to Udam in the praise he received from later scholars, conveying this learning to his nephew, Tasan's great-grandfather Chŏng Hangsin, as well as other relatives. Chŏng Hangsin educated his sons and cousins in the same tradition, including Tasan's father Chaewŏn.

Tasan's father played a major role in his son's early education. Inheriting the academic tradition of Udam, he was well-versed in the classics and histories, and personally taught Tasan to the age of fifteen.

Tasan's father had kept regular company with Southerner scholars since his youth, and was well acquainted with the prominent Ch'ae Chegong (1720–99) and his circle of associates and friends. The two of them formed ties of kinship as well as friendship through the marriage of two of their children. It was Ch'ae who spearheaded the final, brief reaccession to power of the Southerners when he was appointed third state councillor in 1788, the twelfth year of Chŏngjo's reign, and who backed Chaewŏn's appointment to office during this period.[13]

Tasan's mother Yun Sugin was descended from a prestigious family line which was also closely affiliated with the Southerners faction and in consequence had long been involved in factional struggle with the Westerners and their subfaction the Old Doctrine. Tasan's mother's line was distinguished by a number of outstanding scholars, and could trace its descent to the Southerners leader and master of Sijo composition Yun Sŏndo (Kosan, 1587–1671), who, as we have seen, sided with Yun Hyu as a fierce critic of Song Siyŏl's faction during the mourning rites dispute of 1659. Yun Sŏndo's great grandson Yun Tusŏ (Kongjae, 1668–1715), who was also well known for his artistic skills, was none other than Tasan's great-grandfather on his mother's side. This side of Tasan's family also had close links with the family of Yi Ik.

According to Tasan, Yun Tusŏ and his elder brother Yun Hŭngsŏ (1662–1733) handed down the teachings of Yun Sŏndo, and together with the three brothers Yi Ik, Yi Cham, and Yi Sŏ (1662–1723), they breathed new life into the study of the Six Classics, which had hitherto been treated with disdain by the sons of the aristocracy in the capital. The inference here is that, in preparation for the civil service examinations, career-minded youth had engrossed themselves in the mechanical study of the Four Books and Chu Hsi's commentaries, to the neglect of the rest of the Confucian canon. In addition, Tasan indicates, this group of Southerner scholars revived the learning of T'oegye and Hankang (Chŏng Gu, 1543–1620),[14] which had previously been limited to the Yŏngnam region, in their home province of Kyŏnggi.[15] According to Tasan's chronological biography, Yun Tusŏ took a liking to "ancient" learning. He kept a library that was entirely devoted to "administration and practical usage," (*kyŏngje siryong*).[16]

Tasan mentions that, in keeping with the high academic standards of his predecessors, from an early age he had an exceptional ability to read. At the age of six (1768) his compositions already revealed unusually sharp powers of observation and inference, prompting his father to remark that he would "excel in mathematics and calendrical science." By the age of nine (1771) he had already written the "Three Eyebrow Collection" a small volume of poems named after a characteristic scar on his forehead resulting from an early bout with smallpox. By this time he had also begun study for the civil service examinations and was making rapid progress in the study of the classics, histories, and rules of metre.[17]

For the following five years his father continued to distance himself from government, and was consequently able to concentrate on the supervision of his son's intensive studies. During this time Tasan was already receiving praise for his poetry,[18] for which he became well known in later life, and which contributed in making him a favourite of King Chŏngjo (r.1776–1800), who often enjoyed exchanging compositions with him.[19]

At the age of fourteen (1776), not an unusual age for the customs of the time, Tasan married the daughter of a certain Hong Hwabo, a member of the P'ungsan Hong clan who had served as a royal secretary. In the same year he moved to the capital, where his father was reemployed in government as assistant section chief of the Board of Taxation, after the succession of the new king, Chŏngjo.[20] The following year Tasan was introduced to the writings of Yi Ik by Yi's direct descendent and Tasan's companion Yi Kahwan (1742–1801), as well as Yi Sŭnghun (1756–1801), both of whom were related to Tasan. Yi Ik's writings, which were already much talked about, deeply impressed the young Tasan, to the extent that he decided to devote himself to scholarship.[21]

At the age of twenty-one (1783) Tasan passed the literary licentiate examination *chinsagwa*, which qualified him for entry to the *Sŏnggyun'gwan*, the National Confucian Academy. There the quality of his scholarship won him the attention, and consequently the admiration, of King Chŏngjo. In 1784 Chŏngjo presented a list of eighty questions on the *Mean* to the Academy, including one on the subject of T'oegye and Yulgok's expositions of the relationship between principle, material force, the Four Beginnings, and the Seven Emotions. In contrast to his friend and fellow Southerner Yi Pyŏk, who expressed agreement with T'oegye's position, Tasan's views, in his words, "happened to concur with Yulgok's interpretations." On examining the papers, the king highly commended Tasan for "breaking away from vulgar convention" as well as for his accuracy and objectivity, and assigned his work top place. This prompted the Royal Secretary Kim Sangjip to remark that "Chŏng is certain to make a name for himself after receiving such praise."[22] The objectivity that the king had referred to was reflected in Tasan's refusal to blindly follow the established Southerners' tradition of supporting the views of their champion T'oegye over those of Yulgok, who was revered by the Old Doctrine. This tendency for objectivity remained a hallmark of Tasan's work, particularly reflected in his readiness to both praise and criticize certain schools of thought rather than adopt rigid attitudes in favour of one or the other. Nonetheless, it is clear that, on a broad level, he was influenced by his Southerner predecessors. In answer to another question on the *Great Learning,* Tasan had interpreted the meaning of "illustrious virtue" (*ming-te/myŏngdŏk*), a key concept of the classic, to be "filial piety, fraternal respect, and parental love."[23] The king wanted to give Tasan top place, but Ch'ae Chegong, who was supervising the examination, remarked that Tasan's views must have been derived from Yun Hyu, and gave him second place. Ch'ae also mentioned that another leading Southerner figure, Yi Kiyang, had taken the same position, and quoted him as having formerly heaped lavish praise on Yun Hyu.[24]

From then on, Tasan's performance in the various levels of examinations as well as his skill at composition continued to attract the king's attention and special favor. This included the bestowal of royal gifts and personal audiences as well as invitations to the Royal Lectures.[25] Over the years Tasan became a close favorite of King Chŏngjo, and his chronological biography in particular is full of detailed accounts of the formal, informal, and even affectionate exchanges between them. Impressed by Tasan's scholarship, personality, and administrative skills, and most probably a little partial to Tasan's affiliation to the "Expediency Subfaction" (*Sip'a*) of the Southerners,[26] Chŏngjo clearly trusted Tasan and intended to promote him to positions in government of the highest rank.[27] Unfortunately for Tasan, his Old Doctrine colleagues were well aware of these royal intentions.

During his second year (1784) at the Sŏnggyun'gwan Tasan accompanied his friend Yi Pyŏk (1754–86) to Tumi Gorge, where he heard about Western Learning for the first time and obtained a book on its teachings.[28]

Interest in Catholicism among Koreans had started long before. Yi Sugwang had mentioned Matteo Ricci's work on Catholicism one and a half centuries previously. Yi Ik and his followers showed a particular interest not only in the scientific aspect of Western Learning, but also in its religious side. During the reign of Chŏngjo this involvement became more than a passing curiosity for a particular group of Southerner intellectuals, many of whom were affiliated with the school of Yi Ik. In 1784 a member of this group, Yi Sunghun (1756–1801), the son of the newly appointed emissary to the Ch'ing, was baptized by a Western Catholic priest in Peking and returned to Korea with books on Western Learning, the same year that the young Tasan was introduced to the new literature by Yi Pyŏk. On his return Yi Sunghun baptized Kwŏn Ilshin, Kwŏn Ch'ŏlsin's brother, and Yi Pyŏk, and the three of them became founding members of the Korean Catholic Church. Tasan could hardly have escaped the influence of Catholicism, for his colleagues in the Southerners, many of whom were related to him, as well as his brothers, were strongly drawn to it. Tasan, his elder brothers Chŏng Yakchŏn and Chŏng Yakchong, his close associate Yi Kahwan, and Kwŏn Ch'ŏlsin all became involved in the activities of the early Church.[29]

In the conservative atmosphere of Chosŏn Korea, opposition to the new movement was not long in consolidating itself. One year after Yi Sunghun's visit to Peking, in 1785, official repression began with the proscription of Western Learning by Chŏngjo, and in the following year the import of books on Western Learning was banned. Nonetheless, in 1788 the fortunes of the Southerners, who had been excluded from high government position from the end of Sukchong's reign (1674–1720) began to change for the better, with the appointment of Ch'ae Chegong, the Southerners' leader, to the position of Third State Councillor.[30]

In 1789 Tasan took top place in the *taekwa*, the higher level examination for civil service, and as he now had two highly placed supporters in the persons of the king and Ch'ae Chegong, this qualification opened the door for service in a series of important government posts.[31] In 1790 Tasan as well as his cousin Yun Chinul (1762–1815) and four other members of their faction, the Southerners, were offered promotion to key positions in the Office of Royal Decrees by Ch'ae Chegong and the director of the Office of Special Counselors.

This triggered off the fierce protest of the Old Doctrine, who, aware that their monopoly on the Office of Royal Decrees was being eroded, accused the authors of the reshuffle of factional bias. Consequently Tasan, who had been offered the post of diarist in the same office (Sr. 9), refused to take up the position, due to, in his words, "disapproval" in certain quarters.[32] Nonetheless, Ch'ae Chegong had his way, and in spite of continuing pressure from the Old Doctrine, Tasan was appointed to much more senior and influential positions in the same year, including fourth censor in the Office of the Censor-General (Sr. 6) and fourth inspector at the Office of the Inspector General (Sr. 5).[33]

Then in 1791 the so-called "Chinsan incident" brought the Catholic Church into direct confrontation with Neo-Confucian orthodoxy. This provided the Old Doctrine and particularly members of the Old Doctrine "Principle subfaction" (*Pyŏkp'a*) with a pretext for pressuring the king to remove the "pro-Western faction" from power. This was in their political interests as the "pro-Western faction" to which Tasan and his comrades belonged included many young "up and coming" figures in the Expediency subfaction of the Southerners, the historical enemy of the Principle subfaction of the Old Doctrine. A literary licentiate graduate named Yun Chich'ung from Chinsan in north Chŏlla Province, a cousin of Tasan, was executed for refusing, in accordance with a papal ruling implemented in 1742, to prepare an ancestral tablet for his mother. Following this, opponents of Tasan's faction led by an influential member of the Old Doctrine, Hong Nagan, petitioned Ch'ae Chegong, warning him that a group of seven or eight officials who "appeared to be capable and wise" would instigate rebellion. This was an indirect reference to Tasan and his "pro-Western" colleagues. Nonetheless the sympathies of Ch'ae Chegong, who was a leading Southerner figure himself, and the king, lay with the pro-Western faction, who came out of the confrontation ruffled but intact.[34]

Chŏngjo's tacit support for Tasan and his close colleagues was not unrelated to their factional affiliation. During the reign of the previous monarch, Yŏngjo (1724–76), the so-called "Four Colors" (the Southerners, Northerners, Old Doctrine, and Young Doctrine) were further split into subfactions over another fierce controversy that revolved around the problem of succession, in this instance the issue of Crown Prince Sado's death.[35]

Sado (1735–62, later named Changhŏn), the second son of Yŏngjo, became Crown Prince on account of his elder brother's early demise. The prince came to be at loggerheads with his young stepmother Kim (Queen Chŏngsun) as well as the king's favourite concubine, and his behavior came increasingly under question. Consequently, a memorial was presented to Yŏngjo accusing his son of gross misconduct, including the killing of palace concubines, the invitation of Buddhist priests to the palace, and the importation of literature on Western Learning. These accusations were prompted by a group of Old Doctrine officials including the father of Queen Chŏngsun. Finally, under increasing pressure from his palace entourage as well as Old Doctrine officials, Yŏngjo put his son to death. This act split officialdom into two groups, the Principle group, which condoned Yŏngjo's behaviour, and the Expediency group, which strongly opposed it. Consequently, over the factional conflict between the "Four Colors" yet another bitter rivalry was superimposed, the conflict between the Expediency subfaction and the Principle subfaction, which persisted through Chŏngjo's reign to the early years of Sunjo (1800–34).[36] Although the Old Doctrine were split down the middle by the affair, most members of the Southerners supported Prince Sado and considered themselves members of the Expediency subfaction.[37]

When Chŏngjo took the throne, he tried to fulfil his role as a filial son by attempting to vindicate his father Sado.[38] Consequently, the fortunes of the Expediency subfaction, and particularly the Southerners Expediency subfaction, gradually improved at the expense of their rivals, the Principle subfaction. On account of this, as well as the enforcement of the so-called "policy of impartiality", Southerner officials found themselves in the top ranks of government for the first time since the reign of Sukchong. The Old Doctrine were particularly dismayed to see a Southerner leader, Ch'ae Chegong, appointed as chief state councillor in 1793, and did their very best to discredit him and his colleagues.[39] The involvement of Tasan and his friends in Western Learning provided them with the best of pretexts to do so. Tasan himself, in the center of the factional turmoil—as a key figure in the Southerners Expediency subfaction "pro-Western group" and a strong sympathizer of Prince Sado and his son, Chŏngjo—was not immune to factional antipathies. On occasion, when pointing out the political intrigues of the Old Doctrine Principle subfaction, he would refer to them as the "evil party."[40]

In 1792, after the turmoil produced by the Chinsan incident had subsided, Tasan was appointed sixth counselor in the Office of Special Counselors (Sr. 6). In the winter of the same year, the king, impressed by the successful construction of a floating bridge over the Han River, master-minded by Tasan, requested him to submit detailed plans for the construction of the walls at the emergency capital in Suwŏn. The cranes and systems of pulleys that Tasan devised for this project, using various sources including Chinese manuals that were based on Western texts, were given the highest praise by the king, who claimed that Tasan's scientific expertise had considerably reduced the cost of construction.[41]

In 1794 Tasan was appointed to the position of lecturer at the National Confucian Academy (Sr. 5), and then to fifth and sixth counselor in the Office of Special Counselors (Sr. 5, 6). Very soon after, the king personally conferred him with the trusted position of the king's secret envoy to Kyŏnggi Province, where he was responsible for investigating irregularities in local administration.[42]

In 1795, the sixtieth anniversary of the birth of Prince Sado, the king planned to grant an honorific title to the prince as well as his queen. The honorific title to be conferred was to reflect Sado's character and status, and not surprisingly, the choice of names became a focus of conflict between the Expediency subfaction and the Principle subfaction, his supporters and opponents respectively. Tasan drew attention to this event in both of his self-written epitaphs, providing considerable detail in the epitaph for his collected works as well as a mention in the much briefer epitaph to be placed in his grave. According to Tasan's account, Ch'ae Chegong, Yi Kahwan, as well as himself, played leading roles in determining the appropriate titles. In particular, Yi Kahwan and Tasan defended the name of Chŏngjo's lineage by arguing that Sado and his queen be referred to in the most honorific terms possible.[43]

It was not long before Tasan's enemies, determined to put a stop to the rise of the Southerners, and wary of Tasan's increasing influence as a close favourite of the king, found another pretext to discredit him and his colleagues. In the same year word got out that a Chinese priest named Chou Wen-mo (1752–1801) had secretly entered Korea and was actively engaged in gaining support for the newly founded Catholic church. Chou managed to evade the authorities, but three of his followers, including Yun Yuil (1760–95), whom Tasan had previously befriended as a member of the "pro-Western" group before the persecution, were arrested and killed. The King refused to accept rumors, instigated by the Old Doctrine Principle subfaction, that Tasan and his friends had been backing Chou's activities. Nonetheless, to pacify the indignation of the Principle subfaction, he sent Tasan to Kŭmjŏng, South P'yŏngan Province, as superintendent of post stations (Jr. 6).[44] This also provided Tasan with an opportunity to prove that he had renounced any lingering affiliation he might have had to Catholicism. Many of those working at the post stations in Kumjŏng had embraced the new religion, and, following the personal instruction of the king, Tasan did his best to enforce the ban on Catholicism and encourage them to return to their Confucian ways and perform the ancestral rites.[45]

In 1796 Tasan was again promoted, this time to his highest post yet, fourth minister at the Board of War (Sr. 3), and then to the equally influential positions of fifth and fourth royal secretaries. In the following year, in the face of the repeated accusations of his opponents, Tasan turned down a further position in the Royal Secretariat and instead accepted a post away from the capital, in Koksan, Hwanghae Province.[46] During his service as county magistrate in Koksan, as well as during his previous period of office as secret envoy in Kyŏnggi Province, Tasan had first-hand experience of *yangban* excesses and the fierce public resentment they fed.[47]

In 1799 Tasan found himself back in the capital. For a time he was appointed to the position of Third Minister of the Board of Punishments, where on the recommendation of the king he took up many of the responsibilities of the ageing minister himself.[48] But the following year, troubled by continuing accusations and rumours of his affiliation to the church, he retired with his family to his home in Mahyŏn ri. On the insistence of the king he returned to the capital shortly after, but this period in office did not last long. In the summer of 1800, the day after he had presented Tasan with a collection of books and requested his participation in an editorial project, Chŏngjo took ill. A month later he died, leaving the country in the hands of

Yŏngjo's queen, Queen Dowager Kim, who had become regent to Chŏngjo's young son, Sunjo.[49]

Tasan, deprived of the protection of Chŏngjo as well as that of the influential Ch'ae Chegong, who had died the previous year, was exposed to the opportunism of the Old Doctrine Principle subfaction, who were profiting from their close ties to the Queen Dowager, secured during the reign of Yongjo. Shortly after her accession to power, the Queen Dowager ordered that all Catholics be severely dealt with, initiating what came to be known as the Catholic persecution of 1801.[50] Yi Sŭnghun, Tasan's brother Chong Yakchong and his close friend Yi Kahwan were put to death. Chong Yakchŏn, Tasan's second eldest brother, was exiled to Hŭksando off the southwest coast, and Tasan exiled to Kangjin, in south Chŏlla Province.[51]

In 1803 Queen Dowager Kim issued a special decree to free Tasan, but this was opposed by State Councillor Sŏ Yongbo.[52] Sŏ was the powerful Old Doctrine (Principle subfaction) official whose questionable dealings in Kyŏnggi Province had been reported to Chongjŏ by Tasan during his service as the king's secret envoy.[53]

In 1808 Tasan moved to a hill near Kangjin overlooking the south coast, called Tasan, or "Tea Mountain". There he was granted use of a pavilion (later named "Tasan ch'odang") belonging to Yun Tan (1744–1821), a member of his mother's line, the Yun clan of Haenam.[54] It is no wonder that Tasan was named after this place, for this was where he spent one of the most significant periods of his life. He landscaped the site with trees, a pond, and a waterfall, and built two thatched cottages, one of which he used for studying. Soon after he built them, he began lecturing a small group of students on the *Classic of Changes*. On the vertical face of a boulder nearby he wrote two characters meaning "Chŏng's stone," which are still visible today. Having created a suitable atmosphere for study and reflection, Tasan established a personal library of about a thousand volumes and, in the absence of the many distractions surrounding his years in politics, set about writing what were to become his major and most celebrated works.[55] The enthusiasm and methodical attitude with which he set about the study of the Confucian classics is best conveyed in his own words:

> Once I was banished to the coast I said to myself, "I set my mind on learning in my youth, but for twenty years I became enmeshed in secular affairs and was not able to discover the great Way with which the sage-kings of old governed the empire. Now I have the leisure to do so."
>
> Consequently I was filled with happiness. I immersed myself in research on the Six Classics and the Four Books. I collected and investigated the whole range of Confucian commentaries supplementing the words of the Classics, from the Han and Wei to the Ming and Ch'ing, and correcting errors and distortions, as well as noting down selected passages, set out my personal views.[56]

Tasan's work on the classics, which filled 232 fascicles, compared with a total of 262 fascicles taken up by his other works, drew on Japanese as well as Chinese and Korean sources, and was characterized by the broad variety of commentaries which he quoted, and in turn commented upon. His other writings include three major treatises on central institutional reform, local administration, and the legal system, entitled *Kyŏngse yup'yo* (Treatise on Government), *Mongmin simsŏ* (Reflections on fostering the people), and *Hŭmhŭm shinsŏ* (New Treatise on the Legal System), respectively. Summarizing the significance of these writings, Tasan stated,

> By means of the Six Classics and the Four Books the person is cultivated, and by means of the one *p'yo* [the *Kyŏngse yup'yo*] and the two *sŏ* [the *Mongmin simsŏ* and *Hŭmhŭm shinsŏ*], the world and nation are served. Thereby the root and the branches are provided for.[57]

This remark provides insight not only into the functions which Tasan ascribed to his major writings, but also into the extent to which his work was governed by the traditional Confucian worldview, which saw the learning of the scholar as revolving around the dual and interrelated goals of self-development and the ordering of society.[58]

As well as the political treatises and classical commentaries mentioned, Tasan's encyclopedic writings covered such varied subjects as economics, national defense, geography, philology, education, and medicine.

Tasan additionally wrote a series of epitaphs, on himself as well as his close relatives, colleagues, and prominent figures of his time, which remain valuable historical sources. He also wrote a great deal of poetry dealing with his personal circumstances as well as the social and political life of the country. The vivid imagery he used in his many allegories on Chosŏn society and its ruling elite, particularly during his period in exile, indicate the sympathies he had for the economic and social difficulties experienced by the peasantry, with whom he was now in closer contact. They also reveal his equally strong disapproval of the so-called in-law government imposed during the reign of Sunjo.[59] Concentration of power in the Andong Kim clan, centering on the in-laws of the young King Sunjo, had led to greater corruption among government officials and irregularites in the Three Administrations responsible for the collection of taxes. The Hong Kyŏngnae rebellion of 1811 was just one expression of the resulting popular unrest affecting many rural areas. Keen awareness of the abuse of political authority, which he had now seen from both sides of the political divide, and the living standards of the local populace, was reflected not only in the "social poetry" of Tasan, but also in the detailed measures for local administrative reform set out in his *Reflections on Fostering the People* (*Mongmin simsŏ*).

Tasan's critique of orthodox Neo-Confucian thought, the focus of this book, is to be found mainly in his commentaries on the classics, but another important source for his opinions on a wide variety of subjects, including Neo-Confucianism as well as Han Learning, are a series of short essays (*non*) which are considered to have been written during his period of government service under Chŏngjo.[60] Nonetheless, perhaps on account of their brevity, they are not mentioned in his self-written epitaph or chronological biography, which include summaries of all his major works. Including his poems, letters, and other assorted writings, Tasan's complete works, in the form of literary Chinese, take up almost 14,000 pages. Translated into English, they would take up approximately seventy volumes averaging three hundred pages in length.

In 1818, by dint of a memorial presented by Yi T'aesun of the Office of Royal Decrees protesting his continued exile, Tasan was allowed to return to his hometown in Kyŏnggi Province after eighteen years of isolation. In the following year, attempts to reinvest him with a government post were thwarted by the powerful Old Doctrine state councillor Sŏ Yongbo, and a similar request was again turned down in 1827.[61] Consequently, the last fourteen years of Tasan's life were also spent out of office, during which he produced several more major works, including his studies on the *Classic of Documents* and his self-written epitaph (*Chach'an myojimyŏng*). The account of Tasan's life presented in this chapter, as well as the list of his major works set out in the appendix, are based mainly on his epitaph, both the shorter (*kwangjungbon*) and longer (*chipchungbon*) versions, as well as a chronological biography (*Saam sŏnsaeng yŏnbo*) written by Chŏng Kyuyŏng, Tasan's fourth-generation descendant, who had access to materials lost shortly after the biography was written.

3

Tasan's "Classical Learning"

As mentioned in the introduction, Tasan is widely reputed to be a giant of "Sirhak" or "Practical Learning," largely on account of his detailed work on the political and economic order. Nonetheless, to paraphrase Tasan himself,[1] these proposals on administrational reform tell only half of the story. As the following pages indicate, he was profoundly interested in another kind of reform, the cultivation of the self, without which he regarded any attempt at institutional reform to be meaningless. Tasan had mixed feelings about Chu Hsi's philosophy for this very reason. On the one hand, he deeply respected Chu Hsi for having given unprecedented attention to the issue of self-cultivation. On the other hand, he felt that Chu Hsi had badly misinterpreted some of the early Confucian teachings on this very subject, particularly regarding the closely related issue of human nature. This chapter examines his critique of Chu Hsi's influential views, based on a detailed reappraisal of the relevant classical texts.

Tasan's characteristically methodical and exhaustive scholarship, armed with a rigorous means of textual analysis imported from the Ch'ing, provides new and valuable insight into the teachings of Confucius and Mencius. At the same time, he was clearly a philosopher as well as a philologer, keen to reflect on the implications of his intellectual archaeology for the issues that he felt were relevant to his time. Although he criticized Chu Hsi's Neo-Confucian teachings, he showed great interest in the very issues Chu had sought to resolve, including Heaven and human nature, topics that Confucius rarely, and when he did, cryptically, touched upon.[2] It was over these very issues that the major controversies in Korean Confucianism took place, including the so-called "Four-Seven" and "Horak" debates.[3] The reason for the intense involvement of the Korean Confucians in these issues was not, according to a popular misconception, simply due to a penchant for idle speculation on abstract questions, but because they had a direct bearing on methods of self-cultivation and the attainment of sagehood. In the sense that he was fascinated by the question of human nature and its implications for self-cultivation, Tasan was indeed treading in the footsteps of generations of Korean Neo-Confucians before him. What is remarkable is that he used his exhaustive analysis of the classics to provide very different perspectives on the same questions, and to unravel Chu Hsi's sophisticated system in the process. As he reflected on the philosophical implications of his Classical philology, Tasan was simultaneously recreating the tradition, and the resulting innovative aspects of his work are also explored in the following chapters.

As we have seen, both Yi Ik and Tasan used the expression *susahak*, referring to the pristine Confucian teachings, to describe their learning. It was on the basis of a reexamination of the "classical learning" that Tasan surreptitiously but radically challenged the authority of the Ch'eng-Chu school, indicating that this prevailing "orthodoxy" was, in important ways, unorthodox.

The greatest innovations that Ch'eng I and Chu Hsi had introduced into Confucian scholarship were in the area of metaphysics, and particularly their development of the concept of *li*, a metaphysical principle, which they associated with Heaven and human nature. In view of this it is no surprise that in 1789, before his ideological inclinations came under the close scrutiny of his political opponents, Tasan remarked that

> There are three reasons why people at present cannot achieve sagehood even though they desire to do so. One is that they think Heaven is principle,[4] another is that they think humanity [*jen/in*] is the principle of living things,[5] and the third is that they consider the Mean [*yung/yong*] to be normality.[6]

As a Confucian it would be difficult to make a stronger refutation of the central tenets of Chu Hsi's philosophy, particularly in view of the importance attached to the quest for sagehood. Although such undiplomatic pronouncements on the teachings of orthodox Neo-Confucianism are hard to find in Tasan's later writings, the philosophical orientations underlying these criticisms are well defined, and further developed, in his commentaries on the classics written in succeeding years.

The above quotation indicates that two of the three reasons for Tasan's dissatisfaction with the Neo-Confucian outlook of his time were directly related to Chu Hsi's concept of *li*, principle. Furthermore, because Chu Hsi had attempted to ground the whole body of the Confucian teachings on his principle-material force (*li-ch'i*) cosmology, the implications of Tasan's critique of Ch'eng-Chu metaphysics were very broad. It is these implications, expressed in Tasan's formulation of an alternative worldview, that we will examine in this chapter. The particular topics that will be discussed include Tasan's theory of human nature, his concept of moral activism upon which it was grounded, and their impact on his political philosophy.

Human Nature as Proclivities

One of the most original contributions that Tasan made to Confucian philosophy was his interpretation of human nature as proclivities or appetites, which provided the psychological basis for his outward-looking theory of self-cultivation.

Traditional Views of Human Nature

Pre-Sung Perspectives. Considering the importance of ethics in Confucian thought, it comes as no surprise that the question of human nature, granted only a terse yet thought-provoking mention in the *Analects*,[7] developed into a major topic of discussion among Neo-Confucians in China, and dominated Confucian scholarship in the early Chosŏn dynasty. The classical beginnings of the debate, which centered on the question of whether human nature was intrinsically good or not, are found in the dialogue between Mencius, who believed in the original goodness of human nature, and Kao Tzu, who maintained that it had no particular inclination either to good or evil. Kao Tzu compared human nature to swirling water, which is indifferent to direction, but flows to where it is guided.[8] On the other hand, as we shall see, Mencius argued that certain tendencies were fundamental to human nature, and that all people could attain sagehood by giving these feelings full development in their interactions with others. It is because these tendencies are universally present and capable of development that "The sage and I are the same in kind."[9]

Sung Dynasty Neo-Confucian Perspectives. Chu Hsi had attempted to answer the inevitable question raised by the Mencian concept of the goodness of the original nature, that is, the source of evil, by applying the principle-material force (*li-ch'i*) cosmology to the make-up of man himself. At the center of Ch'eng I's and Chu Hsi's attempt to integrate traditional ethical theories into a cosmological framework lay their identification of human nature (*jen-hsing*) with principle.[10] For this reason the Neo-Confucian tradition was referred to as *hsing-li-hsüeh*, "the study of human nature and principle," or the relationship between human beings and the cosmos. Principle was, in its entirety, also equated with the ultimate source of change and transformation, the "Great Ultimate" (*T'ai-chi*) by Chu Hsi.[11] It is the ultimate, unifying principle of the universe, and yet is endowed in its entirety to each of the myriad things of the universe. It is the one differentiated into many, rather as the moon is reflected in countless rivers and lakes.[12] It is also the natural law, providing the pattern for the dispersion and conglomeration as well as all manifestations of material force (*ch'i*), which is the cosmic "stuff" with which the myriad things are made. Endowed in man, *li* becomes both a natural and a normative standard, and constitutes his original nature (*pen-jan chih hsing*). This nature is implanted in *ch'i*, to which he owes his corporality and individuality, and so his physical nature (*ch'i-chih chih hsing*), which is the source of his bodily desires, consists of *li* and *ch'i* combined. According to Chu Hsi, the cravings of the physical nature issue from a distortion of *ch'i*, the extent of which varies between individuals.[13] The relative goodness or evil of individuals is explained in terms of the purity or impurity of *ch'i* in their physical nature, and intellectual differences are ascribed to its clarity or turbidity.[14]

Chu Hsi concurred with the Mencian argument that the nature of human beings was basically good, but he qualified this by saying that "there are those who are good from their birth and those who are evil from their birth," and ascribed this to differences in the material force with which they were endowed. The goal of personal development is the removal of this distortion and the cultivation of a clear, pure endowment.[15]

In using the concepts of principle and material force to account for the contradictory tendencies in human nature, Chu Hsi was confronted by a problem that was too essential to be ignored, that is, the problem of the bifurcation between what is "above physical form" and what has physical form. In order to resolve this problem he used the concept of the Great Ultimate, which was mentioned in the *Classic of Changes* as the source of yin and yang and all transformations, and had been developed by the early Neo-Confucian Chou Tun-i (1017–73) in his *Treatise on the Diagram of the Great Ultimate* (*T'ai-chi-t'u shuo*).[16] The diagram itself, which is said to have been inspired by a similar diagram authored by the Taoist priest Ch'en Tuan, consists of a series of circles depicting the make-up of the cosmos. The Great Ultimate is represented by the uppermost circle, followed below by three other large circles representing the interaction of yin and yang, male and female, and the production of all things, respectively. Chou's treatise refers to the uppermost circle as "The Ultimate of Non-being and also the Great Ultimate" (*wu-chi erh t'ai-chi*).[17] According to Chou, through movement the Great Ultimate generates yin (passive cosmic force) and yang (active cosmic force). The interaction of these cosmic forces produces human beings, who are their most intelligent manifestation, and all things.[18]

Unlike earlier commentators, Chu Hsi equated the Great Ultimate with principle, claiming that it was the principle of heaven and earth and the myriad things. At the same time, each thing is endowed with the Great Ultimate in its entirety. The Great Ultimate is above forms, for it existed "before Heaven and Earth," and yet it produces yin and yang, and activity and tranquillity, which exist only after physical form, and are a manifestation of *ch'i*, or material force. Chu Hsi attempted to resolve the apparent dualism by explaining that the Great Ultimate, as principle, "attaches itself to yin and yang as a man rides a horse," and remained the principle of activity and tranquillity, rather than being activity and tranquillity itself. In terms of the relationship between principle and material force, principle is the source of unity, and material force is the basis of the diversity of all things, in which the one principle is reproduced. Chu Hsi tried to eliminate the Taoistic nuances of the concept "Ultimate of Non-being" by indicating that this represented a complementary phase of the "Great Ultimate," as the principle of activity and tranquillity.[19]

Tasan's Critique: Principle and Human Nature

A classical locus of Confucian perceptions on the relationship between human nature and Heaven can be found in the seventh chapter of the *Mencius*, where it is stated,

> Those who fathom their minds know their nature. Those who know their nature know Heaven. To preserve one's mind and nourish one's nature is the way to serve Heaven.[20]

Ch'eng I had spoken of the mind, nature, and Heaven as manifestations of the "one principle" that penetrated them all.[21] Taking up Ch'eng I's theme of a universal principle shared by human beings and Heaven, Chu Hsi had interpreted Mencius' words to mean that one should thoroughly comprehend the principle embodied by the mind in order to attain a broad understanding of all things, including Heaven.[22]

Confronting Chu Hsi head on, Tasan maintained that the association of an all-embracing principle with Heaven and human nature, one of the theoretical pillars of the Ch'eng-Chu school, was originally derived from Buddhism:

> The scholars of later times [the Neo-Confucians] took Heaven, Earth, the myriad things, the formless and the substantial, the spiritual, perspicacious and bright as well as the ignorant, and reduced them all to the one principle [*li*].... The expression "It begins with the one principle, then it spreads out to embrace all things, and finally returns and gathers them all under the one principle"[23] is identical to Chao Chou's theory of the "ten thousand principles returning to the one."[24] Because the scholars of the Sung all indulged in the study of Ch'an Buddhism in early years, after returning [to the Confucian Way] their theories of human nature and principle still did not escape this influence.[25]

The last sentence in this passage refers to Sung scholars such as Chang Tsai (1020–77), who turned to Buddhism and Taoism before he produced his work on the classics, as well as to Chou Tun-i, who was also attracted to Buddhism and is considered to have incorporated Taoist theory into his metaphysics. According to Tasan, the influence of Buddhism on these early Sung metaphysicians extended to their students, the Ch'eng brothers, as well as to Chu Hsi, who used the doctrines of the Ch'an master Chao Chou to develop his theory of a principle that was unitary and simultaneously inherent in all things, as depicted in his introduction to the *Mean*. The focus of Tasan's critique of Ch'eng-Chu metaphysics was thus the implication that its philosophy of principle was not based on the Confucian classics. It was in this way, by indicating that the Chosŏn "orthodoxy" was not entirely "orthodox" that Tasan challenged the authority of Sung Confucianism.

Furthermore, by introducing a new interpretation of human nature which disassociated it from the *li-ch'i* duality, Tasan attempted to unravel the Neo-Confucian system by grasping its central thread, which linked human nature with principle. His contrasting outlook on principle, human nature, and the relationship between them is thrown into relief in his discussion of one of Mencius' characteristically vivid analogies. This passage draws parallels between the physical and moral inclinations of human beings:

> There is a common taste for flavor in our mouths, a common sense for sound in our ears, and a common sense for beauty in our eyes. Can it be that in our minds alone we are not alike? What is it that we have in common in our minds? It is the sense of principle (*li*) and integrity (*i*). The sage is the first to understand what is common in our minds. Therefore principle and integrity please our minds as beef and mutton and pork please our mouths.[26]

In his commentary on the same passage Chu Hsi had quoted a rather cryptic statement by Ch'eng I that "Principle refers to what exists in things, and integrity refers to the management of things. They are referred to as substance [*t'i*] and function [*yung*]."

Tasan was unhappy with this ontological interpretation of principle, which depicted an abstract term as a cosmological entity. He maintained that no corroboration could be found in the classics for this view.[27] According to the etymology of the *Shuo-wen*, *li/i* or principle referred to the patterns followed by the veins in jade. This pattern had to be carefully observed and followed when the jade was cut or "ordered" (*chih/ch'i*), and thus through the passage of time li came to be associated with the idea of ordering or governing (*chih/ch'i*).[28] Tasan claimed that the references to *li* in the classics all referred to either "pattern" (*mai-li/maengni*), "order" (*chih-li/ch'iri*), or natural law (*fa-li/pŏmni*), and that there was nothing in the classical sources that bore out the Ch'eng-Chu teaching that "human nature is principle."[29] The principle that "pleases the mind" referred to by Mencius is heavenly principle (*t'ien-li/ch'ŏlli*) or moral principle (*tao-i/to'ŭi*). Just as people take pleasure in satisfying their physical appetites, they also derive satisfaction from acting in accordance with moral principles, and the "nature" that Mencius so often alludes to, particularly in his discussions with Kao Tzu, is simply a term for these predilections.[30] Ch'eng I and Chu Hsi had apparently misunderstood Mencius. Principle, the "pattern" of human relations prescribed by Heaven, could not "exist within things," including human nature. The characteristic human tendency to derive satisfaction from acting in accordance with heavenly principle, and performing good deeds, should not, from this point of view, be confused with these moral principles or patterns of moral behavior themselves.

In Tasan's view, Ch'eng I had missed the point, a point that was highly relevant to the central thesis identifying the sage and the rest of humanity. Mencius' analogy, which drew parallels between the physical and moral tastes characteristic of human beings, implied that instinctive and moral behavior are closely related: they are both motivated by affective inclinations. The former involves the appreciation of sensual pleasures, whereas the latter involves the appreciation of harmony and integrity in human relations. Both of these are inclinations that seek to derive pleasure; it is only the objects of these inclinations that are different.

Shang-ti versus the Great Ultimate. Tasan was not content to simply disassociate human nature from the concept of principle, but intended to free it from the Neo-Confucian cosmology as a whole:

> Nowadays people revere the word "nature," elevating it as something great like heaven. They confuse it with theories of the Great Ultimate and yin and yang, and mix it up with discussions of the original and physical [natures]. It is distant, vague, abstruse, and dazzling. They consider themselves to be making fine distinctions and minute analyses, and to have fathomed the hidden secrets of the world. But in the end they have contributed nothing to the practice of daily affairs, so what profit is there in this? I feel compelled to point this out.[31]

In refuting the identification of nature with Heaven or ultimate being, Tasan was not denying the existence of a relationship between them. On the contrary, Tasan underlined the importance of "serving Heaven" and "attaining the virtue of Heaven" as the goal of self-cultivation.[32] But he intended to free the Confucian concept of human nature, and thus self-cultivation, from the particular metaphysical moorings that the Ch'eng brothers and Chu Hsi had tied it to. Central to his redefinition of the human status lay his rejection of Chou Tun-I's concept of the Great Ultimate itself:

> The uppermost circle in [Chou Tun-I's] *Diagram of the Supreme Ultimate* cannot be found in the Six Classics. Is it something highly intelligent? Or is it something unknowing, or something vacant and abstruse which cannot be deliberated upon? Of all the formless things in the universe, none can be the supreme being.[33]

Chou designated the "uppermost circle" of the diagram as "the Ultimate of Non-being, and also the Great Ultimate." Tasan was not rejecting the concept of the Great Ultimate itself, which is described in the *Classic of Changes* as the source of yin and yang and the trigrams.[34] What he was averse to was the use of the cryptic term "the Ultimate of Non-being" to refer to the Great Ultimate. It was not simply the ambiguity of the expression that he was reacting to. In his commentary on the *Classic of Changes*, Tasan clarifies the reasons for his rejection of the Neo-Confucian Great Ultimate:

> Referring to the Great Ultimate of the *Classic of Changes*, K'ung Ying-ta said that the Great Ultimate was the primary material force that permeated all before the appearance of Heaven and Earth, and that the "One" in Lao Tzu's statement "the Way gives birth to the One" is the Great Ultimate. On the other hand the Neo-Confucians elevated the Great Ultimate, claiming that it was principle rather than material force, and that it was above forms. Moreover they placed the Ultimate of Non-being above the Great Ultimate, saying that it was the "Ultimate of Non-being and also the Great Ultimate." If this were so, then the Great Ultimate must have come into being spontaneously. It would be preferable to say that the "one" Lao Tzu referred to is the Great Ultimate, and then the "Tao" that "gives birth to the one" would be the source of generation that gave rise to the Great Ultimate. To express the view of the Neo-Confucians certainly indicates ignorance of the

> original meaning of the *Classic of Changes* and does not measure up to Lao Tzu's explanation.[35]

Whereas the T'ang commentator K'ung Ying-ta (547–648) had interpreted the Great Ultimate of the *Classic of Changes* to be the primary material force, thus locating it in the universe, Chou Tun-i's usage of the expression the "Ultimate of Non-being," originally a Taoist concept, to describe the Great Ultimate, could be taken to mean that it was simultaneously being and non-being, or "above forms" as well as having form. This implied that it was self-generating, excluding any conception of a supreme being or creator presiding over the world of form. Chu Hsi went one step further than Chou by equating the Great Ultimate with principle, for in doing so he was clearly treating it as an existence which was "above form." Tasan was vigorously opposed to the idea of elevating principle, originally a term referring to the innate pattern of things, to the status of an ultimate, transcendent source of change and transformation. From this point of view, Lao Tzu's concept of a Way giving birth to the "one," assuming the "one" referred to the Great Ultimate, was more acceptable than its Neo-Confucian counterpart. Among Confucians, this unfavorable comparison with the views of Lao Tzu amounts to more than a mild refutation. The reason for this sharp criticism is that Tasan considered *Shang-ti/Sangje*, a personal, supreme being, to be the author of the universal order and the overseer of the cosmic interactions between yin and yang.[36]

Tasan pointed out that *Shang-ti*, or "supreme ruler," was a term in common use prior to the late Chou, as indicated by mentions in the *Classic of Odes*, *Classic of Documents* and *Rites of Chou*. The *Shang-ti* that was sacrificed to by the rulers of the early Chou is depicted by Tasan as a transcendent being, distinct from human beings, the spirits, and the myriad things and yet ruling them as their source of harmony and growth.[37]

Tasan classified the "Heaven" (*t'ien/ch'ŏn*) mentioned in the classics into two main divisions, the "boundless, substantial firmament" or universe, and the "sublime, spiritual ruler," the former being a natural manifestation and the latter none other than the *Shang-ti* mentioned above.[38] *Shang-ti* came to be referred to as "Heaven" just as the ruler of a state was referred to simply as "state" in Chinese, the impersonal nature of the appellation "Heaven" eventually becoming attributed to its ruler.[39] Tasan's conception of Heaven as a personal supreme being, and the importance he ascribed to "knowing Heaven" and "serving Heaven" as the basis of self-cultivation and the goal of sagehood, are strikingly reminiscent of the views of Yun Hyu discussed above.[40] If there is a difference between their respective views, it would be Tasan's added emphasis on serving Heaven through human relations, that is, by fulfilling one's ethical responsibilities.[41]

Heaven and human nature are closely linked in Confucian philosophy, and nowhere more directly than in the opening sentence of the *Mean* which states: "What Heaven has imparted is called [human] nature."[42] Because of this, in the Confucian tradition perceptions of Heaven are closely linked to views on human nature, and Tasan's philosophy is no exception. Tasan's monotheistic intepretation of *Shang-ti* as an entity with ethical predelictions responsive to, and involved in, human affairs,[43] provided the ontological foundation for his theory of human nature as proclivities or appetites.

Human nature as moral and physical appetites

Whereas Chu Hsi interpreted human nature in ontological terms as principle embodied in man, Tasan transferred human nature from the metaphysical to a more dynamic, psychological sphere. He was convinced that the classical and particularly Mencian usage of the term referred to it in the sense of innate proclivities or appetites (*shih-hao/kiho*):[44]

> The word "nature" (*hsing/sŏng*) should be read as in "the nature of pheasants," "the nature of deer," "the nature of grass" and "the nature of trees." Originally the word was coined to refer to appetites. One should not interpret it as something lofty, distant and vast. According to the *Chao-kao*,[45] "In regulating the nature, one must exert daily efforts". In the *Wang-chih*[46] it is written, "Through cultivation of the six arts, the nature of the people is regulated," and the *Mencius* speaks of "stimulating the mind and hardening the nature."[47] These all refer to the appetites as nature.[48]

In the above passages quoted by Tasan nature is described as an appetite that should be carefully controlled.[49] On the other hand, in the celebrated opening passage of the *Mean* nature is depicted as a heavenly endowment that should be followed:

> What Heaven has imparted is called [human] nature; the following of this nature is called the Way; training in the Way is called education.[50]

Tasan is in agreement with Chu Hsi when he recognizes that the "heavenly nature" referred to in this passage, which is also an ancient concept originating in the *Classic of Documents*, is something that should be followed rather than regulated. Then how does Tasan resolve the contrast between the "nature" described here in the *Mean* and the more earthy kind of nature described in other classical passages?

Tasan repeatedly spoke of human beings as a subtle combination of spirit and physical form, their natures being the appetites or propensities exhibited by these dual aspects.[51] Specifically, he saw human nature as being characterized by two kinds of propensity: The physical propensities people are equipped with for their survival, such as the desire for food and sex, which they share with the animals, and the spiritual propensities (K: *yŏngji chi kiho*) with which they are uniquely endowed, exemplified by their love of virtue and shame of depravity.[52] This latter inclination is the heavenly endowment referred to in the *Mean*, that should be followed in the cultivation of the Way.

At this point Tasan introduces a further level of differentiation, which appears to be based on his own reflection rather than any specific portion of the classics. Each of the aforementioned appetites, that is, the physical and the moral appetites, in turn, exhibits two complementary aspects:

> Appetites have two aspects [*tuan/tan*].[53] One is the appetite for pleasurable things which are immediately visible, as when we say that it is the nature of pheasants to like mountains, the nature of deer to like the plains, and the nature of drunkards to like wine; this is one kind of appetite. The other is the appetite for things necessary for life and growth, which give eventual fulfillment, as when we say that it is the nature of rice to like water, the nature of millet to like dry soil, and the nature of spring onion and garlic to like chicken droppings. This is another kind of appetite.[54]

Here Tasan appears to be defining two kinds of appetites found in the animal and plant kingdoms. The former class of appetites are characterized by a somewhat aesthetic appreciation of things experienced in the environment, and the latter group of appetites show an inclination for the more essential nutriments that provide a balanced subsistence. When Tasan talks about "liking" in this context he is obviously referring to the tendency of plants to flourish better in some environments rather than in others. But how do these appetites relate to human moral orientations? This question is answered in a subsequent passage, where he explains:

> As to human nature, it invariably delights in goodness and is ashamed of evil. Consequently if someone performs a good deed he is filled with happiness, and if he performs an evil deed his mind is obscured by melancholy. Even if he has never done anything good and he is spoken well of, he is delighted, and even if he has never done anything bad and he is slandered, he becomes angry. This is because he knows good actions are gratifying and evil actions are shameful. When he sees the good actions of others he regards them favorably, and when he sees evil actions he regards them with distaste. This is because he knows good actions are respectable and evil actions are hateful. All these are appetites for things which are immediately visible.[55]

So all human beings take pleasure in acquiring a reputation for being morally respectable, and appreciate the good actions of others. To use Tasan's analogy, this is the moral equivalent of the pheasant's liking for mountains, and the deer's attraction to plains.

But another aspect of human moral appetite, which requires steady cultivation, seeks the kind of consistent action which brings self-fulfilment:

> The longer someone accumulates [goodness] the more she is filled, her vast flowing energy [*hao-jan chih ch'i/hoyŏn chi ki*] becomes extremely great and its strength fills heaven and earth. Then wealth and honour cannot corrupt her, poverty and obscurity cannot move her, majesty and power cannot defeat her.... She becomes a person of complete virtue. This is because

> her nature is partial to doing good just as rice is partial to water, millet is partial to dry soil, and spring onion and garlic partial to chicken droppings.[56]

This human inclination to perform good deeds is comparable to the inclination of rice to grow in water, an appetite for moral nutriment so basic that if it is not satisfied, full maturity cannot be achieved. Development of personality is stunted or arrested in the same way that the growth of plants is impeded by lack of appropriate conditions and nutriments. The expression *hao-jan chih ch'i/hoyŏn chi ki*, the "vast flowing energy," is taken from a statement by Mencius, where he describes his personal cultivation in terms of nourishing (*yang*) this inherent energy, *ch'i*, through the accumulation of moral practice. "If anything in our conduct dissatisfies the heart," adds Mencius, "it starves."[57] As Kalton indicates, Tasan's concept of nature as tendencies which seek fulfillment through moral action fits in well with the Mencian concept of nourishing *ch'i*, which, Tasan argues, has nothing to do with the *ch'i* of Neo-Confucian *li-ch'i* cosmology.[58]

In the above passages Tasan is arguing that there are two complementary aspects to the moral appetites, one for the appreciation of goodness, and another for the practice of goodness.

But in drawing this double parallel he is, like Mencius, closely associating the moral appetites with the physical appetites, and in doing so, graphically indicating that they belong to the same family or order of existence.

The Problem of Dual Natures

Tasan was opposed to the dualistic overtones of Chu Hsi's conception of "original nature" (*pen-jan chih hsing*) and "physical nature" (*ch'i-chih chih hsing*) on both philosophical and textual grounds.

What were the philosophical reasons why Tasan was so thoroughly opposed to these conceptions? Ontologically speaking, he felt that they denigrated man's status as a unique being with capacities unparalled in the animal and plant kingdoms.[59] On the subject of human uniqueness, Mencius had observed rather cryptically, "That whereby people differ from the lower animals is but small. Common people throw it away, while superior people preserve it."[60] Commenting on this passage, Chu Hsi remarked that,

> At the time of their birth both human beings and things receive the principle of Heaven and Earth, which becomes their nature, and both receive the material force of Heaven and Earth, which becomes their physical form. The difference is that, among them, only human beings receive pure material force. They have the capacity to fully realize their nature, and this is the small difference. Although this is spoken of as a small difference, this is where the distinction between human beings and animals lies. The common people do not know this and throw it away. So although they are people in name, in fact there is nothing that distinguishes them from the animals.[61]

Although Chu Hsi does indicate that the advantage of human beings over the animals is their capacity to fully realize their nature, he implies that principle, that is, original nature, is what they have in common, and that material force is the source of differentiation. Tasan was very much opposed to the implication that human beings and animals were endowed with the same nature, and that the difference between them was the extent to which the nature was obscured by impurities in the material force. According to Tasan, in the respect that their senses and behavior incline toward food and sex, people do not show the slightest difference from the animals. What makes them unique is their moral nature, which is transcendent of form. It has no form and no substance, is spiritual and highly intelligent, and dwelling in the physical form, is in control of it. It is on account of this that the concepts of the "human mind" (*jen-hsin/insim*) and the "mind of the Way" (*tao-hsin/tosim*) have existed from ancient times.[62] Whereas human beings can be said to have these two minds, animals are unidimensional in the respect that they only have a physical nature.[63]

In direct contrast to Chu Hsi's depiction of a principle shared by human beings and animals and a material force that differentiated them, Tasan insisted that it was their physical nature that human beings shared with the animals and their moral nature that set them apart. This difference is concisely summarized in the following passage, but only after Tasan reiterates a claim that lies at the heart of his critique, about the "unorthodoxy" of Chu Hsi's theory:

> Chu Hsi's statements do not square with those of Mencius. In Mencius' time there was no concept of "original nature." How

> can one take a false concept that was developed later in order to clarify the subtle words of the sages? The physical nature is very clearly what is shared by human beings and things, and yet the earlier Confucians [Neo-Confucians] say that it is different in each; the moral nature is very clearly what is exclusively acquired by human beings, and yet the earlier Confucians [Neo-Confucians] say that it is acquired by both. I have serious doubts about this.[64]

Furthermore Tasan strongly argued that the Neo-Confucian concept of dual natures had little basis in the Confucian classics. In a sharp critique of this theory, he explained:

> People do not have two natures. [Their nature] is like the partiality of rice to water and its impartiality to dry soil, like the partiality of millet to dry soil and its impartiality to water. Previous Confucians [the Neo-Confucians] spoke of two natures. One they referred to as the "original nature" and the other as the "physical nature," saying that the original nature is entirely good and that the physical nature can be good or evil....
>
> [Human] nature is appetite. Previous Confucians thought that it referred exclusively to the spiritual substance of human beings. Is this not different?...
>
> More than any other, the theory of original nature has contravened Heaven, spurned the mandate, confused principles and harmed the cause of goodness. Former scholars [of the Ch'eng-Chu school] borrowed the term casually, but present-day scholars carelessly repeat it without understanding its origins. The two characters *pen-jan* (original) cannot be found anywhere in the Four Books, Six Classics, or the writings of the Hundred Schools. They are only mentioned repeatedly in the *Leng yen ching*.[65] How can they hope to find in it complete correspondence with the words of the ancient sages?[66]

According to Tasan, the Sung theories of original and physical nature, introduced by Chang Tsai (1020–77) and developed by Ch'eng I and Chu Hsi, were thoroughly "un-Confucian" and inconsistent with the Mencian perception of nature as appetites or inclinations. And yet they became concepts central to the discussions among Chosŏn Neo-Confucians on the relationship between human nature, principle, and material force.

At the beginning of the passage in question Tasan insists that "People do not have two natures." Dualism runs against the Confucian grain, and like generations of Confucians before him, he sought to resolve the ambiguous legacy of the *li-chi* cosmology. On the other hand, unlike his predecessors, he sought for the solution beyond the *li-chi* cosmology itself. But how would he answer the accusation that he is replacing one dualism with another? Although he clearly indicates that human beings have two distinctive levels of nature, he assigns these levels to the same order of existence by defining both of them as appetites. This did not mean that the two levels of appetites harmoniously coexisted. On the contrary, situations could arise which put them in radical conflict, and one that could only be resolved through an internal struggle.[67] This concept of internal struggle reflected the great, and unprecedented, importance that Tasan placed on the role of free will, and particularly *kwŏnhyŏng*, the faculty or power of deliberation, which gave human beings the power to decide on moral courses of action.

Human Nature and Moral Autonomy

Tasan used the concept of *kwŏnhyŏng* with reference to the unique status of humans as beings with moral autonomy, giving it philosophical prominence by making it the linchpin of his novel solution to the classical debate on human nature.

According to Tasan, it was not simply their moral nature per se that distinguished people from the animals; it was their capacity to make moral choices:

> As for the way human beings relate to good and evil, they can do anything. They act autonomously through their ability to direct themselves. As for animals' relationship to good and evil, they cannot act autonomously because they cannot do other than they do.[68]

It was this idea of moral autonomy, the ability to make moral choices, coupled with his explanation of human nature as tendencies, that provided Tasan with a concise and systematic synthesis of the classical debate on human nature:

> In summary, the spiritual aspect of human beings involves three principles. Regarding their nature, it delights in goodness and is ashamed of evil. This is what Mencius meant when he said that nature was good. Regarding their faculty of deliberation [*ch'üan-heng/kwŏnhyŏng*; lit. "to weigh and compare"], they can do both good and evil. It was on this that Kao Tzu based his analogy of swirling water, and Yang Hsiung based his explanation of a mixture of good and evil.[69] Regarding conduct, it is difficult to do good and easy to do evil. This is what led Hsun Tzu to propound his theory that human nature is evil....
>
> Heaven has endowed human beings with a faculty of deliberation that is able to do good or evil. In addition it endowed the lower aspect with the capacity of doing good with difficulty and evil with ease, and the higher faculty with its nature of delighting in goodness and being ashamed of evil.[70]

It was on the basis of the "faculty of deliberation" that one could decide to follow the essential inclinations of one's higher nature, and perform virtuous deeds in spite of the difficulty involved, or alternatively succumb to one's baser instincts. The usage of the concept of *ch'üan/kwŏn* (to weigh, consider), was perhaps inspired, and at least legitimized, by the *Mencius*, where it receives an intriguing mention with reference to the importance of flexibility, and the consideration of circumstances, in the application of rules:

> Shun-yü K'un asked, "Is it a rule of propriety that men and women should not have contact when they give or receive things?
>
> Mencius replied, "It is a rule of propriety."
>
> "Suppose your sister-in-law is drowning. Wouldn't you rescue her with your hand?"
>
> Mencius said, "Only the likes of a wild animal would not rescue his drowning sister-in-law. It is a rule of propriety for men and women not to touch hands when giving or receiving things, but it is *ch'üan* to rescue one's drowning sister-in-law with one's hands."[71]

Although Mencius uses the term *ch'üan* with reference to the capacity of human beings to make choices between conflicting moral imperatives, Tasan extends its significance to include the special human ability to choose between the often conflicting demands of the moral and physical natures.

The Process of Self-Cultivation

Another important reason why Tasan vigorously opposed Chu Hsi's theory of human nature was its ramifications for the question of good and evil, which in turn had profound implications for the process of self-cultivation.

As described above, Tasan envisioned human nature as a tenuous balance between two kinds of appetites: the physical tendencies people are equipped with for their survival, which they share with the animals, and the spiritual tendencies (*yŏngji chi kiho*) with which they are uniquely endowed, exemplified by their love of virtue and shame of depravity.[72]

As Michael Kalton points out, the theory of tendencies is not simply a transposition of the Neo-Confucian theory of conflicting natures to the psychological level.[73] In the first place, it is not necessarily the Sung Confucians Tasan is indebted to for his idea of dual, potentially conflicting aspects: these two kinds of propensity are described in the *Classic of Documents*, in terms of the "mind of the Way" and the "human mind," and in the *Mencius*, in terms of the "greater substance" (*ta-t'i*) and the "lesser substance" (*hsiao-t'i*).[74] Furthermore, Tasan contradicted Chu Hsi's views by maintaining that the physical nature (*ch'i-chih chih hsing*) had nothing to do with good and evil, although it might have a bearing on the intelligence of individuals.[75] This view was based on his radical premise that human nature itself is neither good nor evil in the strictest sense of the terms, for good and evil are only realized as a result of human action.[76]

Sagehood: Moral Nature or Moral Nurture?

To illustrate his argument that human potentiality for good and evil is not dependent on the relative clarity or turbidity of the "physical nature," Tasan used the example of the sageliness of the legendary kings Yao and Shun and the depravity of the tyrants Chieh and Chou:

> Yao and Shun were not unevenly endowed with a pure and bright physical nature, and neither were Chieh and Chou unevenly endowed with a turbid physical nature. Furthermore, this matter has no bearing on the original goodness or evil of their natures. The arguments of earlier Confucian scholars [the Neo-Confucians] about the purity or turbidity of the physical nature are misleading. If the distinction of good and evil is based on the physical endowment then Yao and Shun were naturally good and therefore we have nothing to emulate from them; and Chieh and Chou were naturally evil and leave us with nothing to be cautious about.... The physical endowment may cause men to be clever or dull-witted, but it cannot make them good or evil.[77]

In short, Tasan is arguing that the greatness of Yao and Shun lay in their actions and not in their endowment. Although individual differences in intellectual ability may be ascribed to the physical nature, so far as the potentiality for goodness is concerned, all people are equal. Whether that potentiality is fulfilled depends entirely on the moral choices they make. Tasan rejected even the implication that some people are born with a greater capacity for good than others, let alone explicit attempts to classify such differences between individuals, such as Han Yü's conception of the three grades of human nature.[78] A principal reason for this was that such ethical determinism would detract from his emphasis on the relevance of moral action, based on free will, to the attainment of sagehood.

According to Tasan, human nature is only potentially good, the substantiation of goodness involving the triumph of the moral nature over the physical inclinations. Consequently the natural tendency to excess shown by the self-centered physical propensities must be brought under control rather than treated as an aberration. Self-realisation was a question of getting priorities right rather than purifying the turbid physical endowment, and this was contingent on the exercise of the faculty of deliberation (*ch'üan-heng/kwŏnhyŏng*).[79] As we have pointed out, it was this ability to make moral choices, and consequently to shape his own moral existence, that placed man in an entirely different category from the animals.[80]

The Role of Desire

In consequence, it is no paradox that, while he put great stock in practical ethics, Tasan also put great emphasis on the role of the mind in the process of self-cultivation, particularly in the struggle to overcome selfish desire. It was on this point that Tasan parted ways with many of the Ch'ing critics of the Ch'eng-Chu school, and was unsparingly complimentary of Chu Hsi's views.

Much of the contention among Confucians over the role of desire in the quest for sagehood has revolved around the following passage in the *Analects*:

> Yen Yüan asked about humanity. The master said, "To subdue oneself and return to propriety [*k'e-chi fu-li*] is humanity. If a man could for one day subdue himself and return to propriety, the whole empire would return to humanity. Being humane depends on oneself [*wei-jen yu-chi*], not on others."
>
> Yen Yüan said, "May I ask what that involves?" The Master replied, "Do not look at what is contrary to propriety, do not listen to what is contrary to propriety; do not talk about what is contrary to propriety; do not make a movement which is contrary to propriety."[81]

Chu Hsi had interpreted the expression *k'e-chi* to mean "conquering (*sheng*) the selfish desires of the self (*shen chih ssu-yü*)," and this rendering is what the outstanding late Ming and Ch'ing critics of the Ch'eng-Chu school, including Yen Yüan (1635–1704), Li Kung (1659–1733), Tai Chen, and Juan Yüan, had strongly objected to. Li Kung had followed Yen Yüan's lead in questioning Chu Hsi's interpretation of *chi* as "selfish desires" (*ssu-yü*), adding that whereas followers of the sages spoke about "using propriety to control the self," Sung Confucians stressed "getting rid of selfishness and studying propriety."[82] Indeed, prior to the Sung, the much-quoted Han commentator Ma Jung (79–166), had glossed *k'e-chi* as *yüeh-shen*, to "control the self." Li also took issue with Chu Hsi for having used different glosses for the same word. Was it permissible, Li asked, for Chu to have translated *chi* in *k'e-chi fu-li* (to subdue oneself and return to propriety) as "selfish desires" and yet to translate the *chi* in *wei-jen yu-chi* (humanity depends on oneself) as "oneself" (*wo-shen*)?[83]

Commenting on the same passage, Tai Chen, one of the more philosophically inclined exponents of Ch'ing Evidential Learning, indirectly compared Chu Hsi's view with that of the Taoists and Buddhists:

> Lao Tzu, Chuang Tzu, and the Buddha [spoke of] "having no desires" [*wu-yü*], not of "having no selfishness" [*wu-ssu*]. The way of the sages and worthies was "to have no selfishness" and not "to have no desires."[84] To equate [the self] with selfish desires is therefore a notion the sages totally lacked.[85]

Tai took Li Kung's implicit affirmation of the positive role of desires a step further, by implying that it was desire that provided the impetus for righteousness:[86]

> When the sages ruled the world they shared the feelings of the people [*ch'ing*] and accorded with their desires [*yü*]. Thus the Kingly Way was established.[87]

Tasan's commentary on the same passage takes a very different tack:

> The self has two substances, and also two minds. The mind of the Way subdues the human mind, and thus the greater substance subdues the lesser substance....[88] To subdue the self by means of the self; this is the subtle, essential teaching secretly and exclusively handed down to posterity by a thousand sages and a hundred kings. If one understands this, one can be a sage or worthy. If one is ignorant of this, then one is akin to the birds or beasts. The reason why Chu Hsi is the founder of the revival of the Confucian Way is only this: He was able to impart this truth when he wrote his preface to the Mean.[89]

These are strong words; and they reflect the great significance that Tasan attached to Chu Hsi's teachings on the "mind of the Way" and the "human mind," and the relationship between them. In his introduction to the *Mean*, Chu had emphasized that the "vacuous spirituality" and consciousness of the mind was one and undivided, but at the same time it was imperative to discriminate between the rectitude of the Heavenly Mandate and the selfishness of the physical form. In the same vein, and in answer to the question raised by Li Kung about the meaning of "self" (*chi*), Tasan argued that the "greater substance" and the "lesser substance" Mencius had spoken of were both aspects of the self (*chi*); and yet they were involved in a struggle with each other. In the language of the *Classic of Documents,* the human mind was moved by the inclinations of the senses, and it was the mind of the Way that restrained it when these inclinations did not accord with propriety.[90]

Consequently Tasan refrained from speaking positively about desire per se, as certain of his Ch'ing contemporaries had done in reaction to the Ch'eng-Chu "principle of Heaven/human desire" dualism. He retained a certain asceticism in his notion that man's natural tendency to follow the dictates of his senses should be strongly controlled by an equally natural tendency to "love virtue and be ashamed of depravity." But although he vigorously spoke out in favor of Chu Hsi's rendering of *k'e-chi* as "conquering [*sheng*] the selfish desires of the self," on the issue of desire in general, his position lay somewhere between Ch'eng-Chu learning and the views of most of its Ch'ing critiques. For at the core of his theory of human nature lay the assumption that a certain stratum of affective tendencies, which could be interpreted as the desire for moral fulfillment, provided the main impetus for "cultivating one's flood-like *ch'i*". This is one reason why Tasan took issue with a central tenet of Chu Hsi's theory of self-cultivation, his concept of "investigating things" (*ko-wu*).

The Meaning of *Ko-wu*

Let us take a closer look at Chu Hsi's concept of self-cultivation, which is clearly outlined in his commentary on the *Great Learning*. The first chapter of this classic contains one of the most concise and systematic statements on the subject in the Confucian canon:

> Only after things are comprehended [*ko-wu*] is knowledge completed [*chih-chih*]; only after knowledge is completed may the will become sincere; only after the will becomes sincere may the mind be rectified; only after the mind is rectified may the person become cultivated; only after the person is cultivated may harmony be established in the household; only after household

> harmony is established may the state become well-governed; only after the state is well-governed, may the empire become tranquil.[91]

Chu Hsi called these progressively inclusive steps, from the comprehension of things to the ordering of the empire, the "eight items," the first five representing the "inner dimension" of self-cultivation, and the last three representing the charismatic effect of such cultivation on the social milieu. Following the precedent set by Ch'eng I, he made *ko-wu*, which he interpreted to mean the "investigation of the principle in things," and *chih-chih,* the "extension of knowledge,"[92] the centerpiece of the his theory of self-cultivation. He also added a chapter of commentary on the subject to the body of the classic itself, suggesting that the relevant chapter had been lost. This addition to the text reads:

> What is meant by "the extension of knowledge lies in fully investigating the principle in things" is that, if we wish to extend our knowledge to the utmost, we must probe thoroughly the principle in those things we encounter. It would seem that every man's intellect is possessed of the capacity for knowing and that everything in the world is possessed of principle. But, to the extent that principle is not yet thoroughly probed, man's knowledge is not yet fully realized. Hence, the first step in instruction in greater learning is to teach the student, whenever he encounters anything at all in the world, to build upon what is already known to him about principle and to probe still further, so that he seeks to reach the limit. After exerting himself in this way for a long time, he will one day become enlightened and thoroughly understand [principle]; then, the manifest and the hidden, the subtle and the obvious qualities of all things will all be known, and the mind, in its whole substance and vast operations, will be completely illuminated. This is called "fully investigating the principle in things." This is called "the extension of knowledge."[93]

Ch'eng I's doctrine of the investigation of things, here refined and developed by Chu Hsi, represented a new emphasis on the role of man's cognitive faculties in self-cultivation. Constant investigation of the innumerable manifestations of principle in things and affairs would eventually lead to a sudden, intuitive understanding of the principle endowed in its entirety to each individual by the Heavenly Mandate. In contrast, the positive role the feelings (*ch'ing*) might play in personal cultivation was de-emphasized. According to Chu, nature is substance, the state before activity begins, and the feelings are function, the state when activity has started. Mind includes both of these states.[94] He vividly illustrated this distinction by analogy with the behavior of water, comparing nature to the tranquillity of still water, feeling to the flow of water and desire to waves. Ch'eng I and Chu Hsi both maintained that human beings had good desires which emanated from their humanity, and bad desires akin to "wild and violent waves."[95] Nevertheless, feelings, being function, were not directly associated with nature in its pristine state, and were thus regarded as an object of constant vigilance since they included the distortion-prone material force. As we shall see, this position was also implied by Chu Hsi's interpretation of the Mencian argument on the innate goodness of human nature involving the concept of the four *tuan* or "beginnings." Consequently, emphasis was placed on the suppression of the "human [selfish] desires [*jen yü*]" through an inner union with principle.

Conversely, Tasan's theory of tendencies had identified human nature with the affective capacities. In contrast to the Ch'eng-Chu emphasis on the control of feelings based on the cognition of normative principle, he portrayed the feelings that characterized the moral tendencies as being themselves normative, insofar as they represented a spontaneous but appropriate response to situations. As the nature endowed by the Heavenly Mandate, it was the moral tendencies that provided the impetus for self-realization.

Tasan wrote a detailed commentary challenging Chu Hsi's classification of investigating things (*ko-wu*) and extending knowledge (*chih-chih*) as the first two of "eight items" in self-cultivation and the ordering of society described in the *Great Learning* (and quoted above). Instead he argued that the *Great Learning* as well as the *Mean* clearly gave primacy to sincerity of the will (*ch'eng-i*), the third item in Chu Hsi's schema. Whereas Chu Hsi's emphasis on investigating things set up the cognitive faculties as the starting point of the whole process of self-realization, Tasan's emphasis on sincerity of the will placed volition in the forefront. So how did Tasan reconcile this view with the fact that the *Great Learning* mentioned the dual tasks of investigating things and extending knowledge immediately prior to the sincerity of the will? To understand his argument, we should first look at his interpretation of *ko-wu* (comprehending things) and *chih-chih* (extending knowledge) and at the context within which these concepts are mentioned in the classic:

1. Things [*wu*] have their roots and branches; affairs [*shih*] have a beginning and an end. One comes near the Way in the knowledge [*chih*] of what to put first [*hsien*] and what to put last [*hou*].
2. Those of antiquity who wished to manifest their illustrious virtue to the empire put governing their states well first [*hsien*]; wishing to govern their states well, they first established harmony in their households; wishing to establish harmony in their households, they first cultivated themselves; wishing to cultivate themselves, they first rectified their minds; wishing to rectify their minds, they first made their will sincere, wishing to make their will sincere, they first extended their knowledge; the extension of knowledge lies in comprehending things.
3. Only after [*hou*] things are comprehended is knowledge completed.[96]

According to Tasan the "things" (*wu*) mentioned in the expression "things have their roots and branches" are the very things mentioned in the expression "comprehending things" (*ko-wu*). These are simply the "things" or nouns mentioned in the so-called "items": the will, mind, self, household, state and empire. The "root" of things thus refers to the will, the mind and the self, and the "branches" of things refer to the household, state and empire. Both of these groups are further subdivided into root and branches, sincerity of the will being the root of self-cultivation, and establishing harmony in the household being the root of bringing tranquillity to the empire. They interpenetrate and connect with each other, each of the Items being the basis of its successor.

The "affairs" (*shih*) mentioned in the expression "affairs have a beginning and an end" are the activities involved in the Items, which are making sincere, rectifying, cultivating, establishing harmony, governing well, and bringing tranquillity. Thus the "beginning" of affairs is making sincere, rectifying, and cultivating, and the "end" of affairs is establishing harmony, governing well, and bringing tranquillity.

Along the same lines, the "knowledge" (*chih*) mentioned in the expression "the knowledge of what to put first and what to put last" is the very knowledge mentioned in the expression "the extension of knowledge" (*chih-chih*), which is the knowledge of the order of the Items.[97]

Thus Tasan's interpretation of "comprehending things" and "extending knowledge" throws into relief the relationship between these three passages (which are numbered and set off from each other as separate paragraphs above): The last passage is not simply a reiteration of the second passage, but a reiteration in reverse. The second emphasizes precedence, or what should be put first among the steps or items, and the third emphasizes consequence, or what should be put last. According to Tasan, the leading passage simply expresses the importance of understanding the order of precedence of the Items in the following two passages.

Particularly since Chu Hsi's edition of the *Great Learning*, the interpretation of the character *ko* in *ko-wu* has been a subject of intense discussion among Chinese philosophers, not least on account of the diversity of the contexts it has appeared in among the classics. Tasan maintains that the meaning of *ko* can only be discussed after defining its object *wu*, largely on account of this diversity of usage. He recognizes that Ch'eng I's interpretation of *ko* as *lai* (to come) and Chu Hsi's interpretation of *ko* as *chih* (to arrive at, to reach) both have some basis in ancient usage. But when used in conjuction with *wu* in the context of the self and human relations, *ko* clearly means *liang-tu/yangdo* (to fathom, to comprehend).

Seen from this perspective, "comprehending things" (*ko-wu*) and "extending knowledge" (*chih-chih*) are not two separate steps prior to the sincerity of the will, but refer to the importance of knowing the order of the Items themselves, including the primacy of the sincerity of the will. It is the importance of this specific knowledge, claims Tasan, that is underlined in the preceding passage on "the root and the branches," and not a broad knowledge of all the things to be found in the world as interpreted by Chu Hsi.[98]

Tasan's interpretation of *ko-wu* is somewhat similar to that of Li Kung, who maintained that *wu* referred to the activities mentioned in the eight steps.[99] An even closer similarity is found in his description of Kwŏn Ch'ŏlsin's reading of the passage. According to this description, Kwŏn argued that the "things" (*wu*) to be comprehended were nothing but the "things" in the expression "things (*wu*) have their roots and branches; affairs have a beginning and an end" and the knowledge (*chih*) to be extended was simply the "knowledge" mentioned in the expression "one comes near the Way in the knowledge [*chih*] of what to put first and what to put last."[100]

Consequently, Tasan argues that "comprehending things and extending knowledge" are not part of the process of self-cultivation itself, but are a precondition to it, involving careful reflection on the process by which self-cultivation is achieved. This idea of the importance of reflection prior to moral practice is, according to his rendering, introduced in the second passage of the "Text" itself, which precedes the enumeration of the Items:

> Knowing where to come to rest, one becomes steadfast; being steadfast, one is able to find tranquillity; being tranquil, one is able to find repose; finding repose, one is able to reflect; through reflection one is able to attain understanding [*te*].[101]

According to Tasan, "knowing where to come to rest [*chih-chih*]" means to know about the perfection of virtue through human relations; that is, to understand the meaning of filial piety, fraternal respect and compassion. Once this is achieved one is able to find steadfastness and singleness of purpose, and having this, one gains the wherewithal to reflect deeply on what is essential and come to grasp (*te*) what is prior and what is secondary in striving for the attainment of such virtue. This in turn is nothing but the realization that the sincerity of the will is the point of departure in self-cultivation, and self-cultivation is the point of departure for the task of bringing peace to the empire.[102]

For Tasan, the above passage on "knowing where to come to rest" is essentially an elaboration of the meaning of *ko-wu chih-chih*.[103] Commenting on the relationship between *ko-wu chih-chih* and the Items he asserted that

> Self-cultivation takes the sincerity of the will as its primary task. This is the point of departure. Prior to sincerity, how can there be an additional two steps of moral effort? This [referring to *ko-wu chih-chih*] simply means that in all affairs there must first be deliberation [*tu/to*] and reflection .... knowing where to rest, one

can attain steadfastness [*ching/chŏng*] of purpose, and attaining steadfastness of purpose, one can reflect on affairs. To completely grasp the things [*wu*] and affairs that one deals with, to deliberate on the roots and the branches and ascertain the beginning and the end, and then to follow the branches, and tracing them toward their origin, arrive at sincerity of the will - this is the first step taken in affairs. Only consideration and inference take place before engaging in affairs. Why, then, are the two Items "comprehending things [*ko-wu*]" and "perfecting knowledge [*chih chih*]" placed prior to them [affairs]? "Things" [*wu*] are these very things, and "knowledge" [*chih*] is this very knowledge. Then what have "all the things in the world" and "what is known about the principles of the world" [paraphrase of Chu Hsi's commentary on *ko-wu*] got to do with this?[104]

It appears that, according to Tasan's interpretation, there are only six main "affairs" or "activities" in self-cultivation and the ordering of society, and the first of these is sincerity of the will. Nonetheless, Tasan refrains from using the expression "six items" to refer to them, as he considers sincerity of the will to be the basis of them all, and in a category all of its own. This is why, he argues, the *Mean* states that "sincerity is the beginning and end of things."[105] This is also why the very first commentary in the original *Record of Rites* text of the *Great Learning*[106] is on the sincerity of the will, and furthermore is set off from the other commentaries on the Items.[107]

The primacy of "sincerity of the will"

As with the frequently discussed concept of *jen* or "humanity," which provides a key to understanding Confucius' teachings on ethics in the *Analects*, the concept of *ch'eng* or "sincerity" is pivotal to an understanding of both the *Great Learning* and the *Mean*, and yet at the same time one of the most elusive.

In a short essay where he attempts to clarify the meaning of *ch'eng* or "sincerity," Tasan admits that no clear explanation of the etymology of the character can be found in any of the classical lexicons. Nonetheless, using an expression taken from the *Mean*, he claims that it represents the "beginning and the end of things," in the respect that all affairs, from self-cultivation to the ordering of society, can only be fulfilled through sincerity.[108]

In its commentary on the "Items" the *Great Learning* links sincerity of the will with the attitude of "being watchful when alone."[109] This concept is also mentioned in the opening passages of the *Mean*:

> There is nothing more visible than what is hidden, and nothing more manifest than what is subtle. Therefore the superior man is watchful over himself when he is alone.[110]

In his interpretation of this passage, Tasan skillfully wove together the teachings of the *Great Learning* and the *Mean*, by linking the three concepts "knowing Heaven," "being watchful when alone," and "sincerity":

> The *Mean* takes "knowing Heaven" to be the basis of self-cultivation.... Knowing the visibility of what is hidden and knowing the manifestation of what is subtle is to "know Heaven." To "know Heaven" is to be "watchful when alone," and to be "watchful when alone," is to be sincere.[111]

Behind Tasan's emphasis on the central role of sincerity in the *Great Learning*, and his concomitant rejection of the elevated status Chu Hsi ascribed to *ko-wu*, lay the importance he placed on "knowing Heaven."

In his conception of personal cultivation as depicted by the *Great Learning*, Tasan endowed sincerity of the will with the same comprehensive importance that Chu Hsi had placed on the investigation of things and the extension of knowledge, concluding that, "sincerity of the will and rectification of the mind are the main items of the *Great Learning*."[112] Previous to Tasan, Yun Hyu had also maintained that sincerity of the will was the basis of all the Items in the *Great Learning*. Both of them implied that Chu Hsi's reordering of the *Great Learning* as it had originally appeared in the *Record of Rites* had shifted the focus of attention away from sincerity of the will by giving prominence to *ko-wu*.[113] Two other Southerner philosophers, Yi Ik and Kwŏn Ch'ŏlsin, had also opposed Chu Hsi's amendments to the *Great Learning* mostly on account of his interpretation of *ko-wu*.

Wang Yang-ming, who had long before refuted Chu Hsi's emendments to the *Great Learning*, maintained that "seeking the sincerity of the will" was the central theme of the *Great Learning* as well as the *Mean*, and similarly, that it was the starting point of the entire task of study and self-cultivation. But unlike Tasan, he thought that sincerity of the will was equivalent to *ko-wu*, which he interpreted to mean the active rectification of thoughts—thoughts about experiences as well as inner states of mind—and not a cognitive task prior to self-cultivation.[114]

"Sincerity of the will" in Chu Hsi's edition of the Great Learning. Tasan maintained that the order as well as the phrasing of the *Record of Rites* version, that is, the earlier version, of the *Great Learning* clearly bore out the central role he ascribed to sincerity of the will. In his definitive edition of the Four Books, Chu Hsi had effected changes to the original text of the *Great Learning*, which together with the *Mean* had originally been written as one of the chapters of the *Record of Rites*. In so doing, he followed the lead of the Ch'eng brothers, claiming, as they had, that the bamboo slips on which the text had been written had become disordered, and that Tai Sheng (who was traditionally regarded to be the compiler of the *Record of Rites*) had failed to set it out in the order in which it had been written.[115] Tasan implied that the changes effected by Chu Hsi, in content and particularly in order, shifted the focus of emphasis of the text, apportioning the leading role among the Items to the "investigation of things and the extension of knowledge" in place of sincerity of the will. To understand Tasan's reasons for preserving the order of the *Great Learning* as it had appeared in the *Rites* in his *Impartial Discussion on the Great Learning* (*Taehak kongŭi*), and particularly the importance he ascribed to sincerity of the will, we must clarify the nature of the changes Chu Hsi had effected to the text in his *Ta-hsüeh chang-chü* (The *Great Learning* in chapters and verses).

Chu Hsi completed a total of four types of change to the "Old Text" of the *Great Learning*. First, he divided the text into a classic (*ching*) portion or main text, which he took to be the words of Confucius transmitted by his student Tseng Tzu, and a commentary (*chuan*) portion of ten chapters, which he took to be the interpretations of Tseng Tzu recorded by his followers. Second, he revised the order of the text. Third, he added a supplementary chapter of commentary (*pu-chuan*) on the two Items "investigating principle" and "extending knowledge" (*ko-wu chih-chih*), claiming that part of the text had been lost, and fourth, he emended and suggested emendations to a number of characters.

Among these changes, the two that most radically altered the logical sequence, and with it the philosophical import, of the text as it had been set out in the *Record of Rites*, were the relocation of the commentary on the sincerity of the will and the inclusion of a new chapter on *ko-wu chih-chih* (see diagram).[116] Whereas he could find portions of commentary that seemed to correspond to the so-called "Three Principia" (*kang-ling*)[117] and six of the Items, there was no portion of commentary devoted to an explanation of the two Items *ko-wu* and *chih-chih*. From Tasan's point of view, the reason why there was no separate commentary on *ko-wu chih-chih* was because they were not Items. But Chu Hsi was unable to overlook the lack of a commentary since it was these very concepts upon which he founded and structured his theory of self-cultivation. Consequently, he transferred the phrase "This is called 'knowing the root'. This is called 'the extension of knowledge'" from its position in the so-called "Text of Confucius," using it to constitute a new commentary on *ko-wu chih-chih*, to which he appended his own commentary on the topic. Whereas the expression "This is called 'knowing the root'" had previously followed a passage which referred to self-cultivation as the root, it was now made to refer to the particular tasks of *ko-wu* and *chih-chih*, "investigating things" and "extending knowledge." An additional problem was caused by this relocation, since this expression was now preceded by the last sentence of chapter four, which happened to be exactly the same expression. Dissatisfied by this repetition, Chu Hsi mentions that "Master Ch'eng said, 'This is superfluous text.'" The commentary explaining the sincerity of the will was removed from its leading position at the head of the commentaries, directly adjacent to the main "Text of Confucius," to become the sixth chapter of commentary. It was now superseded by the new section on *ko-wu chih-chih*, which had been absent in the *Record of Rites* version.[118]

According to Tasan, the special status of sincerity of the will is indicated by the fact that, in the *Record of Rites* version of the *Great Learning*, it is the topic of the very first piece of commentary. This commentary on sincerity of the will does not have a particular bearing on the passages immediately before and after, unlike the other commentaries on the Items, which appear after a discussion on the Three Principia (see figure 3.1.).[119] Conversely, this very lack of immediate relation to adjacent passages had provided Chu Hsi with a pretext for relegating the commentary on sincerity of the will to a lowlier position in his edition of the *Great Learning*, following the Three Principia and his commentary on *ko-wu chih-chih*.

Sincerity of the will" and the order of the Items. Discussing the pivotal role of sincerity in the Great Learning, Tasan argued,

FIGURE 3.1

Chu Hsi's Revision of the Great Learning

RECORD OF RITES VERSION
a. The Three Principia
b. On knowledge of priority
c. The Items
d. The Items (reverse order)
e. (1) On self-cultivation as the root. (2) "This is called knowing the root, (3) this is called the extension of knowledge"
1. Commentary on sincerity of the will
2. On self-cultivation (*Book of Poetry*) On the virtuous example of the sages (*Book of Poetry*)
3. Commentary on manifesting virtue (first Principium)
4. Commentary on renewal (second Principium)
5. Commentary on dwelling [in goodness] (third Principium)
6. On hearing litigations e(2) "this is called knowing the root"
7. Commentary on cultivation of the person
8. Commentary on establishing harmony in the household
9. Commentary on governing the state
10. Commentary on bringing tranquillity to the empire

	CHU HSI'S EDITION
	The Classic of Confucius
	a. The Three Principia
	b. On knowledge of priority
	c. The Items
	d. The Items (reverse order)
	e. On self-cultivation as the root.
	The Commentary
1	3. Commentary on manifesting virtue (first Principium)
2	4. Commentary on renewal (second Principium)
3	5. Commentary on dwelling [in goodness] (third Principium)
3	2. On self-cultivation (*Book of Poetry*) On the virtuous example of the sages (*Book of Poetry*)
4	6. On hearing litigations e(2) "this is called knowing the root"
5	e(2) "This is called knowing the root" e(3) "this is called the extension of knowledge" (Chu Hsi's commentary on *ko-wu chih-chih*)
6	1. Commentary on sincerity of the will
7	7. Commentary on cultivation of the person
8	8. Commentary on establishing harmony in the household
9	9. Commentary on governing the state
10	10. Commentary on bringing tranquillity to the empire

Note: To illustrate the extent and nature of the emendments effected by Chu Hsi to the text of the *Great Learning*, the original *Record of Rites* version depicted in the left hand column has been divided into ten separate sections according to subject matter. The enumeration of these sections is retained in Chu Hsi's edition of the *Great Learning* depicted in the right hand column, to indicate the shift in their respective positions. Chu Hsi's enumeration of chapters is indicated by the numbers adjacent to the right hand column.

> Sincerity penetrates the beginning and end of things. By means of sincerity one makes the will sincere, by means of sincerity one rectifies the mind, by means of sincerity one cultivates the self, by means of sincerity establishes order in the household and the nation, and by means of sincerity brings tranquillity to the empire.[120]

By this Tasan did not mean that sincerity of the will was achieved on an individual level prior to the ordering of society. He perceived the order of the Items or steps to be logical rather than temporal, and the relationship between the rectification of the mind and the conduct of human affairs to be a synergistic one. The activities or affairs involved in the Items took place simultaneously:

> If we speak of the principle of "making the will sincere and rectifying the mind," then there is clearly a sequence, but if we speak of the time, there is no delay [involved].[121]

This relationship between sincerity of the will and rectification of the mind extended to the other Items. Sincerity was not achieved prior to moral action, but through it:

> To earnestly serve one's parents is to make [the will] sincere and rectify [the mind] through filial piety; to earnestly serve one's elders is to make [the will] sincere and rectify [the mind] through fraternal respect; to earnestly foster the young is to make [the will] sincere and rectify [the mind] through parental love. One makes [the will] sincere and rectifies [the mind] by regulating the family, makes [the will] sincere and rectifies [the mind] by ordering the state, and makes [the will] sincere and rectifies [the mind] by pacifying the world. Sincerity and rectification always depend on the conduct of affairs, and they are always contingent on human relations. There is no method of [achieving] sincerity with only the will; no technique to achieve rectification with only the mind. To omit the conduct of affairs and reject human relations, and yet to seek the mind's repose in perfect goodness: this is not the original method of the early sages. The key to "preserving the principle of Heaven and subduing human desires" lies in people's dealings with each other. Quiet-sitting

> and self-contemplation should also involve a careful examination of one's contacts with others. Sincerity and rectification are then made possible since they have a basis.... Without recourse to human relations, simply to take hold of the will and seek for a means to make it sincere; or take hold of the mind and seek for a means to rectify it, results in a very confused and indistinct state of affairs.[122]

The implication is that the introspective methods of self-cultivation that appear to have been the order of the day among the orthodox Neo-Confucians of the late Chosŏn, were the result of a misconception that the order of the Items was a temporal one. Tasan went one step further, or should one say one step back, in arguing that Chu Hsi himself was prey to the same misconception, implying that his interpretation of the Items, and particularly *ko-wu chih-chih*, was largely responsible for this state of affairs:

> The things of the earth are so plentiful, extensive and elaborate that they cannot be enumerated, and their principles cannot all be understood. Even if the sages Yao and Shun were granted the longevity of P'eng Tsu,[123] they would be unable to thoroughly know all their causes. If one chose to wait until these things were comprehended and this knowledge was perfected before making the will sincere and cultivating the self, one would have a lot of waiting to do.... How much time would it take to thoroughly examine the principles of the myriad things in the world? It is not only the comprehension of things and perfection of knowledge that take up no time; neither do sincerity of the will and rectification of the mind require one to spread out a mat or prepare a seat and spend time studying.[124]

It could be argued that Tasan had misinterpreted Chu Hsi when he claimed that, according to Chu Hsi, there was a cognitive stage in self-cultivation prior to moral practice. Chu Hsi did not explicitly depict the order of the steps as being temporal as well as logical. On the contrary, in the *Chu-tzu yü-lei* (Conversations with Chu Hsi, categorized) Chu Hsi indicates that the order of the Items delineated in the *Great Learning* is not to be regarded in terms of a clearly defined consecutive progression.[125] Indeed, Chu Hsi's philosophy dwelt on the close relationship between knowledge and action, a theme so pervasive in Chinese thought that it imbued the sayings of Confucius and Mao Tse-tung alike.[126] Nonetheless Chu Hsi is somewhat ambivalent on the question of temporal and logical priority, as the following passage suggests:

> Knowledge and action require each other. It is like a person who cannot walk without eyes although he has legs, and who cannot see without legs although he has eyes. With respect to order, knowledge comes first, and with respect to importance, action is more important.[127]

Although Tasan may have misrepresented Chu Hsi's ambiguous conception of priority, one could also point out that Chu Hsi's interpretation of *ko-wu chih-chih* might lead to introspective attitudes in self-cultivation, by dint of the very ambiguity on the question of priority mentioned. Indeed, Tasan's mentor Kwŏn Ch'ŏlsin intimated that ambiguity and vagueness in the writings of Chu Hsi, particularly in discussions of the concept of virtue and self-cultivation, could be very misleading.[128]

One could easily conclude that the main difference between Tasan and Chu Hsi on their interpretation of the Items of the *Great Learning* is that Chu Hsi regarded *ko-wu chih-chih* to be the starting point of self-cultivation, whereas Tasan simply interpreted it to be the task of understanding the process of self-cultivation.[129]

But again, Chu Hsi appears to be somewhat ambivalent about the relationship between *ko-wu chih-chih* and self-cultivation. For although he gave prominence to the role of *ko-wu chih-chih* through his rearrangement of the order of the *Great Learning* as well as the sheer volume of his commentary on the subject, he still strongly emphasized the importance of sincerity of the will, maintaining that it was "at the forefront of self-cultivation." In agreement with the vast majority of commentators, Chu Hsi himself implied that the concept of sincerity occupied a key position in the teachings on personal cultivation of the *Mean* as well as the *Great Learning*.[130] He could hardly have done otherwise, for the concept is mentioned seven times in the *Great Learning*, a considerable number of allusions in view of the diminutive size of the classic, and seventeen times in the *Mean*, where, explicitly or implicitly, it is given prior consideration in numerous discussions on ethical conduct and the cultivation of desirable virtues.

Although Tasan's reading of *ko-wu chih-chih* would have been considered controversial by followers of the Ch'eng-Chu school, they would have found it difficult to fault him for giving prominence to the role of sincerity in personal cultivation, not only in his work on the *Great Learning* but also in his commentary on the *Mean*. Through his emphasis on sincerity of the will as the first item, Tasan underlined the leading role of volition in personal development, a role that was consistent with his interpretation of human nature as tendencies.

The Concept of Virtue

Tasan's identification of human nature with the affections lay the groundwork for a concept of virtue diametrically opposed to Chu Hsi's view. The lines of battle are clearly drawn in their respective interpretations of a crucial passage from the Mencius, which became a classical locus for all discussions on the relationship between nature, feelings and virtue.

This is what Mencius had originally said:

> Nobody is devoid of a heart sensitive to the suffering of others. Such a sensitive heart was possessed by the Former Kings and this manifested itself in compassionate government. With such a sensitive heart behind compassionate government, it was as easy to rule the Empire as rolling something on your palm. My reason for saying that nobody is devoid of a heart sensitive to the suffering of others is this. Suppose someone were, all of a sudden, to see a young child on the verge of falling into a well. He would certainly be moved to compassion, not because he wanted to get in the good graces of the parents, nor because he wished to win the praise of his fellow villagers or friends, nor yet because he disliked the cry of the child. From this it can be seen that whoever is devoid of the heart of compassion is not human, whoever is devoid of the heart of shame is not human, whoever is devoid of the heart of courtesy and modesty is not human, and whoever is devoid of the heart of right and wrong is not human. The heart of compassion is the beginning [*tuan*] of humanity; the heart of shame, of integrity; the heart of courtesy and modesty, of propriety; the heart of right and wrong, of wisdom. Man has these four beginnings [*tuan*] just as he has four limbs... When

> these are fully developed, he can tend the whole realm within the Four Seas, but if he fails to develop them, he will not be able even to serve his parents.[131]

Mencius was arguing that certain feelings are fundamental to man's nature, and that all men can attain sagehood by giving these feelings full development in their interactions with others.[132] It is because these tendencies are universally present and capable of development that "The sage and I are the same in kind."[133] These four *tuan* or "nascent moral sprouts," as P. J. Ivanhoe puts it, are the source of four essential ingredients of character: humanity, integrity, propriety, and wisdom.[134] In the classics the word *tuan* was commonly used in the sense of *fa-tuan*, meaning "beginning" or "origin," or *tuan-hsü*, meaning "the extremity of a thread," or, by analogy, "clue" in the sense that the extremity of a thread provided the key to unravelling a knot.[135] Chu glossed it to mean *tuan-hsü* arguing that, being emotions, the four tendencies were external manifestations of the virtues, which were innate attributes of the nature.[136] This interpretation reflected the distinction he drew between nature, or principle, as substance, and the emotions as function.[137]

On the other hand, the majority of commentators prior to the Sung took the term *tuan* in this context to mean "beginning" or "source," which would signify that the virtues were a development of the incipient tendencies. Tasan did the same, claiming that the Neo-Confucians had put the cart before the horse:

> In the *Mencius* it is said that humanity, integrity, propriety, and wisdom are rooted in the heart. These can be compared to blossoms. It is only their root which is in the heart. The heart of compassion and the heart of shame issue from within; humanity and integrity are realized without. The heart of courtesy and modesty, and the heart of right and wrong issue from within; propriety and wisdom are realized without. Present-day scholars understand it [the *Mencius*] to mean that humanity, integrity, propriety, and wisdom are four kernels located within man's belly like his organs.[138]

Tasan insisted that virtue (*te*) could only exist as a result of ethical conduct.[139] This reflected its etymology. The phonetic compound of *te* consists of the character *chih*, meaning "upright" or "honest," and *hsin*, meaning "heart" or "mind." The radical signifies a "small step" or "pace."[140] He was obviously taking this etymological meaning into consideration when he claimed that:

> Originally there is no virtue within the heart, only the upright nature. What is meant by "virtue" is action in accord with the upright heart. The term "virtue" is applicable only upon the completion of good deeds. How can one have "illustrious virtue" before there is action?[141]

The "illustrious virtue" that Tasan mentions here is a reference to one of the so-called "Three Principia (*kang-ling*)"[142] of the *Great Learning*, describing the essential teachings of the Classic:

> The way of the *Great Learning* lies in manifesting illustrious virtue [*ming ming-te*], loving the people, [*ch'in-min*] and resting in the highest good [*chih yü chih-shan*].[143]

Confucius and Mencius frequently pointed to the realization of virtue as the task of self-cultivation, and the manifestation of virtue as the mark of sagehood. It comes as no surprise, then, that the *Great Learning* makes the manifestation of virtue the foremost of the "Three Principia."

Tasan, in keeping with his interpretation of virtue as being acquired *a posteriori*, saw the "illustrious virtue" as being nothing but the result of filial piety, fraternal respect, and parental compassion, the primary virtues extolled by the *Great Learning*. He indicated that his viewpoint was not a particularly original contribution, mentioning that it reflected the interpretation of the Yüan scholar Lu Yü-ch'i as well as that of his predecessor, Yun Hyu.[144]

Chu Hsi's interpretation of the "illustrious virtue" (*ming-te*) of the *Great Learning* is consistent with his idea of virtue as principle existing *a priori* within the nature. Illustrious virtue is not accumulated; it exists in the mind from the moment of birth. Its presence simply needs to be manifested by a concentrated effort to release it from the encroaching endowment of material force or *ch'i*.

> Illustrious virtue is what people acquire from Heaven. It is vacuous, perspicacious, and bright, and thus embodies all the manifestations of principle and responds to the myriad affairs.

> But it may be restricted by the endowment of *ch'i* or concealed by human desire, so occasionally it will become obscured. Never, however, does its essential brightness cease. In view of this the student should concord with its emanations and seek to manifest it, thereby restoring its original condition.[145]

Tasan takes issue with this interpretation of illustrious virtue on philological grounds. Chu Hsi's interpretation of illustrious virtue as a natural endowment is poorly corroborated by the classics. There is no evidence that any metaphysical significance was ascribed to the idea of virtue as it was taught in the *T'ai Hsüeh* or Confucian Academy of pre-Ch'in times,[146] or that concepts such as "principle" (*li*) or "material force" (*ch'i*) were taught there.[147] The *Mencius* states that during the Three Dynasties education provided at all institutions of higher learning was intended to "make clear the human relations [*ming-lun*],"[148] revealing that it was essentially ethical in character, and that, at least in the educational curricula of the period, *ming* was used in an ethical rather than a psychological or metaphysical context.[149] Describing the educational program of the *T'ai Hsüeh* in particular, the *Rites of Chou* reveals that the Director of Music instructed the eldest sons of the aristocracy in the Six Virtues, which are enumerated as moderation, harmony, reverence, impartiality, filial piety, and fraternal respect, indicating that the curriculum focused on the cultivation of acceptable attitudes and moral conduct.

In view of this, Tasan concludes that "virtue" in its classical sense is nothing but the practice of social norms such as filial piety and fraternal respect.[150]

Tasan's theory of virtue closely resembles Kwŏn Ch'ŏlsin's interpretations, which take issue with Chu Hsi's metaphysical orientation in no uncertain terms. According to Kwŏn,

> Among the people of antiquity there was not one person who referred to the inwardly present mind and nature as virtue. That which is not manifested in actual affairs cannot be virtue.[151]

There was also a philosophical reason why Tasan rejected the concept of innate virtue. On the assumption that virtue was by definition good, Chu Hsi's conception of virtue implied that goodness could exist in the mind prior to moral action, a position unacceptable to someone whose fundamental axiological premise was that the distinction between good and evil could only be made in the context of human relationships.[152]

Nevertheless, Confucius appeared to be depicting virtue as a natural endowment when he claimed that "Heaven produced the virtue that is in me: what can Huan T'ui do to me?"[153] This concept of virtue obviously does not correspond to the acquired virtue described by Tasan above. Tasan called this natural attribute the "virtuous nature [*te-hsing/tŏksŏng*]" and drew a sharp distinction between this and virtue itself:

> Without personal practice, how can virtue exist? Consequently, it is called the virtuous nature. The nature originally takes pleasure in the good. When it responds to emotional stimuli and is aroused, it becomes the good heart. The extension of this heart may be regarded as humanity, integrity, propriety, and wisdom. Therefore this nature is called the "virtuous nature."[154]

Here the virtuous nature is being identified with the moral nature (*yŏngji chi kiho*), the human proclivity for goodness. Its aroused state is the good heart, which corresponds to the "upright heart" mentioned by Tasan above. However it is only the "extension" or objectification of the upright heart through ethical practice that can be called virtue. Consequently virtue is realized *a posteriori* as opposed to being endowed by the Heavenly Mandate.

The idea of virtue as being realized *a posteriori* appears in the *Record of Rites*, which states, "All that which is acquired through Rites and Music may be called virtuous. Virtue is an acquirement."[155] Chu Hsi drew the same conclusion in his commentary on the *Analects* where he quoted the *Record of Rites*, stating that "Virtue is an acquirement. When the Way is practiced something is acquired by the mind."[156]

The question of Chu Hsi's seeming ambivalence on the nature of virtue as innate or acquired attribute can be resolved in terms of the substance-function (*t'i-yung*) dichotomy that he applied to key philosophical concepts such as humanity (*jen*). The "substance" of virtue would be the natural endowment and its "function" would be its expression in moral practice. Nonetheless, it would be misleading to equate Tasan's "virtuous nature" with Chu Hsi's portrayal of virtue as substance, since the two concepts are entirely heterogeneous. Tasan's frame of reference was psychological rather than ontological, seeing innate attributes and their behavioral expression in terms of psychological tendencies and their fulfillment rather than as substance and function. In his eyes the idea of virtue as substance preexisting its expression as function risked being misconstrued as meaning that it is capable of cultivation independently of moral conduct, thus perpetuating the idea of self-cultivation through introspection to which he was so opposed.

Chu Hsi had advocated a two-tiered system of self-cultivation reflecting Ch'eng I's formula "integrity to square the external life and seriousness to square the internal life."[157] This represented an affirmation of the importance placed on ethical practice by classical Confucianism, to which was added a new internal dimension based on the premise of virtue existing within the mind, as substance.

Conversely, by stripping virtue of any ontological status and making its realization solely contingent on the fulfillment or objectification of the moral tendencies, Tasan restricted the medium of self-cultivation entirely to the sphere of practical ethics.

Tasan's dynamic interpretation of human nature and virtue thus provided the basis for his outward-looking theory of self-cultivation, succinctly formulated in his exposition of the *Great Learning*. Tasan refuted Chu Hsi's presentation of the classic as having been intended as "learning for adults," and took great pains to demonstrate philologically that it had indeed, as the Late Han classicist Cheng Hsüan (127-200) and the T'ang commentator K'ung Ying-ta (547-648) had maintained, originally been intended as a textbook for the education of the sons of the aristocracy. In doing so he was not implying a rejection of the "new" status imparted to it by Chu Hsi, that of a guide to self-cultivation intended for a wide readership. He was pointing out that it was not a treatise on self-cultivation simply for its own sake. It was learning for government and the ordering of society, and this was the context in which the principles of self-cultivation were taught to the sons of the ruling elite in the ancient *T'ai-hsüeh*, or Confucian academy.[158] By definition, the self-cultivation of the *chün-tzu/kunja*, a person of moral nobility, was not possible apart from the ordering of society, since cultivation was only achieved through the fulfillment of moral responsibility.

This approach to self-fulfillment and learning, according to Tasan, sharply contrasted with the detached, speculative attitude of Korean scholars at the turn of the nineteenth century. The self-esteem of the literati, absorbed in the search for quiescence and new insight into the mysterious harmony between principle and material force, seemed to grow in inverse proportion to their social involvement. A refusal to serve the ruler and sully one's hands with the affairs of state was regarded as a mark of sagehood, and rustic literati (*sallim*) commanded more respect than high officials.[159] Yet this was a time when their scholarly energies and public influence were urgently needed in the service of reform.

Self-Cultivation and the Ordering of Society

In view of his consistently critical attitude toward Ch'eng-Chu learning, whose worldview he held largely responsible for the ineptitude of the scholar-bureaucrats, it might seem ironic that Tasan described the learning of the *chün-tzu*, the person of moral nobility, as "nothing but self-cultivation and the ordering of society,"[160] using the very expression Chu Hsi had coined to describe the teachings of the *Great Learning*.[161] This reveals the admiration that he admittedly felt for Chu Hsi, whose commentaries had guided his early studies of the classics. Nonetheless, the conception of learning as incorporating the dual goals of personal realization and the public good goes much farther back than Chu Hsi. The teachings of Confucius and Mencius were built around the ideal of the "sage-king" or "scholar-politician." These two aspects are interrelated in a passage of the *Spring and Autumn Annals* (*Ch'un-ch'iu*) which defines the business of government as abundant provision for the needs of the people (*hou-sheng*) and the profitable use of resources (*li-yung*), within the dictates of the rectification of virtue (*cheng-te*).[162] This early emphasis on the cultivation of the individual as a necessary condition for the establishment of a prosperous society is echoed in the words of Confucius. When pressed by Yen Yüan to describe the superior man he answered that "He cultivates himself so as to give all people security and peace."[163] This formula describing the dual responsibility of the sage became a defining characteristic of the structure of Confucian thought, reflected in the order of the celebrated "Eight Items" or "Steps" of the *Great Learning*,[164] and resurfacing in a multitude of forms in the thought of Neo-Confucian thinkers. Chu Hsi consequently enshrined this teaching in his introduction to the *Great Learning* with the statement that the classic, along with his commentary, should show the student how to "cultivate the self (*hsiu-chi*) and bring order to society" (*chih-jen*).

Not only did Tasan categorize his writings in terms of these dual goals of Confucian learning, but his philosophical system itself was built around the idea of their interrelatedness, which he felt had been obscured by introspective tendencies in Sung philosophy.[165] He attempted to bridge the gap between the personal and interpersonal, to redefine the idea of self-cultivation in terms of social involvement through moral practice.

Discussing the issue of self-cultivation in the Neo-Confucian tradition, Tu Wei-ming has referred to the first four Items of the *Great Learning* as the "inner" dimension of self-cultivation and the last four as their "outer manifestations."[166] Tasan saw the relationship between the Items more in terms of an interdependency, and indeed, it was the Neo-Confucian conception of a cause-effect relationship between the former and latter Items that he refuted in his discourse on the *Great Learning*:

> Former Confucian scholars [scholars of the Ch'eng-Chu school] understood this classic to be [a treatise on] the method of regulating the mind and the nature. But the Sages of old considered the regulation of the mind and nature to consist in the practice of affairs, and the "practice of affairs" involves nothing but human relations.[167]

"Establishing harmony in the household" and "ordering society" were not simply the result or expression of individual cultivation, but were the medium through which sincerity of the will and rectification of the mind were to be accomplished. Tasan had effectively replaced Ch'eng I's formula of "straightening the internal life" to "square the external life"[168] with the concept of "regulating the exterior to bring peace and order to the interior."[169]

Jen and the "Three Virtues"

By interpreting the elusive concept of *jen*, or humanity—a value that had come to symbolize the Confucian ethos—as the fulfilment of moral responsibility, Tasan made it the crucial bridge linking the dual ideals of Confucian learning. In doing so he attempted to resolve a conflict in the minds of the literati between the demands of these ideas, that is, "self cultivation," or sagely learning, on the one hand and the "ordering of society," or public office, on the other.

In ancient Seal Characters, *jen* was represented by a pictograph of a human being adjacent to the symbol for the number two.[170] Tasan was again giving prominence to etymology when he argued:

> *Jen/in* is the association of two people. Treating one's elder brother with fraternal respect is *jen*. Elder brother and younger brother are two people. Serving one's king with loyalty is *jen*. King and minister are two people. Ruling the people with compassion is *jen*. Ruler and citizen are two people. The fulfilment of respective duties in relationships between all pairs of people, including spouses and friends, is *jen*.[171]

Rejecting the metaphysical significance that the Neo-Confucians had ascribed to it, Tasan regarded the *jen* of Confucius and Mencius to be a generic term for the virtues, claiming that "*Jen* is the `illustrious virtue' of human relations, the collective name for filial piety [*hsiao/hyo*], fraternal respect [*t'i/che*] and compassion [*tz'u/cha*]."[172]

The three virtues mentioned above assumed a pivotal role in Tasan's philosophical system. They were far from being a random sample taken from the virtues mentioned in the classics: according to the ninth chapter of commentary of the *Great Learning*, they were the specific virtues the ruler should exemplify in his government of the state:

> What is meant by "to govern the state, it is necessary first to establish harmony in the household" is this: no one is able to teach others who cannot teach his own household. Therefore, the ruler does not leave his household, yet his teachings are accomplished throughout the state. Filial piety becomes the means to serve the ruler; fraternal respect becomes the means to serve elders; compassion becomes the means to treat the multitude.[173]

Two fundamental assumptions made here, characteristic of early Confucian political thought, are that the virtuous conduct of the sovereign exerts a charismatic effect on the state, and that ideal political relationships are an extension of family ethics. Accordingly, the ruler who exemplifies the three primary virtues of filial piety, fraternal respect, and compassion (or parental love) will, through moral example, inspire the ministers and high officials to adopt the same attitude in their respective social circles and extend them in the government of the state. Since, by extension, the Three Virtues (which is how we shall refer to them henceforth) represent the key to ideal government, they provide the link between the family and its political macrocosm, the state. In Tasan's worldview they also provided the link between the two poles of the *Great Learning*, self-cultivation and the ordering of society, since, as we have seen, he also regarded practical ethics to be the means of self-cultivation.

He summarized the integrative role played by the Three Virtues in the following comment:

> Filial piety, fraternal respect, and compassion are the teachings of the *Great Learning*. It is through the practice of filial piety, fraternal respect, and compassion that one governs family and nation. There is no need to pursue other virtues. One simply has to extend and apply these three. Among these, the virtue of compassion (*tz'u*) is the means of fostering the people.[174]

For Tasan filial piety symbolized the conduct required of inferiors toward superiors, fraternal respect the mutual relationships between siblings and equals, and compassion the conduct of superiors toward inferiors.[175] An indication of the essential role he ascribed to the Three Virtues is the fact that he equated them with the Five Relations—the archetypal ethical principles of pre-Ch'in Confucianism—and used these two terms interchangeably. He justified this with an intriguing explanation of the origins of the "Five Relations." According to the *Classic of Documents*, Tasan points out, the legendary ruler Shun had instructed his minister of education to "promulgate the five teachings [*wu chiao*],"[176] and that, as a result, they came to be universally observed.[177] Mencius interpreted these to be the five relations governing the relationships between father and son, sovereign and minister, husband and wife, old and young, and friends.[178] But Tasan accepted an older explanation of the "five teachings," given in *Tso's Commentary on the Spring and Autumn Annals,* as being paternal duty, maternal love, fraternal affection (on the part of the elder brother), fraternal respect (on the part of the younger brother), and filial piety.[179] The ninth chapter of the *Great Learning* had simply abbreviated the first four relationships described by Tso, referring to them as compassion and fraternal respect.[180] The Three Virtues were thus a condensation of the five teachings of Shun, symbolizing the entire range of Confucian ethics.

The Significance of "Compassion" (*Tz'u*)

Notwithstanding the significant status given it in the *Great Learning* passage quoted above, in the context of the whole Confucian canon the concept of *tz'u* (compassion) enjoys sparse attention in contrast to the abundance of references to *hsiao* (filial piety) and *t'i* (fraternal respect).[181] This reflects a general tendency in the Confucian tradition to stress the moral responsibility of inferiors rather than that of superiors in the family ethical system, and by extension, in the political sphere. It is this very imbalance that Tasan redressed by assigning *tz'u* such a central position in the Confucian ethical constellation.

Tasan frequently referred to *tz'u* as the guiding ethic and motive of true leadership (*mumin/mongmin*, "fostering the people").[182] On being questioned why the ninth chapter of the *Great Learning*—which dealt with the government of the state—dwelt particularly on the meaning of *tz'u* as opposed to the other virtues, Tasan replied,

> Among the three [virtues] only compassion is easily experienced. Therefore it is through this that one comes to appreciate and practice filial piety and fraternal respect. The ancients used to say that only when one raises children does one come to understand parental affection. This is how one comes to appreciate filial piety.[183]

The feeling of compassion, one of the "Four Beginnings" described by Mencius, was considered by Tasan to be the most basic of all.[184] "Sensitivity to the suffering of others" was the spontaneous tendency that Mencius had depicted, in the allegory of the child by the well, to illustrate the innate goodness of human nature. When extended, it became the key to humanity (*jen*) and ideal government—to use his expression, translated literally, the "practice of government sensitive to the suffering of others." In the same vein, the concept of *tz'u* mentioned in the *Great Learning* and elucidated by Tasan, symbolized the spirit of Mencian political humanism *par excellence*—the attitude of the ideal ruler, and in particular his identification with the sufferings and needs of the people. In a discussion on the tenth chapter of the *Great Learning* Tasan contrasted the spontaneous nature of compassion with the conditional nature of filial piety and fraternal respect, which, as responses elicited by parental affection, required cultivation.[185] By analogy, on a political level, the implication was that if the ruler did not embody compassion in his leadership, then he could not expect the people to treat him with genuine loyalty or respect. This idea of reciprocity inherent in the concept of the Three Virtues applied not only to the "vertical" relationship between parent and child, or ruler and ruled, but to the "horizontal" relationship between siblings and equals, since *t'i*, the second of the Three Virtues, symbolized both fraternal respect for seniors and fraternal affection for juniors.[186]

Leadership through Moral Example

Through his discussion of "ruling the state" as described in the *Great Learning*, and particularly in his treatment of the Three Virtues, Tasan underscored a prominent theme in classical Confucian thought, that the ordering of society was achieved through the power of moral example. He considered the *Great Learning* to be a treatise on personal cultivation, and the charismatic effect of such cultivation on leadership, rather than a treatise on the administrative aspect of government per se. Consequently, one finds very little discussion on the technicalities of government in his commentary on the classic.[187] In line with this emphasis, he rejected the vaguest suggestion that the classic implied that the role of the ruler as moral exemplar be supplemented by an actively didactic one. This was a principal reason why he opposed Chu Hsi's suggested emendment to the expression *ch'in-min* (loving the people) in the *Record of Rites* version of the *Great Learning*. Chu's emendment proved to be particularly controversial, especially because it involved one of the so-called "Three Principia" described in the very opening statement of the classic (see page 105), a statement which delineated the subject matter of the whole text.

Chu Hsi had followed the precedent set by Ch'eng I in suggesting that the character *ch'in* (to love, to feel affection for) of *ch'in-min* (loving the people) be replaced with *hsin* (to renew), resulting in the expression *hsin-min* (renewing the people). The evidence he provided to justify this change were the three somewhat disjointed passages on the theme of renewal in chapter two of the Tseng Tzu commentary, which was supposedly a commentary on *hsin-min*.[188]

Like Yang-ming, Tasan considered Chu Hsi's suggested emendation to *ch'in-min* to be unwarranted. Yang-ming had insisted that the expression *ch'in-min*, "loving the people," was no erratum. It implied the practical involvement of the ruler with the day-to-day necessities of his people as well as his responsibility to educate them, whereas the expression *hsin-min*, "renewing the people," referred only to the charismatic side of leadership. But Tasan's reasons for preferring the expression *ch'in-min* were rather different. For him the import of *ch'in-min* revolved entirely around moral example and had nothing to do with the ruler's active involvement in the inculcation of values or the provision of resources.[189] The didactic overtones of the expression *hsin-min* or "renewing the people" did not tally with the essential message of the *Great Learning*, that of leadership through the power of moral example.[190]

This difference of interpretation with Chu is brought into focus by Tasan in his commentary on the third principium, "resting in the highest goodness" (*chih yü chih-shan/chi ŏ chisŏn*):

> Although the Way of the Sages treated the completion of the self and the completion of things as the beginning and end [of all affairs], completion of the self is achieved through self-cultivation and completion of things is also achieved through self-cultivation. This is the meaning of the expression *shen-chiao* [teaching by example].... Once I have attained the highest goodness the people will follow me of their own accord and attain goodness. So the highest goodness of the people is not something which I can forcefully demand of them. "The practice of humanity depends on oneself. Does it depend on others?"[191]

Here again Tasan is linking the teachings of the *Mean* and the *Great Learning*. Chapter 25 of the *Mean* explains that the completion of things is achieved through the completion of the self, and Tasan uses this concept to press his point home, which is that the ordering of society is naturally achieved through the self-cultivation of rulers.

In short, the idea of affection and harmony conveyed by the use of the character *ch'in* in the *Record of Rites* version of the *Great Learning* was consistent with Tasan's conception of the *Great Learning* as a treatise on practical ethics.

Philologically, he saw his adoption of the expression *ch'in-min*, and in particular his position that *ch'in-min* was nothing but the practice of filial piety, fraternal respect, and parental love, to be justified not only by the references to the Three Virtues in the *Great Learning*, but also by references in other classical texts. He pointed to an abundance of passages in the *Analects*, the *Mencius* and the *Classic of Filial Piety* implying a causal relationship between the manifestation of virtue (*ming-te*) on the part of rulers and the affection the people showed for each other (*min-ch'in*).[192] According to a representative passage in the *Mencius*,

> The object of them [the schools of the Three Dynasties] was to make clear [*ming*] human relations. When human relations are thus manifested by superiors, then the common people below will have affection [*ch'in*] for one another.[193]

In view of this causal relationship, Tasan speaks of *ch'in-min* in the sense of "causing the people to love each other," rather than "loving the people" as the great majority of commentators understood it to mean. Remarkably, except for the sentence in the *Great Learning* under discussion, very few of the passages in the classics extolling or exhorting virtuous conduct on the part of rulers use the transitive expression *ch'in-min*, but only the reverse, *min-ch'in*, in the intransitive sense that the people themselves are stirred into showing affection for each other through the example of the ruler's virtue.[194] This fact provides the philological basis for Tasan's position that the "*ch'in-min*" of the *Great Learning* does not mean "loving the people," but "causing the people to love each other" a natural result of the ruler's self-cultivation through virtuous conduct. This is why Tasan speaks of both *ming ming-te*, "manifesting illustrious virtue," and *ch'in-min* as involving the practice of the Three Virtues, the former on the part of the ruler, and the latter on the part of the people.[195]

This idea of leadership through moral example suggested by the *Great Learning* is far from being a philosophy of government through inaction, and indeed Tasan vigorously denies that Confucius taught such a "Taoistic doctrine" himself.[196] When Confucius said that "A ruler who rectifies [*cheng*] his state by virtue is like the north polar star, which remains in its place while all the other stars revolve around it"[197] he was simply portraying the power and magnetism of moral example. By glossing the character *cheng* as signifying "rectification"—which is one of the meanings it represents in certain classical texts—rather than "government"—which is the meaning it more commonly conveys—Tasan implies that this cannot be taken as a statement on political attitudes. Similarly, Tasan's consistency in limiting his discussion of the *Great Learning* to the moral sphere—bearing in mind his voluminous writings on economic and political administration—indicates his conception of this classic as a treatise dealing primarily with the ethics of leadership rather than the mechanics of government, a subject which is given very little mention in his commentary on the *Great Learning*.

The fact that Tasan deems Chu Hsi's emendment to *hsin-min* unnecessary does not mean that he rejects the idea of the people's being "renewed" through the example of the sovereign. He acknowledges that the two characters *hsin* (to renew), and *ch'in* (to love), resemble each other graphically and have related meanings, in the sense that if the people love each other, then they are renewed. This similarity of appearance and meaning is a possible explanation for the references to renewal in Tseng Tzu's commentary,[198] but hardly justifies an alteration to the "Main Text."[199]

The point of contention however, is not Chu Hsi's suggestion of renewal itself, but the nature and process of renewal that he describes as taking place. According to his commentary in the *Great Learning, in Chapters and Verses*,

> Hsin means "to remove the old" [*ko ch'i chiu*]. It is said that, once one has personally manifested one's illustrious virtue, one must then extend it to others, so that they too might have the means to expel their "long-stained impurities" [*chiu-jan chih wu*].[200]

The expression "long-stained impurities" (*chiu-jan chih wu*) is inspired by a statement in the *Classic of Documents* that "those who have long been stained by filthy manners will be allowed to renovate themselves."[201] It is the existence of these "long-stained impurities"—which Chu Hsi equates with the turbidity of the physical endowment—that necessitates a renewal, accomplished through the cultivation of one's own inborn illustrious virtue. After renovating oneself in this way, one then brings about the same renovation in others through the extension of the illustrious virtue.

Tasan responds by challenging a key premise of Chu Hsi's idea of renovation—his concept of "long-stained impurity"—and the assumptions about human nature that lie behind it:

> There are two ways of being stained. One derives from familiarity with wicked people and the other from practicing evil customs. This is what Confucius meant when he said "By nature men are alike. Through practice they have become far apart."[202] How can ignorance requiring the education of correct principles be "stained"? At the age of eight, students entered the School of Lesser Learning [*Hsiao-hsüeh*], practiced sprinkling, sweeping, and polite conversation, familiarized themselves with ritual, music, calligraphy and mathematics, and were cultivated in the practice of reverence. Those who had laid the foundation to qualify for the Confucian Academy [*T'ai-hsüeh*] entered it at the age of fifteen. How could they possibly have been tarnished with "long-stained impurities"? What Chu Hsi refers to as "old stains" [*chiu-jan*] are not the old stains mentioned by Ma in the *Classic of Documents,* where he says that "those who have long been stained [*chiu-jan*] by filthy manners will be allowed to renovate themselves." The "stains" of the physical endowment and human desire cannot be absent even in a so-called *shang-chih/sangji* [a very wise man].[203]

Chu Hsi is evidently using the expression "old stains" to describe the turbidity of the physical endowment, which in varying degrees is present in the mind from birth, and the removal of which he considers to be the task "manifesting illustrious virtue" *(ming ming-te)* and "renewing the people" *(hsin-min)* are addressing. In the last sentence of the above translation the word "stains" is placed in quotation marks as Tasan is obviously poking fun at Chu Hsi's idea that the physical endowment or human desires are themselves stains that obscure the original nature. According to Tasan, the concept of "renewal" mentioned in the *Great Learning* has nothing to do with the removal of the stains acquired through the years of degenerate behavior that Ma is referring to in the *Classic of Documents*, considering the youth and limited social exposure of the students at the *T'ai-hsüeh* (at whom the teaching of the *Great Learning* was supposedly directed).

Tasan regards the lucidity or turbidity of the physical endowment as representing only a potential for good or evil. The only kind of "stain" he recognizes is that which is acquired through conduct. The notion that human desires and the physical endowment impose restrictions on the free expression of "original nature" prior to conduct, is more reminiscent of Buddhist doctrine than the Confucian Way:

According to the *Leng yen ching* "The nature hidden in the Thus-come *[ju-lai/tathāgata]* is pure and natural." This is the "original nature." If the original nature becomes stained by new obscurity *[hsin-hsün]* then it loses the original substance of Suchness *[chen-ju/tathatā]*. This is a theory repeatedly mentioned in the [Buddhist] doctrines of Wisdom *[po-je/prajñā]* and the Awakening of Faith *[ch'i-hsin]*. If we say that it is newly obscured, then the original substance, vacuous and bright though it may be, is newly covered by the obscurity and stains of the physical endowment. Therefore "new obscurity" is [what Chu Hsi refers to as] "old stains," and "old stains" are nothing but "new obscurity." If one speaks of it in relation to the original nature then one refers to it as "new obscurity," and if one speaks of it in relation to present conditions then one refers to it as "old stains." Profound truth though this may be, it is certainly not what is meant by *ch'in-min* and *hsin-min* in the *Great Learning*.[204]

The origin of Chu Hsi's concept of the turbid material force (or "old stains," as he puts it in the passage above quoted from the *Great Learning, in Chapters and Verses*) covering the original nature, is here being attributed to the Buddhist doctrines of the *Prajñāpāramitā* and Śraddhotpāda shastras. The idea of turbid material force obscuring the "illustrious virtue" is parallel to the concept of "new obscurity" which is said to cause the loss of the original substance of Suchness.

Tasan is thus criticizing Chu Hsi for indulging in philosophical speculation and introducing extraneous concepts without reference to the context of the *Great Learning*, which is essentially a treatise on practical ethics. The clue to the meaning of "renewal" is found in a passage on the charismatic effect of the ruler's virtuous conduct, in the ninth and tenth chapters of the *Great Learning* itself:

It is said in the *Great Learning,* "Through the benevolence of one family, the whole state becomes benevolent, and through its courtesy the whole state becomes courteous" and also "When the ruler treats the aged as they should be treated, then the people will be aroused [*hsing*] toward filial piety. When the ruler treats his elders as they should be treated, then the people will be aroused [*hsing*] toward fraternal respect." *Hsing* means "to renew," to eliminate the old and to be newly aroused. This is

> what is meant by "renewing the people". How could this possibly mean that the "vacuous perspicacious substance [of the mind]" is newly illuminated?[205]

In other words, the idea of "renewal" implied in the *Great Learning* has nothing to do with the removal of obscure material force (*hsün-ch'i*)—it is a moral renewal inspired by the example of the sovereign and reflected in the "arousal" (*hsing*) of the people toward filial piety, fraternal respect, and parental love.

Political Implications

So far as political philosophy is concerned, as opposed to problems of metaphysics and human nature, Tasan rarely confronted the opinions of the Ch'eng brothers and Chu Hsi directly. This is not surprising when one considers that the major innovations of the Ch'eng-Chu school were in the field of human nature and principle, rather than in the more down-to-earth areas of rites, music, and government. Nonetheless, Tasan was ready to differ when their metaphysics and ethics bore implications for political leadership, as we have seen in the case of Chu Hsi's views on the subject of *hsin-min*, the renewal of self and society. Furthermore, one reason why Tasan had so vehemently opposed Chu Hsi's theory of self-cultivation was the implication that intellectual attributes, and in particular the cognitive refinement required for the "investigation of the principle in things and affairs" played a major role particularly in the initial stage of self-cultivation. This perspective could be interpreted as lending legitimacy to the traditional assumption that the educated class had a head start in the pursuit of virtue and thus enlightened leadership. Conversely, Tasan's emphasis on the affective character of the moral inclinations, as well as his emphasis on sincerity of the will as the starting point for moral enlightenment, relegated the cognitive powers to a position, albeit still a significant position, of secondary importance. This change in emphasis furnishes a further explanation for Tasan's unprecedented confidence in the ability of the uneducated majority to choose virtuous leaders.

Tasan's advocacy of the extension of family ethics, particularly compassion, to the sphere of government, begs the question of whether he simply intended to draw attention to the ethical basis of benevolent monarchy originally suggested by Mencius. But behind Tasan's call for a return to practical ethics lay the conviction that any attempt to promote concrete reforms under the prevailing system of government would prove fruitless without an accompanying change in attitudes on the part of the leadership. This concern is particularly understandable in view of the apparent ease with which policies and administrational safeguards implemented to stem exploitation and corruption had been circumvented due to a susceptibility of later Chosŏn *yangban* politics to the abuse of power. Nevertheless there is evidence that Tasan favored systems of government built upon populist principles that would discourage such abuse, but he did not give such ideas concrete expression in his proposals for reform, presumably as he knew that they would be far from welcome. His *Treatise on Ideal Government* (*T'angnon*) clearly reveals an aspiration not only for qualitative change in political attitudes along the lines of classical political humanism, but change in the system of government itself:

> How did the emperor come to exist? Was he sent down and inaugurated by Heaven? Or did he become emperor by springing up from the grassroots?
>
> Five houses formed a hamlet [*lin*], and the leader selected by these five became a hamlet chief. Five hamlets formed a village [*li*], and the leader selected by these five became a village chief. Five towns [*pi*] formed a district [*hsien*], and the leader selected by these five became a district chief. The representative selected by the district chiefs became a feudal lord, and the representative selected by the feudal lords became the emperor. The position of emperor was established by the people.... In ancient times those below selected those above—this accords with the Way. Nowadays those above select those below—this contravenes the Way.[206]

With unexpected candor, and yet in the typically Confucian manner of appealing to ancient tradition, Tasan is suggesting the desirability of reform by contrasting a somewhat idealized interpretation of the Chou dynasty system of leadership with that of the late Chosŏn. Here he is clearly talking about political power wielded by the people on a more institutionalized basis than the temporary right to revolution suggested by Mencius.[207] This confidence in the choice of the people may well originate in Tasan's conception of human nature, particularly his belief that, not only are human beings able to attain the "virtue of Heaven," but that even those who remain a long way from achieving this end are endowed with a faculty enabling them to make enlightened moral choices. Seen in this light, the opening words of the above passage could hardly be interpreted as a manifesto for secular government, as opposed to government in accordance with the Heavenly Mandate. On the contrary, Tasan is equating the two in the Confucian equivalent of *vox populis vox dei*. This was of course the spirit of the Mencian political teachings, but Tasan took the unprecedented step of giving it concrete, and lasting, institutional expression in his "bottom-up" theory of government.

Tasan failed to elaborate and build on the radical implications of his intriguing "bottom-up" theory of government, as well as equally provocative proposals on land reform also written during his early years before or shortly after taking up government office.[208] Most likely his time in office, spent under the close and envious scrutiny of his conservative Old Doctrine opponents, would have been even shorter had he ventured to do so.

But there is perhaps another reason why such lofty idealism becomes harder to find in his later works, a reason barely concealed between the lines of a poem written during his period of exile:

> In my youth I thought about sagehood
> In middle age I hoped to be a wise man
> In my old age I ended up siding with the common people
> Fretting about what is to become of them, I can't even sleep[209]

Exile in one of the most destitute corners of the peninsula had dealt a stunning blow to Tasan's youthful idealism. Perhaps this is why one no longer sees him writing about the radical changes hinted at in the brief essays mentioned on page 65, but rather on the more specific and sober proposals for reform detailed in his later masterpieces such as the *Reflections on Fostering the People* (*Mongmin simsŏ*) and *Treatise on Government* (*Kyŏngse yup'yo*), which focus on change within the basic framework of existing Chosŏn institutions. He could hardly have predicted that, two hundred years later, when the socioeconomic context of such reforms had been utterly transformed, the spirit behind them would have a far greater impact on the national consciousness.

4

Tasan's "Classical Learning," Ch'ing Evidential Learning, and Tokugawa Ancient Learning

In a thought-provoking paper entitled "Korea's Role in the History of East Asian Philosophy," Fred Sturm of the University of New Mexico underlines the need to examine further international "influences and consequences" in East Asian intellectual history.[1] This approach is particularly productive in the study of Tasan's thought, which was influenced by two principal currents of reaction to the Ch'eng-Chu school in China and Japan, to be found within the Evidential Scholarship (*K'ao-cheng hsüeh*) of the Ch'ing "Han Learning" movement, and the so-called "Ancient Learning" (*Kogaku*) of the Tokugawa.

Tasan and the Evidential Learning of the Ch'ing

It appears that no detailed discussion has yet been published on the impact of Ming and Ch'ing scholarship on Tasan's work.[2] Research on this topic is complicated by the fact that Tasan rarely mentioned the philosophical views of particular thinkers of the Ch'ing,[3] in spite of the fact that he had access to a large amount of literature from this period.[4]

The obvious reason for this lack of mention, particularly in the case of Tasan's commentaries on the Four Books, is that the blatantly anti-Ch'eng-Chu stance of many Ch'ing Confucian thinkers met the disapproval of their conservative Korean counterparts. But it was not simply a reluctance to be associated with such outright opposition to Chu Hsi's teachings that discouraged Tasan from quoting and discussing their work. He himself disapproved of what he saw as unqualified criticism of Sung Neo-Confucianism made by Ch'ing philosophers such as Mao Ch'i-ling.[5]

Tasan also disapproved of certain tendencies in *hsün-ku-hsüeh* or "philological learning," a systematic approach to glossing texts championed by the "Han Learning" scholars of the Ch'ing, including Mao, in their attempt to analyse classical literature. The term *Han-hsüeh* or "Han Learning" originally referred to a school of scholarship that was pioneered by Hui Tung (1697–1758) in Soochow during the eighteenth century, and taken up by Wang Ming-sheng (1722–98), Wang Ch'ang (1725–1807), and Ch'ien Ta-hsin (1728–1804) at the illustrious Tzu-yang Academy. Their scholarship was often referred to as "ancient learning" (*ku-hsüeh*), and they "sought the truth in actual facts" (*shih-shih ch'iu-shih*).[6] The movement focused on Han dynasty commentaries and exegesis, and particularly those of the earlier Han. These were regarded as valuable sources for research on the classics, especially because their authors had access to early versions of classical texts, and were less speculative in approach than the Sung commentators. The expression *Han-hsüeh* or "Han Learning" later became almost synonymous with *K'ao-cheng-hsüeh* or "evidential learning," although, as Benjamin Elman points out, the methodology of Evidential Learning was not monopolized by Han Learning, but used in many other fields of study, such as history, astronomy, geography and epigraphy.[7] Evidential Learning itself was a new mode of scholarship that emerged in the late Ming, which gave priority to verification and proof, made systematic use of sources, and shunned speculation. These are all characteristics of the approach of the "Han Learning" scholars, which Tasan referred to as *Hsün-ku-hsüeh*, or Philological Learning.

In a revealing passage of his *Treatise on the Five Schools* (*Ohang-non*), Tasan argued that the original pursuit of Philological Learning was to clarify the meanings of terms in the classics in order to discover the essence of the Way, but that the Philological Learning of his time had deviated from this ideal.

According to Tasan, the commentaries of the great T'ang classicists K'ung Ying-ta and Chia Kung-Yen had been very influential, but they had only succeeded in analyzing the meaning of words and phrases and failed to clarify the profound teachings and way of the Early Kings and sages. Chu Hsi, concerned about these developments, had sought for meaning beyond the glosses of the Han and Wei, and brought about a revival of the Confucian Way through his work on the classics, a contribution far superior to that of his Han predecessors. It was up to contemporary scholars to examine the glosses in the Han commentaries, and then to search for the meanings and principles in the works of Chu Hsi, and finally to assess reliability and accuracy by directly consulting the classical texts. Then they should put what they have thus learnt into practice, "below" in establishing harmony in their households and bringing order to the state, and "above" by attaining the virtue of Heaven and returning to the Heavenly Mandate.[8]

Nonetheless, Tasan maintained that in his time, although Philological Learning proponents claimed that their learning was a combination of Han and Sung scholarship, it actually followed the Han tradition by limiting itself to the detailed exegesis of minutiae.[9]

In other words, the Philological Learning scholars occupied themselves with philological inquiry into the meaning of words and phrases, while shunning the Sung tradition of fleshing out the broader philosophical issues such terminology was used to discuss. For Tasan the analysis of phrases and concepts was a means to the end of clarifying the philosophical import of the Confucian teachings, particularly regarding such key issues as self-cultivation and the ordering of society, and he deplored what he considered to be the establishment of philology as an end in itself devoid of reference to philosophical implications. Whereas the work of such early Ch'ing scholars as Yen Jo-chü (1636–1704) and the School of Han Learning focused on philological research and left little room for theoretical discussion, Tasan used the new methods of linguistic analysis and etymological research to enlarge on traditional philosophical questions and provide alternatives to Chu Hsi's theories.

To illustrate opposing extremes within Han and Sung Confucianism, Tasan borrowed two expressions from a saying by Confucius, "Learning without thought is labor lost; thought without learning is perilous."[10] On the one hand, the Han Confucians had focused on the study of ancient texts without making "clear distinctions," and were thus unable to avoid the influence of divination and the influx of corrupt doctrines. This was a case of "study without thought." On the other hand the Neo-Confucians had placed emphasis on the plumbing of principle and the study of annotations, and were thus prone to mistakes and inaccuracies. This showed the weakness of "thought without study."[11]

Although both Han and Sung scholarship come in for criticism in his commentaries as well as his *Treatise on the Five Schools*, Tasan's deep respect for Chu Hsi for having revived the Confucian Way as a living tradition is unmistakeable, and what is also clear is that he regards the inaccuracies of the Sung teachings as less destructive than the empty academicism of Philological Learning.

Such criticisms of Philological Learning may be applicable to a sizeable proportion of mainstream Ch'ing proponents of Han Learning who paid little attention to the cultivation of virtue, but they could hardly have been directed at a group of later Ch'ing scholars, whom Elman has referred to as "*k'ao-cheng* philosophers," such as Tasan's contemporary Tai Chen, as well as Juan Yüan and Chiao Hsün (1763–1820). As Elman has argued, these thinkers brought out certain implications of the new philology for traditional philosophical issues.[12] These implications were especially productive in their philosophical critiques of orthodox Neo-Confucianism. It is in this respect that Tai Chen and Juan Yüan's work on the classics paralleled the scholarship of Tasan, and it was this characteristic of their scholarship that was criticized by less philosophically oriented exponents of Han Learning.[13] In spite of these parallels Tasan only mentions Tai Chen's work twice in his classical commentaries, and only with reference to the *Classic of Documents*. As we shall see, in the case of the Tokugawa Ancient Learning scholars, the coverage given to them in Tasan's commentaries appears to be in inverse proportion to the sympathy that he showed for their views, and the fact that Tai Chen is only rarely quoted reveals little about Tasan's attitude toward his work. Juan Yüan and Chiao Hsün receive no mention, possibly because their work was not yet accessible.[14]

Nonetheless, there are significant differences between Tasan and his late Ch'ing counterparts in terms of scholarly methods as well as the critical approaches they took toward Ch'eng-Chu Learning. Tasan, Tai, and Juan shared the techniques of Philological Learning in their etymological and phonological research on certain key concepts appearing in the *Analects* and *Mencius* to show that Neo-Confucian interpretations had injected extraneous modes of thought. But despite

Tasan's misgivings about Philological Learning, he seems to have been significantly more indebted to its methods than Tai Chen, and even Juan Yüan. Whereas Tai and Juan often used the essay-type approach in their discussion of these concepts, Tasan introduced his interpretations in the form of highly detailed commentaries on the classics. In his verse-by-verse analysis of the Four Books, for example, Tasan cited numerous commentaries on each passage, particularly those of Han, Wei, T'ang, Sung and Tokugawa scholars, providing subcommentaries supplementing or criticizing their views, as well as appending his conclusions. Various shades of meaning and differences in usage of particular concepts were discussed by citing references in other texts, including early sources such as the *Classic of Odes*, and lexicons for treatments of etymology and phonology.[15]

Tasan retained the more rigorous and objective philological approach of the mainstream Han Learning proponents in his discussion of Confucian philosophy. Although he was opposed to the uses to which the Han Learning school had applied Evidential Learning, he recognized its value as a tool in the analysis of the classics:

> The merit of Ch'ing scholarship lies in its examination of evidence (*k'ao-chü*). This approach is characterized by detailed philological inquiry and scantiness with regard to moral principles....[16]

In his "Introductory Remarks to `Ancient Glosses on the Classic of Documents'" Tasan showed familiarity with the methods of Evidential Learning in the following analysis of its various manifestations:

> With regard to differences between characters, one refers to *k'ao-i* [examination of differences]; with regard to mistaken meanings one refers to *k'ao-wu* [examination of errata]: with regard to corroboration using other sources, one refers to *k'ao-cheng* [examination of evidence]; with regard to the fair evaluation of opinions, one refers to *k'ao-ting* [evaluative examination]; and with regard to the comparative study of disputations, one refers to *k'ao-p'ien* [examination of arguments].[17]

This multifaceted philology provided the foundation for Tasan's critique of Chu Hsi, as well as his elaboration of alternative philosophical views. In this regard another significant difference between Tasan's work and the Ch'ing "evidential philosophers" mentioned is that he was more sympathetic toward Chu Hsi, particularly for his attempts to clarify the "hidden import" of the sages' teachings for the problem of self-cultivation, and especially with respect to the relationship between the "mind of the Way" and the "human mind," and the related problem of selfish desire, as discussed in chapter 3. Tai's work on the classics in particular, including his *Evidential Analysis of the Meanings of Terms in the Mencius* (*Meng-tzu tzu-i shu-cheng*), was more stridently anti–Chu Hsi, with stronger political overtones.[18]

Another significant difference is that Tasan appears to be more inclined to elaborate on his critiques and build alternative frameworks of interpretation. Although Tai and Juan were quite ready to point out the "speculative extravagancies" of the Neo-Confucians, including their ontological interpretations of human nature and the Investigation of Things,[19] they appear less ready than Tasan to use the implications of these conclusions in developing novel constructions, such as Tasan's theory of *kiho* or "appetites," to resolve the ambiguities of the classical teachings.

Tasan and the Ancient Learning proponents of the Tokugawa

Although it is still hard to find systematic work on the impact of Ch'ing scholarship on Korea, interest is growing in the links between Chosŏn and Tokugawa Confucianism. In this context it is significant that at least seven Korean-language articles and one book have been published during the last decade or so which provide a detailed discussion of the views of Korean "Sirhak" thinkers on Japanese culture, politics, and Confucian thought.[20]

Tasan discussed various aspects of Japanese culture as well as literature on Japan in at least eight different works, including his *Essay on Japan* (*Ilbonnon*).[21] In this short essay Tasan indicated that he was impressed by the works of Itō Jinsai and the classical commentaries of Dazai Shundai and Ogyū Sorai, three outstanding Japanese thinkers associated with the so-called "Ancient Learning" of the Tokugawa.

Furthermore, the writings of these thinkers appear to have reassured Tasan of the civilized and peaceful intentions of the Japanese people, and in the remainder of the essay he speculated on the decline of Japanese militarism and its implications for future relations with Korea.[22]

Previous to Tasan, Yi Ik, whose work he greatly admired, had shown an interest in Japanese Confucianism, and in particular an appreciation of the social and political impact of the work of Yamazaki Ansai (1618–82) and his followers. This marked a departure from the indifference or disdain shown by Yi Ik's Neo-Confucian predecessors toward Japanese scholarship. Although it is not known on which particular sources Yi Ik's information was based, we do know that his disciple An Chŏngbok (1712–91) had studied the work of Itō Jinsai, which was first introduced to Korea through the embassy to Japan in 1719. An had also read of Japanese reactions to Itō Jinsai's scholarship in the report of Yu Hu, a secretary who had accompanied the Korean emissaries to Japan in 1748.[23] An Chŏngbok appeared especially impressed by Itō Jinsai's *Boy's Questions* (*Dōjimon*) and the epilogue to the same work written by Hayashi Keihan, commenting that, "On the whole, he [Itō Jinsai] deeply respects Mencius, while at times he disparages Ch'eng I. His writings are excellent and contain many valuable sayings. It is unexpected that such a man of letters should exist in an uncultivated island nation."[24]

As we shall see from the analysis below, Itō Jinsai's work appears to have made a still greater impact on the views of Tasan, who was more receptive to Itō's critique of orthodox Neo-Confucian learning than his philosophically conservative fellow Southerner, An Chŏngbok.

In view of the interest in Japanese scholarship shown by the School of Yi Ik, it is hardly surprising that Tasan obtained, among other Japanese works, Jinsai's *Ancient Meaning of the Analects* (*Rongokōgi*), Sorai's *Evidential Study of the Analects* (*Rongochō*), and Shundai's *External Transmission of Ancient Glosses on the Analects* (*Rongokokun gaiden*).[25] Chŏng Chong has made a detailed study of the structure and content of Tasan's voluminous *Commentaries on the Analects, Old and New* (*Nonŏ kogŭmju*). In a statistical analysis of previous commentaries quoted in this work, Chŏng noted that a commentator named "Sun," or Dazai Shundai, is quoted 82 times, making him the ninth most frequently quoted. Another commentator referred to as "Chŏk," or Ogyū Sorai, is quoted 37 times, putting him in twelfth place, whereas "Tŭng,"—Itō Jinsai—is quoted twice.[26] The most quoted of all commentators is of course Chu Hsi with 398 passages. Curiously, the number of quotations attributed to these Japanese scholars appears to be inversely proportional to the amount of sympathy Tasan felt for their views. One possible reason is that he often quoted glosses he disagreed with to highlight his own contrasting interpretations.

In an article dealing principally with Tasan's *Essay on Japan*, Yi Ŭrho defines four trends characterizing the thought of the Tokugawa scholars Itō Jinsai, Dazai Shundai and Ogyū Sorai, which also appear in the work of Tasan.

First, Yi maintains that the "Ancient Learning" scholars' veneration of the "Way of the Early Kings" is reflected in Tasan's advocacy of a return to the teachings of Yao, Shun, the Duke of Chou, and Confucius.

Secondly, they opposed a "rationalistic" tendency exhibited by the Ch'eng-Chu school and attempted to reinvest the emotions (*ch'ing/chŏng*) with the more elevated status they had enjoyed in the classical Confucian teachings. This trend is apparent in Tasan's theory of natural inclinations (*sŏngkiho sŏl*), his "dynamic" interpretation of human nature as psychological tendencies.

Thirdly, they rejected Neo-Confucian quietistic tendencies and the principle/material force (*li-ch'i/i-ki*) dualism, focusing instead on practical ethics and the more substantial issues of rites, music, and politics. This tendency is reminiscent of the Korean Sirhak school's emphasis on ethical practicality and social utility in the form of administration and practical usage (*kyŏngse ch'iyong*).

Fourthly, Yi argues, a tendency for *kyŏnghŏmnon chŏk kwahak sasang* or empirical, scientific thinking, and a sympathy for the concerns of the urban professionals and merchants, which was a manifestation of a utilitarian attitude.[27]

Such attempts to draw concise parallels between the approaches of "Ancient Learning" and "Sirhak" thinkers may provide thought-provoking frameworks for comparative research, but they can be misleading. This is due not least to the very divergent forms of social practicality advocated within the Ancient Learning and Sirhak schools—if such broad spectrums of thought can be called schools—that grew out of the reaction to political realities as well as perceived quietistic and introspective tendencies within the Ch'eng-Chu school. On the one hand Jinsai, particularly in his later works, concentrated on practical ethics as the basis of self-cultivation, whereas Sorai and Shundai were more involved in political philosophy and institutions. I would further qualify the above comparison by adding that, although the scholarship of both Tasan and the Ancient Learning proponents was marked by philological inquiry and exegetical research of a more methodical and rigorous nature than that of their Neo-Confucian predecessors, none of them were empiricists in a strictly philosophical or scientific sense.

With this in mind I have attempted to outline several common themes in the work of Tasan on the one hand, and Jinsai and Sorai on the other:

First, in their commentaries on the classics they studied the "ancient meanings" of terms in order to rediscover the teachings of the early sages which were considered to have been obscured by Sung and Ming "speculative" philosophy, by means of thorough exegesis and philological research. This trend was accompanied by a rejection of any reliance on the authority of particular commentaries. Tasan and Sorai criticized the usage of certain philosophical categories, for example, the principle-material force (*li-ch'i*) metaphysical framework and substance-function (*t'i-yung*) dualism, imposed by the Ch'eng-Chu school proponents in their attempt to systematize the classical teachings.

Secondly, on the basis of the above-mentioned empirical approach and the resulting insight they considered themselves to have gained into the pristine Confucian message, they emphasized the practical spirit of pre-Ch'in Confucianism in its various manifestations. This was accompanied by a criticism of the emphasis on quietistic introspection they attributed to Neo-Confucian techniques of self-cultivation, and considered to have originated from Buddhism and Taoism. In contrast they emphasized that personal realization could only be achieved through interpersonal relationships, governed by practical ethics and ritual conduct.

Thirdly, they rejected dualistic tendencies and Buddhist influence in Ch'eng-Chu metaphysics and their application to the human condition in the theories of "original nature" (*pen-jan chih hsing*) and "physical nature" (*ch'i-chih chih hsing*).

In the fourth place, they emphasized the positive role the feelings could play in self-cultivation, or the capacity of the feelings and desires to reflect principle, insofar as they formed the basis of man's potential to do good.

Not surprisingly, these are themes that had previously emerged or been hinted at in certain branches of Ming and early Ch'ing Confucianism. Their empirical methodology, their affirmation of the positive role of the emotions and desires, and their emphasis on the practical value of scholarship were preceded by the work of Late Ming and early Ch'ing thinkers such as Lo Ch'in-shun (1465–1547), Yen Yüan (1635–1704), and Li Kung (1659–1733).

It was on the basis of the Evidential Learning methodology, used by Ch'ing scholars to formulate their critiques of Neo-Confucian orthodoxy, that Tasan introduced certain novel perspectives which echoed developments in the Jinsai-Sorai schools:

First, Tasan, Jinsai, and Sorai drew from the religious orientation of the Shang and Early Chou to develop a more personalized, dynamic conception of Heaven.

As with Tasan, a prominent characteristic of the thought of Sorai and Jinsai was their opposition to the Sung view that Heaven was principle.[28] Jinsai replaced the idea of an impassive principle with his idea of Heaven's Way (*tendo*) as a living and active entity (*katsubutsu*), arguing that Heaven and earth is one great living thing.

> How could the term li be enough to be the source for the endless changes of this living organism? *Li* is in fact a term of death. It is within things, but does not rule things.[29]

The two points of contention raised here are that the term li conveys the idea of inanimacy, being simply the inner pattern of the conglomeration and dispersion of ch'i, and furthermore that being intrinsic it cannot play the role of ruler or overseer of things ascribed to Heaven by writers of the Chou. In contrast, Jinsai referred to the Way of Heaven as the constant flux of the cosmos, and to the Heavenly Mandate as the command of an entity who responded to the human order and took an active role in human affairs, "observing the good and evil, integrity and corruption of men."[30] He also compared Heaven to a ruling prince, and its mandate to his command.[31]

This idea of Heaven as an entity responsive to, and involved in, human affairs, is given only passing mention in Jinsai's criticism of the Ch'eng-Chu depiction of principle and his discussion of the distinction between the Way of Heaven and the Mandate of Heaven. On the other hand, the conception of a transcendent, active Heaven played a central part in the philosophy of Sorai, who censured Ch'eng Hao for claiming that Heaven and Earth did not have a mind. The Way of the Early Kings was the ultimate standard to be followed, and this was "entirely based on reverence for Heaven."[32]

Tasan and Jinsai's personalization of Heaven as an entity with ethical predelictions served as the ontological basis for their emphasis on self-realization through ethical practice. Conversely, Sorai's depiction of Heaven as an unfathomable object of reverence external to man, and the basis of the authority of the Early Kings, had decidedly political implications.[33] On the one hand, explicitly in the case of Tasan, the potential of human beings to "communicate directly" with Heaven and "attain the virtue of Heaven" signified a subjective, creative role in the interpretation and application of ethical norms.[34] But in the case of Sorai, the separation of man from an unknowable, transcendent Heaven, and his advocacy of Rites and Music as a creation of the Early Kings, implied a reliance on the objective standards set up by a secular authority rather than on the autonomous interpretation of norms. This is one reason why Sorai rejected Jinsai's adoption of "filial piety, brotherly love, benevolence and integrity" as the means to bring "peace and contentment to the world" in favor of the more precise delimitations on behavior required by the rites.[35]

Tasan's depiction of the supreme ruler *Shang-ti* as an object of reverence has generally been ascribed to the influence of "Western Learning", to which he and many other members of the Southerner faction in the eighteenth century were undoubtably attracted. But one cannot discount the possibility that the writings of Jinsai and Sorai also played a significant part in the formulation of his monotheistic version of Confucianism. At the very least, the work of these two Tokugawa scholars must have encouraged him to look back to the *Classic of Documents* and *Classic of Odes* for canonical justification in his rejection of the orthodox Neo-Confucian conception of Heaven as principle.

Secondly, Jinsai's adoption, and Tasan's elaboration, of the early Chou conception of Heaven as a sentient being actively involved in human affairs, provided the ontological foundation of their interpretation of human nature as essentially dynamic.[36] Human nature was the moral tendency to "love goodness" and "hate evil" endowed by Heaven, and consequently Chu Hsi's conception of nature as an "unmanifested" (*wei-fa*) state prior to contact with things was rendered meaningless.[37] This affective interpretation of nature, particularly in the form of Tasan's theory of psychological propensities, represented the philosophical expression of a tendency already present in Ming scholarship to interpret nature dynamically, as a reaction to a perceived quietism within the Ch'eng-Chu school. Lo Ch'in-shun's philosophy, for example, exemplified a monistic tendency to interpret the human nature imparted by the Heavenly Mandate as an expression of material force as well as normative principle, and consequently to envisage feelings as qualities of the Heaven-endowed nature.[38]

Thirdly, Jinsai and Tasan's interpretation of human nature in terms of the innate movement of the mind (*hsin*) toward goodness provided the psychological basis for a rigorous philosophy of practical ethics, characterized by an outward-looking approach to self-cultivation, that is, the perception that personal development took place entirely within the medium of human relationships. This approach drew strength from the argument that self-realization could only be attained if the moral tendencies characterizing the nature could be objectified in ethical conduct.[39] Both of them took upon themselves the task of clarifying a pre-Ch'in emphasis on ethical practice they perceived to have been obscured by an inward trend in the Ch'eng-Chu school. Pointing out that Confucius and Mencius gave greater weight to the nourishment of the moral tendencies rather than introspection, Jinsai sought to unfold the hidden import of the Confucian ethical teachings—and in the process unravel Neo-Confucian metaphysics—through a systematic philology he ingeniously developed well before the Japanese had even set eyes on the works of the *k'ao-cheng* pioneers Ku Yen-wu and Yen Jo-chü. One and a half centuries later, Tasan harnessed the incisive power of a now mature *k'ao-cheng* scholarship in his attempt to "pierce the veil" the Han, Tang and Sung commentaries had cast over the practical ethics of Confucius and Mencius, and unfold their philosophical import.

A fourth tendency, explicit in the philosophy of both Tasan and Jinsai, and implied in the work of Tai Chen,[40] was the sharp distinction they drew between the Way of Heaven and the Way of man. The concept of the Way of Heaven, they argued, had originated in the *Classic of Changes* and indicated purely natural processes such as the fluctations between yin and yang. It had nothing to do with the Way Confucius had spoken of in the *Analects*, which was the Way of man, that is, the path of moral duty that people should follow in their daily existence.[41] In making this distinction they severed the link between cosmology and ethics that had served as the linchpin of Chu Hsi's entire system, and rebuilt a frame of reference for self-cultivation that was entirely based on practical ethics. This objectification of norms—the Way of man—did not signify, however that their ethical theories were teleological, let alone utilitarian. Jinsai held that the Way existed irrespective of the existence of man, and Tasan believed that man's moral inclinations were endowed by a virtue-loving Heaven, Heaven in this context being *Sangje*.[42] This distinction between a natural Way and the Way of man also served, in the case of Tasan, to bring into relief an alternative vision of man as a unique being, endowed with a freedom to make moral decisions that distinguished him from the "birds and the beasts."[43] As we have mentioned, a common theme to be found in the very diverse approaches taken by Jinsai and Tasan on the one hand, and Sorai on the other, is the spirit of "social practicality" as a reaction to inward-looking orientations and subjectivism in Sung and Ming Neo-Confucianism. Tasan and Jinsai's mutual opposition to Chu Hsi's theory of the investigation of things (as a separate step prior to the "sincerity of the will") was derived from the belief that internal and external should be taken care of simultaneously, a view not unrelated to Wang Yang-ming's theory of the unity of knowledge and action.[44] Tasan took this form of ethical activism a step further by reversing Ch'eng I's emphasis on "straightening the internal life" to "square the external life"[45] with the concept of "regulating the exterior to bring peace and order to the interior."[46]

Tasan's radical form of ethical practicality was based on the idea that virtue was only realized through upright deeds, a view echoing the standpoint taken by Sorai in his criticism (albeit unsubstantiated) of Jinsai's interpretation of virtue as referring "merely to what exists before virtue is achieved."[47] Furthermore, his conception of "regulating the exterior to bring peace and order to the interior" is curiously reminiscent of Sorai's constant emphasis on the realization of virtue through the practice of rites and music. Although Sorai advocated the practice of ceremonial forms principally in the context of "pacifying the world," he simultaneously presented it as the classical approach to self-cultivation in contrast to the idealistic, subjective Neo-Confucian theories of "plumbing principle and extending knowledge," which were nothing more than efforts to "control the mind by means of the mind." I would hesitate to speculate whether Sorai's depiction of rites and music as a means of self-cultivation was entirely a tactical justification in the pursuit of political goals. In view of this, instead of characterizing the transition from the Jinsai to the Sorai school primarily as the increasing separation of inner and outer, or moral cultivation and politics,[48] I would rather stress a tendency toward the objectification and externalization of norms—as a means of self-cultivation as well as social control—in response to subjective trends in the Sung and Ming. To attack the route of introspective cultivation as a method for attaining correct ethical and political action is not equivalent to attacking the union of inner and outer, as Maruyama claimed.[49]

Tasan's conception of virtue as acquirement marked a similar transition in late Chosŏn dynasty thought, though Sorai took the trend toward externalization much further, criticizing the practical ethics championed by Jinsai as representing "a foot without inches, and a measuring rod without notches." Indeed, Tasan and Jinsai left plenty of room for subjective interpretation in their ethical systems, since they were very much concerned with the individual's capacity, as an independent agent, to reinterpret and internalize norms. The fine balance between self-control or motivation on the one hand and social sanction on the other was a perennial concern of Confucians. Mencius vividly exemplified this concern in his disparagement of the "good careful villager" who followed all the conventions and yet remained far from the Way.[50] Sorai's inclination to the social side of the balance was inherited by Shundai, whom Tasan bitterly attacked for considering the common people incapable of the initiative required to become "superior persons."

Enlarging on an enigmatic remark by Confucius that "the common people may be made to follow it (the Way) but may not be made to understand it,"[51] Shundai had claimed that,

> Among the people of the world, there are superior people (*chün-tzu*) and petty-minded people. Only when certain superior people rule the masses is the world put in order. If all individuals and families in the world were enlightened, and all the common people became superior, then there would be no common people left. And without common people, there can be no nation. Consequently even in the age of Yao and Shun the common people were simply common people. Those who are not superior cannot be enlightened. The rulers of the Ch'in treated the common people as ignorant for the same reason.[52]

Claiming that Confucius' remark was simply about the difficulties inherent in conveying abstract truth, Tasan retorted,

> Confucius himself said that "in education there should be no class distinction"....[53] The mind of a sage is highly impartial, having no self-interest. Therefore Mencius said that anyone can become a Yao or Shun. How could one be so intolerant as to treat the common people as ignorant and obstinately bar them from the way of Yao and Shun out of selfish desire?[54]

Behind Shundai's rather transparent defence of feudal mores Tasan saw the self-interests of a privileged class at work. He contrasted this with the egalitarian spirit of Confucian education, at the heart of which lay Mencius' conception of the universal attainability of sagehood. Tasan's faith in the moral initiative of individuals and his resulting disdain for Shundai's elitism was not the expression of a particularly modern form of populism; it reflected the fierce contention that had long raged between Mencian idealists and legalistically inclined Confucians since the establishment of the Ch'in autocracy.

In terms of the relative emphasis placed on the demands of self-cultivation on the one hand, and the political goal of "pacifying the state" on the other, Tasan could be said to take the middle ground between Jinsai and Sorai. He shared Jinsai's intense concern with practical ethics and the nourishment of the moral disposition, and at the same time attempted to develop the implications of these ideas in his political thought. He was more involved in the business of government than Jinsai, who had no links with the world of politics,[55] having served under King Chŏngjo for eleven years before he was exiled to south Chŏlla Province. During this period of service he was shocked by the indifference of many literati toward the affairs of state in a period rife with social unrest. He ascribed this to a tension existing in their minds between the demands of self-cultivation and their duty to the state, which he attributed in turn to Taoist and Buddhist influences on Ch'eng-Chu learning. Consequently, he became very much preoccupied with the problem of reconciling the two great themes of the *Great Learning*, self-cultivation and the ordering of society, and built his philosophical system around the idea of their interrelatedness.

5

Back to the *Su* and the *Sa*—or Forward?

The research conducted in chapter 1 on the distinctive intellectual trends shown by Old Doctrine and Southerner thinkers in the wake of the Rites Disputes, as well as the discussion of Tasan's life and philosophy in chapters 2 and 3, indicates that he did not escape the influence of his factional predecessors' attitudes toward Confucian learning. His usage of the Evidential Learning techniques of the late Ming and early Ch'ing, his emphasis on the study of the Six Classics, his critique of Chu Hsi's edition of the Four Books, his attempt to rediscover the spirit of the Confucian and Mencian teachings by analyzing the ancient meaning of terms and rejecting reliance on particular commentaries, as well as his attraction to the monotheism of the early Chou and Western Learning, all reflect trends that had begun to surface in the writings of Yun Hyu and the school of Yi Ik.

Nonetheless, in applying the new techniques of textual analysis, corroboration, and verification more broadly and thoroughly, Tasan went one step further than his predecessors, by challenging the conceptual framework of the influential Ch'eng-Chu system itself. The analysis of Tasan's philosopy in chapter 3 shows that he took a significant step away from the confines of orthodox Neo-Confucian scholarship in its strict sense of being *hsing-li-hsüeh*, "the study of human nature and principle." As we have seen, he accomplished this mainly through his rejection of the applicability of the principle-material force (*li-ch'i*) cosmology to problems of human nature.

On a philological level, Tasan criticized the original nature—physical nature dichotomy as having no basis in the Confucian teachings, insisting that these concepts were not mentioned in the classics, and that the only references to the physical nature prior to the Sung were in Buddhist works.

On a philosophical level, there were two principal reasons why Tasan rejected Chu Hsi's theory of human nature. One reason was that the conception of principle as being universally present in human beings, animals, and the natural world detracted from the elevated status of humans as beings uniquely endowed with a moral nature that delighted in goodness and was ashamed of evil, and furthermore with a faculty of deliberation that enabled them to follow the inclinations of either the "mind of the Way" or the "human mind."

Another reason why he took issue with Chu Hsi's views was the implication of moral determinism that he considered to be inherent in the concept of the relative clarity and turbidity of the physical nature endowed in individuals. He considered this to be antithetical to the Mencian proposition that all people were potentially sages, and that it detracted from the importance placed on practical ethics by Confucius and Mencius, as it depicted Yao and Shun as sage-kings by nature rather than self-nurture.

At the same time, it could be argued that it is Tasan's very interest in the problem of nurture, that is, self-cultivation, that places him in the Neo-Confucian camp. For it was his interest in the problem of self-cultivation that led him, as it had done with Chu Hsi, to reserve especially detailed commentaries for the *Great Learning* and the *Mean* among all the chapters in the *Record of Rites*, in view of their relatively systematic and detailed treatment of the subject.

But for all the respect that Tasan showed toward Chu Hsi for his attempt to clarify the process of self-cultivation, which lay at the heart of the transmission of the Confucian Way, it remains clear that they had very different opinions on the subject. Not the least of these differences originated in their opposing views on the nature of virtue (*te*). By stripping virtue of any ontological status and making its realization contingent on the objectification of the moral tendencies, Tasan restricted the medium of personal cultivation entirely to practical ethics. For this reason, he also vigorously opposed any suggestion, or any ambiguity that might lead to the suggestion, that *ko-wu* (the comprehension of things) represented the initial step in the process of self-cultivation itself.

This did not mean that Tasan was de-emphasizing the role of the mind in self-realization. It was precisely in this area that he considered Chu Hsi to have revived the stagnant Confucian Way and handed down one of his greatest contributions to Confucian philosophy, which was the importance he placed on the problem of the mind of the Way (*tao-hsin*) and the human mind (*jen-hsin*), and the relationship between them, with respect to self-cultivation.

As we have seen, Tasan called his scholarship *Susa* learning, referring to the rivers *Su* and *Sa*, near the banks of which Confucius was said to have taught his students. In the tradition of the Tokugawa exponents of "Ancient Learning" Itō Jinsai and Ogyū Sorai, and in the same vein as his contemporary, the Ch'ing philosopher Tai Chen, Tasan put the new Evidential Learning methods to good use in attempting to uncover the meaning of key concepts in the pre-Ch'in Confucian teachings, and used the resulting insight as the basis on which to challenge many of Chu Hsi's interpretations. In this way he claimed to have "pierced the veil" that the Han, T'ang, and Sung commentaries had drawn over the pristine teachings of Confucius and Mencius, and to have uncovered their significance.

He was certainly not setting a precedent in making this claim. Many of the writers of the very commentaries he criticized, such as Han Yü, Ch'eng I, and Chu Hsi, had also claimed to be preserving the hidden import of the classical teachings, which they considered to be in danger of becoming further obscured by the influence of extraneous teachings. And yet it was Ch'eng I and Chu Hsi who, in their attempt to give the Confucian ethical teachings a metaphysical grounding, formulated the new correlative cosmology based on principle and material force, and complementary theories on human nature based on the relationship between the original nature (*pen-jan chih hsing*) and physical nature (*ch'i-chih chih hsing*), applying concepts that were either foreign to the language of the *Analects* and *Mencius*, or used in entirely different contexts. And it was Confucius, who, self-effacingly referring to himself as a transmitter rather than a creator in the respect that he was simply conveying the teachings of the Duke of Chou and the Early Kings, introduced decidedly novel views on, for example, such important subjects as the qualifications of leadership, the meaning of propriety, and the essence of humanity.[1]

In view of this, the question we should ask is, to what extent was Tasan simply resolving the ambiguities, clarifying the assumptions, and fleshing out the meaning of the Confucian teachings, and conversely, to what extent, in the time-honored tradition of East Asian Confucianism, was he indulging in *t'o-ku kai-chih*, smuggling in the new in the guise of the old? It is clear that Tasan was not content to simply be a philologer or historian, but was a dedicated philosopher in the Confucian sense, in that he was subjectively involved in the task of clarifying the process of personal cultivation and the ordering of society. This is why he was so opposed to what he saw as the one-sided involvement of the school of Han learning in purely philological questions without consideration of the philosophical implications. Rather than simply analyzing and expounding on the meaning of ancient words and phrases, he was attempting to systematize anew the terse, cryptic teachings of Confucius, and in so doing he was naturally recreating the tradition. The principle–material force system synthesized by Sung scholars was used to provide answers to more abstract questions that the early Confucians either did not try to grapple with, or answered inconclusively, and in proposing alternative views on such problems as human nature and methods of personal cultivation, Tasan was also ready to indulge in philosophical speculation, informed speculation though it was, on the basis of philological inquiry. Nonetheless, having pointed the finger at Chu Hsi for introducing concepts extraneous to the Confucian tradition for the purpose of clarifying it, Tasan was reluctant to do the same. But in at least several instances, namely in his systematic usage of the concepts *kiho* (appetites) and *kwŏnhyŏng* (faculty of deliberation), his philosopher's urge to resolve major controversies through conceptual innovation, or, at the least, the creative extension of traditional concepts, got the better of his desire to retain, in its entirety, the classical framework of interpretation. Although we are indebted to Yi Ŭrho for having drawn attention to the historical significance of Tasan's usage of the term *susahak*, or "Classical Learning" to describe his approach to Confucian scholarship, one would be hard put to conclude that Tasan had simply provided a clearer window on the original form and significance of the pristine teachings. He was clearly not satisfied to simply analyze and deduce in the tradition of the Han philologists, leaving philosophical dilemmas unresolved, for he was involved in the traditional pursuit of transmitting the Way, that is, clarifying the Confucian teachings, spoken and implied, as a code of conduct, for people of subsequent ages far removed from the time of Confucius.

One notable aspect of the synthesis that Tasan tried to formulate in place of the Neo-Confucian cosmology was the level of integration he achieved between his ontological and ethical perspectives, namely, his conceptions of *Shang-ti*, human nature and the realization of virtue, the goal of self-cultivation. His depiction of *Shang-ti* as a personal being with ethical predilections provided the ontological basis for his novel perception of human nature as affective tendencies, which, being endowed by Heaven, also "took pleasure in the good and were ashamed of evil." This dynamic perception of human nature was in turn consistent with the conception of virtue as something acquired only as a result of ethical conduct. The concept of a higher order of appetites that could only be satisfied through moral action reinforced his philosophy of practical ethics which denied the existence of virtue as an *a priori* endowment.

On the other hand, Tasan seems to have skirted the problem of, in Confucian terms, the relationship between what is "above form" and what is not, a problem that Chu Hsi struggled to resolve through his development of the concept of the Great Ultimate. In particular, he says very little about the nature of the relationship between *Shang-ti* and the cosmos. One explanation for this is that he placed much greater priority on the resolution of ethical problems than on ontological dilemmas, a characteristic he shared with the pre-Ch'in Confucians.

A principal focus of controversy has been the question of the impact of Catholicism on Tasan's thought. The historical record indicates that he was strongly attracted to the Catholic teachings during his early years, and was possibly a convert at least until the persecution of the Old Doctrine threatened to bring his career to an abrupt end. But it would be unwise to draw any definite conclusions about his relationship to Catholicism from his writings, particularly his exposition of the classics. His monotheistic interpretation of Heaven as a sentient being could well have been inspired by his youthful excursion into Western Learning, but on the other hand this tendency was exhibited to a certain extent by the exponents of "Ancient Learning" who certainly influenced him, and yet their views on the subject have not been linked to Catholicism. Furthermore the personalization of Heaven, which Tasan lent respectability to by adducing the monotheistic *Shang-ti* of the early Chou as his source, could have been a counterreaction to the rationalization of Heaven by the Ch'eng-Chu school.

The analysis of Tasan's exposition of the classics carried out in this study indicates that, except perhaps for his ideas on political representation outlined in his *Treatise on Ideal Government* (*T'angnon*), Tasan's work remains solidly within the broad bounds of Confucian tradition. The new methods of evidential research imported from the Ch'ing did not lead him to a historicism that questioned the validity of the classics for his own time. For him the teachings of Confucius and Mencius remained a repository of wisdom for the attainment of sagehood and the pacification of the nation, the traditional occupation of Confucian literati, a dual interest that permeated his writings on both philosophy and administrational reform.

Appendix: Major Works

Mentioned in Tasan's *Self-Written Epitaph* and *Chronological Biography*

Date of Completion	Title and Source
1789	Taehak kangŭi (Lectures on the *Great Learning*), CYC, 2.2.
1798	Magwa hoet'ong (Comprehensive study of smallpox), CYC, 7.1–6.
1804	Sangnye sajŏn (Four commentaries on funeral rites), CYC, 3.1–16 (introduction dated 1804).
1808	Cherye kojong (An examination of ancestral rites), CYC, 3.22.
	Chuyŏk sajŏn (Commentary on the *Classic of Changes*), CYC, 2.37–44.
	Yŏkhak sŏŏn (Introduction to the *Classic of Changes*), CYC, 2.45–48.
1809	Sigyŏng kangŭi (Lectures on the *Classic of Odes*), CYC 2.17–19.
1810	Sigyŏng kangŭibo (Supplement to lectures on the *Classic of Odes*), CYC, 2.20.
	Karye chagŭi (Marriage ritual procedure), CYC, 3.23.
	Sohak chugwan (Elucidation of the *Lesser Learning*), CYC, 1.25.

1811	Abang kangyŏkko (An examination of national territory fortification), CYC, 6.1–4.
1812	Minboŭi (Discussion of national defence), CYC Supplement, 3:333.
	Ch'unch'u kojing (Evidential analysis of the *Spring and Autumn Annals*), CYC, 2.33–36.
1813	Nonŏ kogŭmju (Commentaries on the *Analects*, old and new), CYC, 2.7–16.
1814	Maengja yoŭi (Essential meaning of the *Mencius*), CYC, 2.5–6.
	Taehak kongŭi (Impartial discussion on the *Great Learning*), CYC, 2.1.
	Chungyong chajam (Admonitions on the *Mean*), CYC, 2.3.
	Chungyong kangŭibo (Supplement to lectures on the *Mean*), CYC, 2.4.
	Taedong sugyŏng (Record of Korean rivers), CYC, 6.5–8.
1816	Aksŏ kojon (Examination of documents on music), CYC, 4.1–4.
1817	Kyŏngse yup'yo (Treatise on government), (incomplete) CYC, 5.1–15.
	Sangŭi chŏryo (Essentials of mourning ceremony), CYC, 3.21–22.
1818	Mongmin simsŏ (Reflections on fostering the people), CYC, 5.15–29.
1819	Hŭmhŭm shinsŏ (New treatise on the legal system), CYC, 5.30–39.
	Aŏn kakpi (Correct concepts for the rectification of errors), CYC, 1.24.
1822	Chach'an myojimyŏng (Self-written epitaph), CYC, 1.16.

1834 Sangsŏ kohun (Ancient glosses on the *Classic of Documents*), CYC, 2.21–28.

Maessisŏp'yŏng (An Evaluation of Mei Tse's *Classic of Documents*), CYC, 2.29–32.

Major Works Not Dated

Sohak pojŏn (Supplementary commentary on the *Lesser Learning*).

Chŏllyego (An examination of standard rituals).

Sangnye woep'yŏn (Addendum on funeral rites), CYC, 3.17–20.

Sarye kasik (Four rites, family ceremonies).

Yeŭi mundap (Questions and answers on ritual), CYC, 3.23.

Abang piŏgo (A study of national defense) (incomplete).

P'ungsu chipŭi (Collected discussions on geomancy), CYC, 3.24.

Ŭiryŏng (Supplement on medicine), CYC, Appendix.

Notes

Introduction

1. Michael Kalton has concluded that "Tasan's scholarship was a vast legacy rich in new potential for Confucians, but history has followed rather a different course. Tasan's legacy has been without heirs, a potential never taken up and developed into a living tradition." This is not entirely the case, but nonetheless Kalton has devoted a highly readable, well-documented monograph, from which this passage is quoted, to Tasan's critique of Chu Hsi's philosophy (Michael C. Kalton, "Chŏng Tasan's Philosophy of Man: A Radical Critique of the Neo-Confucian World View," *The Journal of Korean Studies* 3 (1981): 3–37). This monograph, which, among other factors, encouraged me to do further work on the subject, deals with Tasan's critique of Chu Hsi's metaphysics, including his alternative view of Heaven, in connection with his philosophy of man. Consequently, this book places comparatively more emphasis on other aspects of Tasan's critique, particularly his views on self-cultivation, practical ethics, and their sociopolitical implications.

2. Kim Yŏng-ho, "Sirhak kwa kaehwa sasang ŭi yŏngwan munje," *Han'guksa yŏn'gu* 8:63–80.

3. An indication of his influence is the frequency of references to his thought and direct quotations from his writings in memorials presented during the last years of Ch'ŏlchong's reign (1849–63) and the whole period of Kojong's rule (1864–1907). King Kojong himself is reputed to have lamented over the fact that he did not belong to the same generation as Tasan. He is said to have compensated for this by ordering the *Yŏyudang chip* (Tasan's Collected Works) to be copied and regularly consulting it as a guide in his formulation of policy (ibid., 68–69).

4. The *Analects*, the *Mencius*, the *Mean*, and the *Great Learning*.

5. The main source used for Tasan's writings in this book is the *Chŭngbo Yŏyudang chŏnsŏ* (Seoul: Kyŏngin munhwasa, 1981). This edition comprises a photoreprint of the entire *Yŏyudang chŏnsŏ*, which was compiled by Kim Sŏngjin, revised by Chŏng Inbo and An Chaeho, and published in 1934–38 by the Sinchosŏnsa in seventy-six volumes, as well as a number of other writings, including an appendix containing a chronological biography. There are a number of autographs of small portions of Tasan's works and notes in private hands and in the Academy of Korean Studies, but none of those discovered to date include extensive commentaries on the classics. Of greater importance is a transcription of Tasan's collected works said to have been commissioned by King Kojong in 1885, entitled *Yŏyudangjip*. The *Yŏyudangjip*, of uncertain date, is preserved in the Kyujanggak (royal archives), which are housed in Seoul National University.

Kim Sanghong has indicated that the Sinchosŏnsa edition, which includes Tasan's commentaries on the Confucian classics, contains a significant incidence of misprints. He draws this conclusion on the basis of a limited comparison of Tasan's poems published in the Sinchosŏnsa edition with those appearing in the *Yŏyudangjip* preserved in the Kyujanggak (Kim Sanghong, *Tasan Chŏng Yagyong munhak yŏn'gu* [Seoul: Tandae, 1986], 18–38). In view of this, research may well be warranted on the textual accuracy of Tasan's commentaries printed in the *Chŏngbo Yŏyudang chŏnsŏ* edition used for this study. This would be a major task in view of the substantial size of these collected works. Nonetheless, all of the major philosophical points discussed here are outlined in more than one work, and consequently isolated misprints would not have a significant bearing on the arguments put forward here.

6. See, for example, the treatment given to "Sirhak" thought in the standard history text *Han'guk ŭi yŏksa*, by Ha Hyŏngang (Seoul: Sin'gu munhwasa, 1979), 226–34. For an English-language discussion of the subject, see Frits Vos, "The Yangban-Jeon and Some Reflections on the Fate of Korea," *Tongbang hakji* 7 (1963):175–97.

7. The Ch'ing reformer and philosopher K'ang Yu-wei (1858–1927) referred to this subtle mode of innovation as *to-ku kai-chih*, "changing the system by appealing to antiquity."

8. Benjamin E. Elman, *From Philosophy to Philology: Intellectual and Social Aspects of Change in Late Imperial China* (Cambridge, MA: Harvard University Press, 1984), xiii.

9. Benjamin E. Elman, "Criticism as Philosophy: Conceptual Change in Ch'ing Dynasty Evidential Research," *Tsing Hua Journal of Chinese Studies*, new series, 17.1,2 (December 1985): 165.

10. Fung Yu-lan, *A History of Chinese Philosophy* (Princeton: Princeton University Press, 1953), 2:630–31.

11. Wm. Theodore De Bary, ed., *Sources of Chinese Tradition* (New York: Columbia University Press, 1960), 614.

12. See Elman, "Criticism as Philosophy," 165–97, and *From Philosophy to Philology*.

13. Chapter 2 is a revised version of my article "Factional Politics and Philosophical Development in the Late Chŏson," *Journal of Korean Studies*, 8 (1992): 37–80. This article provides a more detailed discussion of political developments, and particularly the momentous Rites Disputes that led to new factional alignments.

Chapter 1. Tasan's Intellectual Heritage

1. Originally Mencius had conferred this title on Confucius (*Mencius*, 5B:1, in HYISIS, supplement no. 17). The same term was also used to describe the role of Chu Hsi in bringing the various trends of Neo-Confucian thought to philosophical fruition.

2. See discussion on the significance that should be ascribed to factionalism in Kang Man'gil et al., *Chŏng Tasan kwa kŭ sidae* (Seoul: Minŭmsa, 1986), 41–43.

3. In his book on the history of Korean Confucianism, Yi Pyŏngdo does discuss the close identification of particular factions with the two main schools of Ch'eng-Chu Neo-Confucianism (revolving around the interpretations of T'oegye and Yulgok respectively). Yet he provides little detail on

factional links with other important streams of Confucian thought that filtered into the peninsula at a later stage, such as the Yang-ming school, or the Han Learning movement of the Ch'ing (Yi Pyŏngdo, *Han'guk yuhaksa* [Seoul: Asea munhwasa, 1987], 261). More specifically, in his ground-breaking study of Tasan's political and economic thought, Hong Isŏp has pointed out that Tasan's views on current affairs, and particularly the epitaphs he wrote for his Southerner colleagues, certainly reflected his factional orientations, but little space is given to the influence such orientations had on his thought (Hong Isŏp, *Chŏng Yagyong ŭi chŏngch'i kyŏngje sasang yŏn'gu* (Seoul: Han'guk yŏn'gu tosŏgwan, 1959) 225–30.

4. Two very readable English-language overviews of this popular subject are provided by Cho Ki-jun, "Silhak Thought in the Late Yi Dynasty and its Socio-Economic Background," *Asea yŏn'gu* 11.4 (December 1968): 95–113 (including an informative bibliography on each major "Sirhak" thinker), and Michael C. Kalton, "An Introduction to Silhak," *Korea Journal* 15.5 (May 1975): 29–46.

5. Yi Usŏng, "Sirhak yŏn'gu sŏsŏl," in *Sirhak yŏn'gu immun*, ed. Yŏksa hakhoe (Seoul: Ilchogak, 1983), 6.

6. Ch'ŏn Kwan-u, "Han'guk sirhak sasang ŭi kujo wa palchŏn," *Sasanggye* 3(1966) :10–17. In a much earlier study Kim Yangsŏn ("Han'guk sirhak paltalsa," *Sŭngdae hakpo* 5 [1957]) identified four stages in the development of Sirhak. The Formative Stage which began in the reign of King Sŏnjo (1567–1608) was catalyzed by the introduction of Western Learning through Yi Sugwang, and characterized by the egalitarianism of Hŏ Kyun and Yu Mongin. The reign of Injo (1623–49) marked the beginning of the Development Stage, during which Western scientific ideas and the Evidential Learning of the Ch'ing were adopted by such scholars as Yun Chŏn and Pak Sedang, and found more systematic expression in the writings of Yu Hyŏngwŏn and Yi Ik. The Maturation Stage which took root in the reign of Yŏngjo (1724–76) saw the appearance of the School of Northern Learning (*Pukhakp'a*), so called because of the influence exerted upon it by Ch'ing intellectual trends, among whose more outstanding members were Hong Taeyong, Pak Chiwŏn and Pak Chega. It was in this period that the various trends of Sirhak were synthesised in the work of Chŏng Yagyong. The Stage of Decline began in the reign of Sunjo (1800–1834) with the Sinyu Supression of 1801, when many Sirhak proponents were executed or sent into exile for

dabbling in the "heterodox doctrines" of Catholicism. Following this Sirhak scholarship was limited to nonpolitical fields, as for example, in the epigraphy of Kim Chŏnghŭi and the encylopedic work of Yi Kyugyŏng.

7. Yi Kwangnin, *Han'guk kaehwasa yŏn'gu* (Seoul: Ilchogak, 1974), 37; *Han'guksa*, ed. Kang Man'gil et al., 27 vols. (Seoul: Han'gilsa, 1994), 11:106.

8. Chu Hsi, *Chung-yung chi-chu*, SPPY edition, 1a.

9. Ch'ŏn Kwan'u, "Han'guk Sirhak sasang ŭi kujo wa palchŏn." *Sasanggye*, 3 (1966):11–12.

10. As Ch'ŏn points out, the *locus classicus* of this expression is found in the *Han-shu*, where it is written that King Hsien of Ho-chien, who took the throne in 155 B.C.E., "restored scholarship and honored antiquity. He sought the truth in actual facts."

11. Ch'ŏn Kwanu, "Yu Hyŏngwŏn, sae hakp'ung ŭi sŏn'guja," *Han'guk ŭi in'gansang*, 4:300–301.

12. Chŏng Kubok, "Yu Hyŏngwŏn ŭi 'Pangye surok,'" in *Sirhak Yŏn'gu immun,* ed. Yŏksa hakhoe (Seoul: Iljogak, 1983), 23–24.

13. The translation of *ch'i* as "material force" is far from satisfactory, particularly because in its more rarified manifestations it has nothing to do with matter. Nonetheless it is so widely used that it would be confusing to use another term.

14. Thanks are due to Stephen Linton for this insight.

15. For a reliable translation of, and commentary on, the pieces of correspondence that constitute the principal exchanges of the *Four-Seven Debate*, see Michael Kalton, with Oaksook C. Kim et al., *The Four-Seven Debate* (Albany: SUNY Press, 1994). For a concise, readable overview of the same debate, see Julia Ching, "Yi Yulgok on the 'Four Beginnings and the Seven Emotions'," in *The Rise of Neo-Confucianism in Korea*, ed. Wm. Theodore de Bary and JaHyun Kim Haboush (New York: Columbia University Press, 1985). For a detailed study of the *Horak* debate, see Michael Kalton, "The Horak Debate: Tensions at the Core of the Neo-Confucian Synthesis," *Journal*

of Korean Thought, 1 (1997). Tasan himself showed considerable interest in the Four-Seven Debate. As described in chapter 2 he seems to have inclined toward the views of Yulgok in his youth. Later on he tried to resolve the conflict between the Yulgok and T'oegye schools by arguing that their seemingly contradictory positions arose from implicit differences in their perceptions of key concepts involved in the debate [see Han Hyŏngjo, "Chu Hsi esŏ Chŏng Yagyong ero ŭi chŏrhak chŏk sayu ŭi chŏnhwan," Ph.D.. diss., Academy of Korean Studies, 1992, 106–114]. In general he refrained from criticizing the essential philosophical positions of either thinker, reserving his attacks on Neo-Confucian metaphysics for Chu Hsi and the Ch'eng brothers.

16. See preface to Chu Hsi's *Ta-hsüeh chang-chü*, SPPY edition, 3a.

17. Pak Sŏngmu, "Tasanhak ŭi yŏnwŏn kwa sidae chŏk paegyŏng koch'al," *Tasan hakpo*, 6 (1984): 18–22; Ha Hyŏngang, *Han'guk ŭi yŏksa* (Seoul: Sin'gu munhwasa, 1979), 226–29.

18. See section below, "The Southerners."

19. Hong Isŏp. "Sirhak e issŏsŏ ŭi Namin hakp'a ŭi sasang chŏk kyebo," *Inmun kwahak* 10 (1963): 191.

20. According to Yi Ik, from the reign of Sŏnjo, the number of applicants who successfully passed the civil service examinations gradually increased until the ratio of graduates to official positions reached extreme proportions (Yi Ik, *Sŏngho chŏnsŏ* [Seoul: Yŏgang, 1984], 7:413.)

21. James B. Palais, "Confucianism and the Aristocratic/Bureaucratic Balance in Korea," *Harvard Journal of Asiatic Studies* 44.2 (1984):459. See also Kang Chujin, *Yijo Tangjaengsa yŏn'gu* (Seoul: Seoul taehakkyo ch'ulp'anbu, 1971), 128, 352–53.

22. *Pungdangnon*, Sŏngho chŏnsŏ, 7:412–13. For the full text of Yi Ik's treatise on factionalism, see my translation in Peter H. Lee, ed. *Sourcebook of Korean Civilization*, Vol. 2, New York: Columbia University Press, 1996.

23. For a brief discussion of the "upward-looking" orientation of Koreans, their concomitant "vertical conciousness" as well as its negative role in factionalism, see Yi Kyut'ae, *Han'gugin ŭi ŭisik kujo* (Seoul: Mullisa, 1977),

1:52–55. Yi maintains that the reason why factional splintering in Korea was more prevalent than in China or Japan was because of the particularly strong inclination of Koreans to be upwardly mobile. When the position of a particular factional leader was weakened, subleaders would fill the power vacuum by becoming leaders in their own right, fostering their own subfactions rather than cooperating to bolster central authority.

24. The Northerners, Southerners, Easterners and Westerners were all named after the approximate areas of the capital their founding members originated from.

25. Yi, *Han'guk yuhaksa*, 261.

26. M. S. Seoh claims that the reason why such a large proportion of outstanding and creative scholars, writers, and philosophers should come from the Southerners is that they were "outraged" over their disadvantage in the realm of central politics from the reign of King Sukchong (r. 1674–1720) (M. S. Seoh, "Yi Ik, an 18th Century Korean Intellectual," *Journal of Korean Studies* 1 (1969): 21).

27. Takahashi Tōru, "Chosen gakusha no tochi heibunsetsu to kyosansetsu," in *Hattori sensei koki shukuga kinen rombunshū* (Tokyo: Tomiyama Fusa, 1936), 615. According to Takahashi, in the supplementary civil examination the government usually passed 33 examinees. But while the Old Doctrine faction were in power, on average one-half of the successful candidates were from their own faction, ten from the Young Doctrine, and the remaining five to six from the Southerners and Northerners.

28. Yi Ik, *Insamun, Saengjae, Sŏngho saesŏl*, 1:272, quoted in Lee Woosung, "Korean Intellectual Tradition and the *Sirhak* School of Thought," in *The Traditional Culture and Society of Korea: Thought and Institutions*, ed. Hugh H. W. Kang (Honolulu: Center for Korean Studies, University of Hawaii, 1975), 134. In this article Lee describes the socioeconomic conditions giving rise to, and the characteristics of, the three streams of thought he has identified within the Sirhak movement (see above, pages 10–11), but curiously avoids any mention of factional associations.

29. Miura Kunio, "Orthodoxy and Heterodoxy in Seventeenth-Century Korea: Song Siyŏl and Yun Hyu," in *The Rise of Neo-Confucianism in Korea*, 427.

30. Han U'gŭn, "Paekho Yun Hyu yŏn'gu (1)," *Yŏksa Hakpo* 15 (September 1961): 7.

31. *Hyŏnjong kaesu sillok*, in *Chosŏn wangjo sillok* (Seoul: Kuksa p'yŏnch'an wiwŏnhoe, 1970–72), 3:28a.

32. *Songja Taejŏn* (Seoul: Han'guk samun hakhoe, 1971), 40.15b.

33. Song compared Yun to the Yin dynasty sage Po-i, who died of starvation rather than live sumptuously under the rule of the newly established Chou dynasty (*Myŏngjae sŏnsaeng yŏnbo hurok*, 2, quoted in Han, "Paekho Yun Hyu yŏn'gu," 16).

34. *Songja Taejŏn*, appendix, 2.32a.

35. *Paekho chŏnsŏ* (Taegu: Kyŏngbuk taehakkyo ch'ulp'anbu, 1974), 3:1893.

36. Ibid., 2:1346. According to Yun, "The ancients regarded heaven and earth as their parents, and lived in accordance with them, showing respect and reverence. They regarded the world as one family, and conducted themselves in it with benevolence and love" (ibid., 3:1891). This perception of the universe as extended family was also reflected in Chang Tsai's celebrated "Western Inscription."

37. *Taehak kobon pyŏllok*, *Paekho*, 3:1501–14.

38. *Paekho*, 3:1505–6.

39. See Han Ugŭn, "Paekho Yun Hyu ŭi sadan ch'iljŏng, insim tosimsŏl," in *Yi Sangbaek paksa hoegap kinyŏm nonch'ong* (Seoul: Ŭryu munhwasa, 1964), 238–48.

40. *Paekho*, 3:1686, quoted in Miura, "Orthodoxy and Heterodoxy," 431. In contrast to the considerable space he devoted to discussion on ancient ritual described in the *Record of Rites* as well as the *Rites of Chou*, Yun reserved no separate commentary for the *Chu Tzu chia-li* (Chu Hsi's Family Ritual), which commanded the attention of most contemporary authorities on the rites.

41. The great historical importance Yun Hyu ascribed to Chu Hsi is obvious in his description of himself as one who lived "three thousand years after Confucius, and five hundred years after Chu Hsi." *Paekho*, 1:75.

42. *Sukchong sillok*, in *Chosŏn wangjo sillok*, 2:14a.

43. *Paekho*, appendix 2, 3:1891.

44. Ibid.

45. *Tohak wŏllyusok*, quoted in Yi Pyŏngdo, *Han'guk yuhaksa*, 332. I have not been able to locate the source of this intriguing passage.

46. Miura, "Orthodoxy and Heterodoxy," 416.

47. JaHyun Kim Haboush, *A Heritage of Kings: One Man's Monarchy in the Confucian World* (New York: Columbia University Press, 1988), 23; Martina Deuchler, "Reject the False and Uphold the Straight: Attitudes toward Heterodox Thought in Early Yi Korea," in *The Rise of Neo-Confucianism in Korea*, 378.

48. *Sukchong sillok*, 4:13a.

49. *Hyŏnjong kaesu sillok*, 3:28b.

50. The study of rites (*Yehak*) assumed such importance that Chŏng Injae has classified the development of Chosŏn Confucianism into three periods, *Sŏngnihak* (Neo-Confucian learning), *Yehak*, and *Sirhak*. This can be misleading in view of the fact that *Sŏngnihak* continued to be a focus of attention throughout the dynasty, whereas the proponents of administrative and economic reform comprising the Sirhak movement were in the minority, albeit a significant one in terms of intellectual development. Nonetheless, the study of rites did flourish during the middle period. According to Yi Pyŏngdo this was a natural step in the maturation of Neo-Confucian institutions, and also in response to the social disorder resulting from the Hideyoshi and Manchu invasions (Yi, *Han'guk yuhaksa*, 297). Another reason for the increased attention given to the study of rites could be ascribed to the impact of the Rites Disputes of 1659 and 1674.

51. *Analects* 2:5, in HYISIS, supplement no. 16.

52. Chu Hsi and Lü Tsu-ch'ien, comp., *Reflections on Things at Hand*, tr. and annotated by Wing-Tsit Chan (New York and London: Columbia University Press, 1967), 202.

53. Five different attires could be worn, the untrimmed mourning dress (*ch'amch'oe*) for the three-year period of mourning, trimmed mourning dress (*chaech'oe*) for the three-year or one-year periods, thick hemp mourning dress (*taegong*) for nine months, thin hemp (*sogong*) for five months, and thin, loosely woven attire (*sima*) for three months, depending on the proximity and nature of the kinship between mourner and deceased, as well as the status of the deceased (*Chu Tzu chia-li*, comp. by Ch'in Chün [reprint prefaced 1701], 4:69b–77b.

54. Haboush, *A Heritage of Kings*, 11–21.

55. *Hyŏnjong sillok*, in *Chosŏn wangjo sillok*, 1:1b.

56. *Paekho*, 3:1907.

57. *I-li chu-shu*, SPPY edition, 29.2a.

58. Initially Yun Hyu maintained that, according to the ritual codes, the three-year mourning attire should be worn for the heir, whether royalty or not (*Paekho*, 3:1907). Later on, during the second Rites Dispute, he pointed out that the *Kukcho oryeŭi* (Five Rites of the Dynasty) described the ritual system of the ruling house, and that it stipulated two kinds of dress: those in mourning for the king should wear the untrimmed mourning dress (*ch'amch'oe*) appropriate for the three-year period of mourning, and those in mourning for the queen should wear the trimmed mourning dress (*chaech'oe*) appropriate for the three-year or one-year periods. A sharp distinction, Yun argued, should be made between these regulations and the five types of dress prescribed for the class of scholar-officials by the *Kyŏngguk taejŏn* (Great Statutes for the Governance of the State).

59. *Paekho*, appendix 2, 3:1907.

60. *Paekho*, appendix 2, 3:1909; *Hyŏnjong kaesu sillok*, 3:29a.

61. Yi, *Han'guk yuhaksa*, 308; Kang, *Yijo Tangjaengsa yŏn'gu*, 192–93.

62. Miura Kunio, "Orthodoxy and Heterodoxy," 422, 416.

63. *Hyŏnjong sillok*, 22:28a–34a.

64. Ibid., 22:35a.

65. *Paekho*, 1:369.

66. *Sukchong sillok*, 1:7b–8a.

67. Ibid., 3:32b.

68. Ibid., 9:31–53.

69. *Han'guk yuhaksa*, 349; *Sukchong sillok*, 3:32b.

70. Yi, *Han'guk yuhaksa*, 315–16; Kang, *Yijo Tangjaengsa yŏn'gu*, 162–65.

71. Kang, *Yijo Tangjaengsa yŏn'gu*, 144–53, 352. See also Han, "Paekho Yun Hyu yŏn'gu," (1), 3–5.

72. *Sukchong sillok*, 2:14a–b.

73. Pak Sedang, *Sijang*, 1a–2a, *Sŏgye chŏnsŏ* (Seoul: T'aehaksa, 1979), 1:21.

74. *Yŏnbo*, 1b, *Sŏgye chŏnsŏ*, 1:22.

75. Ibid., 3a.

76. Ibid., 5b.

77. Ibid., 7a–b.

78. Ibid., 11b–12a.

79. *Tap Yun Chain sŏ*, 11b–13a, *Sŏgye chŏnsŏ*, 1:7.

80. Yun Sasun, "Pak Sedang ŭi Sirhak sasang e kwanhan yŏn'gu," in *Sirhak sasang ŭi t'amgu*, ed. Pak Chonghong et al. (Seoul: Hyŏnamsa, 1983) 32 note 4.

81. Ibid.

82. Yi, *Han'guk yuhaksa*, 338.

83. Martina Deuchler has referred to Pak as the "rebel within" in contrast to Wang Yang-ming and his exponents in *The Rise of Neo-Confucianism in Korea.*

84. *Mean*, 15.

85. *Taehak sabyŏnnok*, in *Han'guk ŭi sasang taejŏnjip* (Seoul: Tonghwa ch'ulp'an kongsa, 1977), 23:500.

86. *Analects*, 14:35.

87. In spite of the fact that hardly any reference to Pak's views can be found in Tasan's classical commentaries, there are intriguing parallels in their work, both in methodology and in content. The approach of "proceeding from the near to the far," and "studying the mundane, and consequently attaining the sublime" pervaded the philosophical writings of Tasan, who contrasted it with the speculative attitude of the Ch'eng-Chu school.

88. Yun, "Pak Sedang ŭi Sirhak sasang e kwanhan yŏn'gu," 90.

89. *Pan'gye chapko* (Seoul: Yŏgang ch'ulp'ansa, 1990), 110.

90. Ibid., 72.

91. Kim Yŏngdong, *Pak Chiwŏn sosŏl yŏn'gu* (Seoul: T'aehaksa, 1988), 161, 319–30.

92. Song was Pak Sech'ae's teacher and the two were also related. Nonetheless after Pak sided with Yun Chŭng, relations between them sharply deteriorated (See Kang Chujin, *Ijo tangjaengsa yŏn'gu*, 326).

93. Ch'ŏn Kwan'u, "Yu Hyŏngwŏn, sae hakp'ung ŭi sŏn'guja," in *Hanguk ŭi in'gansang* (Seoul: Sin'gu munhwasa, 1965) 4:326; Han Ugŭn, *Sŏngho Yi Ik yŏn'gu* (Seoul: Seoul taehakkyo ch'ulp'anbu, 1971), 153; Hong Isŏp, *Chŏng Yagyong ŭi chŏngch'i kyŏngje sasang yŏn'gu* 27–29.

94. See *Hyŏnp'a Yun chinsa haengjang*, *Haengjang*, 29a, CYC, 1:17.

95. The Six Classics are the *Classic of Changes* (*I-ching*), *Classic of Documents* (*Shu-ching*), *Record of Rites* (*Li-chi*), *Classic of Odes* (*Shih-ching*), *Spring and Autumn Annals* (*Ch'un-ch'iu*) and *Rites of Chou* (*Chou-li*). The *Rites of Chou* replaced the *Classic of Music* (*Yüeh-ching*), which was lost, as one of the Six Classics.

96. Two of the Four Books, the *Great Learning* and the *Mean*, were originally two chapters in the *Record of Rites*. In his edition of the Four Books, Chu Hsi had effected significant changes to them, in textual order and in content (see chapter 3). Not surprisingly, many of the Ch'ing Han Learning proponents and Korean Southerner scholars who rejected Chu Hsi's amendments to the classical texts underscored the importance of the study of the Six Classics.

97. *Analects*, 2:11.

98. *Sŏngho chŏnsŏ*, 9:29a–b; 22:37a.

99. *Kunggyŏng, Sŏngho saesŏl*, 27:17a–b, in *Sŏngho chŏnsŏ*, 6:1008–9.

100. *Sŏngho saesŏl yusŏn*, comp. An Chŏngbok (Seoul: Myŏngmundang, 1982), 2:107–110. Yi Ik lent weight to these criticisms by quoting T'oegye as having implied that such additions to the Great Learning were not only unnecessary but counterproductive.

101. *Sŏngho saesŏl yusŏn*, 2:113–14; *Karye*, *Sŏngho saesŏl*, in *Sŏngho chŏnsŏ*, 6:905.

102. *Analects*, 2:16.

103. *Idan*, *Sŏngho sasŏl*, 493.

104. Yi Ŭrho, *Tasan kyŏnghak sasang yŏn'gu* (Seoul: Ŭryu munhwasa, 1981), 20–21.

105. *Nogam Kwŏn Ch'ŏlsin myojimyŏng, Myojimyŏng*, 33b, CYC, 1:15.

106. *Nogam Kwŏn Ch'ŏlsin myojimyŏng*, 34b–35a.

107. *Sŏ*, 39b–41b, CYC, 1:18.

108. Pak Sŏngmu, "Tasanhak ŭi yŏnwŏn kwa sidae chŏk paegyŏng koch'al," *Tasan hakpo*, 6 (1984):15.

109. *Nogam Kwŏn Ch'ŏlsin myojimyŏng*, 34b.

110. Ibid.

111. See Mark Setton, "Tasan's `Practical Learning,'" *Philosophy East and West* 39.4 (October 1989):377–91.

112. *Nogam Kwŏn Ch'ŏlsin myojimyŏng*, 33b; Pak, "Tasanhak ŭi yŏnwŏn," 14.

113. Ch'ŏn, "Yu Hyŏngwŏn, sae hakp'ung ŭi sŏn'guja," 300–301.

114. *Chungyong chajam*, 3b, CYC, 2:3; *Maengja youŭi*, 2:38b, CYC, 2:6. See also Tasan's mention of Yi Ik's transmission of the tradition of *susa* learning to his followers (*Nogam Kwŏn Ch'ŏlsin myojimyŏng*, 33b). In his pioneering work *Tasan kyŏnghak sasang yon'gu* (Seoul: Ŭryu munhwasa, 1981) Yi Ŭrho rightly underlines the importance of the concept *susa* as a key to understanding Tasan's thought, particularly with regard to the insight he provides on the classical meanings of concepts in the Confucian teachings. Nonetheless chapter 5 of this book argues that Tasan's interpretations of some of these concepts were quite creative in certain areas, and represented more than just a window on the early teachings.

115. *Sukchong sillok*, 2:14a–b. Han U'gŭn, *Sŏngho Yi Ik yŏn'gu*, 6–7.

116. *Nogam Kwŏn Ch'ŏlsin myojimyŏng*, 35b.

117. Pak, "Tasanhak ŭi yŏnwŏn", 15. Tasan again took the opportunity of indirectly praising the work of Yun Hyu in an epitaph to Yi Kiyang by quoting him as having said "The writings of Yŏ Kang (Yun Hyu) are like the words of *Chiu-t'ien Hsüan-nü* (who, according to legend, was the Taoist immortal who instructed Huang Ti in military strategy when he fought with Ch'ih Yu). They are like glistening pieces of jade, and hardly what a common stomach could digest" (*Pogam Yi Kiyang myojimyŏng*, *Myojimyŏng*, 32a, CYC, 1:15). Significantly it was Ch'e Chaegong, the leader of the Southerners faction in Tasan's time, who had recalled these words.

118. This is not to say that interest in "unorthodox" tendencies was entirely restricted to the Southerners. Yun Hyu was born into the ranks of the "Lesser North" (*Sobuk*), an offshoot of the Northerners, and was associated with the Westerners before the Rites Disputes drove him into the welcoming arms of the Southerners. Pak Sedang, another early critic of Chu Hsi, and Chŏng Chedu, a leading exponent of the diminutive Chosŏn Yang-ming school, were associated with the Young Doctrine. What these figures have in common, though, are links with opposition to Song and his influential faction, who had invested their grip on power with the legitimacy of mainstream Confucianism, through their whole-hearted and unquestioning espousal of the Ch'eng-Chu teachings.

Chapter 2. The Road to Tea Mountain

1. His personal names were Miyong and Songbo, and his courtesy name Sa'am. He was later named Tasan after the mountain where he lived during his exile in Chŏlla Province.

2. *Chach'an myojimyŏng*, *Myojimyŏng*, 1a, YC, 1:16; SSY, 1.

3. Now Nŭngnae-ri, Choan-myŏn, Namyangju County, Kyŏnggi Province.

4. SSY, 1.

5. *Chach'an myojimyŏng*, 2b.

6. *Chegasŭng ch'waryo*, *Che*, 39b, YC, 1:14.

7. *Kasŭng yusa*, *Yusa*, 16b, YC, 1:17; *Chach'an myojimyŏng*, 2b.

8. *Yŏyudang chŏnsŏ poyu* (Seoul: Kyŏngin munhwasa, 1982), 2:647, quoted in Pak Sŏngmu, "Tasanhak ŭi yŏnwŏn."

9. Ibid., 2:644, 651, quoted in Pak, "Tasanhak ŭi yŏnwŏn."

10. *Tokhaeng Chŏnggong myojimyŏng*, in *Sŏngho sŏnsaeng chŏnjip* (Seoul: Kyŏngin munhwasa, 1974), 2:531.

11. *Udam Chŏngsŏnsaeng myogalmyŏng*, in *Sŏnghosŏnsaeng chŏnjip*, 2:460.

12. *Kasŭng yusa*, *Yusa*, 18b.

13. *Kasŭng yusa*, *Yusa*, 18a.

14. Chŏng Ku followed the teachings of T'oegye, and together with him, is regarded as one of the founding members of the Yŏngnam school.

15. *Hyŏnp'a Yun chinsa haengjang*, *Haengjang*, 29a.

16. SSY, 3.

17. Ibid., 2–4.

18. *Chach'an myojimyŏng*, 6a–b.

19. See, for example, SSY, 49–50.

20. Ibid., 5.

21. Ibid., 5–6.

22. *Chach'an myojimyŏng*, 3a; SSY, 9–10.

23. See discussion of these virtues in chapter 3.

24. *Pogam Yi Kiyang myojimyŏng*, *Myojimyŏng*, 32a–b. Intrigued by Ch'ae's remarks, Tasan personally asked Yi whether all this was true, but Yi seemed inclined to play down his apparent admiration for Yun, putting it

down to a "youthful phase." There could have been ulterior reasons for this change of heart, in view of Yun Hyu's status as a major opponent of the Old Doctrine.

25. *Chach'an myojimyŏng*, 3a.

26. See page 60 for a brief discussion of the origins of the "Expediency subfaction" (*sip'a*) and "Principle subfaction" (*pyŏkp'a*).

27. See SSY, 12–16, 25–27, 31–32, 45, 67.

28. *Chach'an myojimyŏng*, 3a.

29. Ch'oe Sŏg'u, "Chŏng Tasan ŭi sŏhak sasang", in *Chŏng Tasan kwa kŭ sidae*, Kang Man'gil et al. (Seoul: Minŭmsa, 1986), 108–112.

30. In 1793, when he had sufficiently strengthened his position, Chŏngjo promoted Ch'ae Chegong to the highest seat of government, the position of chief state councillor (*Chŏngjo sillok*, in *Chosŏn wangjo sillok*, 37:41a–b). But the opposition of the Old Doctrine was so strong that Ch'ae only retained his position for nine days. This indicates the extent to which the Old Doctrine, and particularly the Old Doctrine Principle subfaction, had obtained a secure grip on power (*Chŏngjo sillok*, 37:51a–52a).

31. SSY, 17–18.

32. The most senior rank in the eighteen ranks of Chosŏn government office is referred to as Sr. 1, the next as Jr. 1 and so on down to Jr. 9.

33. SSY, 21–24; *Chach'an myojimyŏng*, 3b.

34. *Chŏngjo sillok*, 33:44a–b; *Chach'an myojimyŏng*, 3b; SSY, 28, 31.

35. Factional animosities continued to take center stage in the political process, regardless of the implementation of the "Policy of Impartiality" (*T'angp'yongch'aek*), instituted by King Yŏngjo (r. 1724–76) at the beginning of his reign, which required the appointment of officials irrespective of factional affiliation. As it turned out, the "Policy of Impartiality" had not eradicated the potential for conflict between rival groups, partly because previously

disenfranchised factions vigorously sought to consolidate the foothold on power the policy had given them.

36. Chŏng Sŏkchong, "Chŏngjo, Sunjo yŏn'gan ŭi chŏngguk kwa Tasan ŭi ipchang," in *Chŏng Tasan kwa kŭ sidae*, 17; *Chŏngjo sillok*, 25:45a.

37. *Han'guksa*, ed. Chindan Hakhoe (Seoul: Ŭryu munhwasa, 1959), 4:62–63.

38. *Chŏngjo sillok*, 1:5a–b.

39. Ibid., 37:51a–52a.

40. *Chach'an myojimyŏng*, 7a.

41. *Chach'an myojimyŏng*, 4a–b; SSY, 31–38.

42. During his period of service in Kyŏnggi Province, Tasan found that the governor was selling off government grain at extortionate prices, on the pretext of using the gains for building roads. As soon as Tasan returned to the capital, he reported this to the king. The governor in question was none other than Sŏ Yongbo, a leading figure of the Old Doctrine Principle subfaction who eventually became chief state councillor and presided over the purge of Tasan's faction during the following reign (*Myojimyŏng*, 4b–5a).

43. *Chach'an myojimyŏng*, 5a–b; SSY, 45–47.

44. *Chŏngjo sillok*, 43:12a; SSY, 60.

45. *Chach'an myojimyŏng*, 6b–7b.

46. Ibid., 8a; SSY, 84.

47. *Chach'an myojimyŏng*, 3b–9b.

48. Ibid., 9b.

49. Ibid., 10a.

50. *Sunjo sillok*, in *Chosŏn wangjo sillok*, 2:4b.

51. Chŏng Yakchŏn (1758–1816) was also an accomplished scholar of the classics, who wrote several commentaries on the *Classic of Changes* and *Analects*, and during their exile he continued to take an interest in Tasan's work, praising his commentary on the *Classic of Changes* and encouraging him (*Sŏnjungssi myojimyŏng*, *myojimyŏng*, 41a).

52. *Chach'an myojimyŏng*, 12a.

53. See note 42.

54. Situated in Mandŏk-ri, Toam-myŏn, Kangjin County. See Pak Sŏngmu, *Tasan sanmunsŏn* (Seoul: Ch'angjak kwa pip'yŏngsa, 1985) 44.

55. SSY, 150; *Chach'an myojimyŏng*, 12a.

56. Ibid., 12b.

57. Ibid., 18a.

58. These dual goals of Confucian learning were described by Chu Hsi in his preface to the *Ta-hsüeh chang-chü*, 3a.

59. Cho Kwang, "Chŏng Yagyong ŭi min'gwŏn ŭisik yŏn'gu," *Asea yŏn'gu*, 56:81–118; Kim, *Tasan Chŏng Yagyong munhak yŏn'gu*, 130–162.

60. CYC, 1:11–12.

61. *Chach'an myojimyŏng*, 12b.

Chapter 3. Tasan's "Classical Learning"

1. See page 64.

2. See *Analects*, 5:13.

3. See page 20.

4. Ch'eng Hao and Ch'eng I, *I-shu*, 11:11b, in *Erh-Ch'eng ch'üan-shu*, SPPY edition.

5. See ibid., 11:51, where it is stated "The innumerable things all have the nature; these five norms are the nature." The "five norms," which include humanity, were considered by the Ch'eng brothers and Chu Hsi to be basic principles shared by all things, which in human beings were the source of benevolent feelings (see discussion on the concept of virtue in this chapter).

6. *Taehak kangŭi*, 40a.

7. "By nature people are alike. Through practice they have become far apart." *Analects*, 17:2.

8. *Mencius*, 6A:2.

9. *Mencius*, 6A:7.

10. Chu Hsi, *Chu Tzu ch'üan-shu* (Ch'eng-tu shu-chü, 1870), 42:6a.

11. Ibid., 49:8b.

12. Ibid., 49:10b–11a.

13. Ibid., 43:3a–4b.

14. Ibid., 43:8a.

15. Ibid., 45:4b

16. Wing-tsit Chan, *Chu Hsi: Life and Thought*, (Hong Kong: The Chinese University Press, 1987), 113–19.

17. The concept of an "Ultimate of Non-being" can also be found in the *Lao Tzu*, which could well have been the source of the expression in the *Diagram* (see *Lao Tzu*, chapter 28).

18. Chou Tun-i, *Chou Lien-hsi chi*, 1:1–2, in *Ts'ung-shu chi-ch'eng* (Shanghai: Hang-fa kuan-shu yin-wu-shang, 1935).

19. *Chu Tzu ch'üan-shu*, 49:8b–15a.

20. *Mencius* 7A:1.

21. *I-shu*, 22A:14b. See also *I-shu*, 25:4b.

22. *Meng Tzu chi-chu*, SPPY edition, 7:1a.

23. Paraphrase of Chu Hsi's words in his introductory remarks to the *Mean*.

24. A Ch'an master of the T'ang (778–897?).

25. *Maengja yoŭi*, 2:38a.

26. *Mencius*, 6A:7. Quoted, with minor modifications, from Chan, *A Source Book*, 55–56.

27. *Maengja yoŭi*, 2:26a.

28. In a concise but well-corroborated analysis of the etymology of *li*, Allen Wittenborn argues that an earlier meaning of *li*, as it appeared in the *Classic of Odes*, referred to the boundary lines marking off areas in a field, which probably followed the natural lie of the land. The meaning described in the *Shuo-wen*, suggests Wittenborn, is derived from this (Allen J. Wittenborn, The Mind of Chu Hsi: His Philosophy, with an Annotated Translation of Chapters One through Five of the "Hsü Chin-ssu Lu"' Ph.D. dissertation, University of Arizona, 1979, 14–15.

29. The commonly accepted translation of *li* as "principle" reflects the overridingly noumenal quality ascribed to it by the Sung Confucians that Tasan was reacting against, whereas its original, more phenomenological meaning, and the classical references derived from it, would more accurately be described as "pattern" or "grain," as in "going against the grain" (see preceding note). The concept of "pattern" cannot be discussed without

reference to some form of concrete order, whereas the term "principle" is more abstract.

30. *Maengja yoŭi*, 2:26a–b.

31. *Taehak kangŭi*, 2:26b.

32. *Chungyong kangŭibo*, 20b, CYC, 2:4; *Chungyong chajam*, 5b; *Nonŏ kogŭmju*, 1:24b, CYC, 2:7.

33. *Maengja yoŭi*, 2:38b.

34. *Classic of Changes*, Great Appendix A:11, HYISIS, supplement no. 10.

35. Quoted in Sŏng Nakhun, "Yuhak sasang ŭi kŭndae chŏk chŏnhwan: Chŏng Tasan ŭi yuhak ŭl chungsim ŭro," in *Kugyŏk Chŏng Tasan munsŏn*, trans. and ed. Yi Chaeho (Seoul: Yŏkang ch'ulp'ansa, 1987), 303.

36. *Kalton*, "Chŏng Tasan's Philosophy of Man," 22.

37. *Ch'unch'u kojing*, 4:24a, CYC, 2:36.

38. *Chungyong ch'aek*, 30a, CYC, 1:8.

39. *Maengja yoŭi*, 2:38b.

40. *Chungyong chajam*, 19b; *Nonŏ kogŭmju*, 4:13a, 7:32b.

41. *Nonŏ kogŭmju*, 7:44a.

42. *Mean*, 1.

43. *Chungyong chajam*, 29b.

44. D. C. Lau points out that Mencius did not challenge Kao Tzu's remark that "the appetite for food and sex is nature" (D. C. Lau, *Mencius* [Hong Kong: Chinese University Press, 1984], introduction, xiv). The difference between Mencius and Kao Tzu is that the former held that nature

did not solely consist of the physical appetites. This difference is brought into focus by Tasan's concept of nature as consisting of two tiers of appetites.

45. A chapter of the *Classic of Documents.*

46. A chapter of the *Record of Rites.*

47. *Mencius*, 6B:15.

48. *Taehak kangŭi*, 2:25b–26a.

49. The late-Ch'ing thinker Juan Yüan (1764–1849; see chapter 4 for further comparison with Tasan) brought into play a large variety of pre-Ch'in sources to refute Sung dynasty metaphysical interpretations of human nature, arguing along similar lines that these were influenced by the concept of a "Buddha nature," and that in classical Confucianism human nature incorporated both sensual and moral aspects. Juan Yüan quoted numerous passages from the *Classic of Documents*, *Classic of Odes,* and *Mencius* to prove that, in the eyes of the ancients, there were elements in human nature that needed to be controlled. Human nature, which included affections and sensual desires, was conditioned by human circumstances and thus had to be carefully observed and regulated. For this reason Juan Yüan was heavily critical of Li Hsi-chih's influential theory of "returning to the nature," which referred to a nature entirely divorced from the world of human affections. (*Hsing-ming ku-hsun*, *Yen ching shih chi* [Shanghai: Commercial Press, 1937], 10:1–32).

50. *Mean*, 1.

51. *Taehak kangŭi*, 2:25a.

52. *Chungyong chajam*, 2b.

53. Kalton translates *tan* as "sources" which would give Tasan's theory of appetites a dualistic hue. As we shall see in the discussion of the Mencian "Four Beginnings," *tan* is a tricky word to translate. Etymologically it refers to the extremities of a thread, so it can mean both beginning and end.

54. *Taehak kangŭi*, 2:26a.

55. Ibid.

56. Ibid., 26a–26b.

57. *Mencius*, 2A:2.

58. *Maengja yoŭi*, 1:17a.

59. Ibid., 2:19a–b.

60. *Mencius*, 4B:19.

61. *Meng-tzu chi-chu*, 4:17b–18a.

62. The *locus classicus* of these two concepts can be found in the *Classic of Documents*, 4:8b, in SSCCS.

63. *Maengja yoŭi*, 2:20a.

64. Ibid., 2:20b. It should be pointed out that Chu Hsi is ambivalent on the question of whether it is the original or physical nature that is shared by people and things, as Tasan points out in another passage. In the *Meng Tzu chi-chu*, 4:17b–18a, Chu Hsi argues that people and things are similar in respect to principle but different in respect to material force, but in the *Meng Tzu chi-chu*, 6A:3, he mentions that people and things do not seem to be different in respect to material force but that as for the endowment of principle, things can not be said to be endowed with humanity, integrity, propriety and wisdom to the same extent.

65. The *Leng yen ching* is the abbreviated name of the *Shou leng yen ching*, or *Sūrangama sūtra* in Sanskrit, a work of the Tantric school translated into Chinese in 705.

66. *Taehak kangŭi*, 2:26b–28b.

67. *Nonŏ kogŭmju*, 2:44a, 6:2b.

68. *Maengja yoŭi*, 2:19a.

69. According to Yang Hsiung, human nature is a mixture of good and evil, and through personal cultivation people can develop the one or the other potential.

70. *Taehak kangŭi*, 2:28a.

71 *Mencius*, 4A:18.

72. *Chungyong chajam*, 2b.

73. *Kalton*, "Chŏng Tasan's Philosophy of Man," 29.

74. The concepts "greater substance" and "lesser substance," the greater and lesser aspects of a person's nature, are mentioned in *Mencius,* 6A:15, where it is argued that the great person becomes so by following the former, whereas the lesser person tends to follow the latter. Mencius adds that once the greater aspect has been established, the lesser aspect, which is drawn to material things, cannot snatch it away.

75. *Nonŏ kogŭmju*, 9:16b.

76. Ibid., 9:17a.

77. Ibid., 9:12a–b.

78. Ibid., 9:10b–11a. For Han Yu's views, see *Ch'ang-li hsien-sheng chi*, SPPY edition, 11:5b–6a. Chu Hsi does not delineate different grades of original nature, but his depiction of individual differences in the degree of purity of the material force implies individual differences regarding the potentiality to do good or evil (see *Chu Tzu ch'üan-shu*, 45:1a).

79. *Nonŏ kogŭmju*, 9:12a.

80. Ibid.

81. *Analects*, 12:1.

82. Li Kung, *Lun-yü chuan-chu wen*, 21b, in *Yen-Li ts'ung-shu* (Taipei: Ssu-ts'un hsüeh-hui, 1923), vol. 6; Yen Yüan, *Ssu-shu cheng-wu*, 4.5a, in *Yen-Li ts'ung-shu;* Juan Yüan, *Yen ching-shih chi*, 3:162, in *Ts'ung-shu chi-ch'eng*.

83. Li Kung, *Lun-yü chuan-chu wen*, 21b.

84. Confucius and Mencius did not speak of "having no desires" as a means of attaining humanity (see the dryly humorous comment in *Analects*, 14:1) but they did tend to speak of desires in a more negative than positive tone (see *Analects*, 14:12, *Mencius* 7B:35).

85. Tai Chen, *Meng-tzu tzu-i shu-cheng*, 56, quoted in Benjamin E. Elman, "Criticism as Philosophy," 173.

86. See also Ann-ping Chin and Mansfield Freeman, *Tai Chen on Mencius: Explorations in Words and Meaning* (New Haven: Yale University Press, 1990), 53.

87. Tai Chen, *Meng-tzu tzu-i shu-cheng*, 9–10.

88. See note 74.

89. *Nonŏ kogŭmju*, 6:1b–2a.

90. *Nonŏ kogŭmju*, 6:2a–b.

91. A slightly modified version of Daniel K. Gardner's translation in *Chu Hsi and the Ta Hsüeh*, 131–158.

92. Or, in an alternative expression appearing in the above passage, the "completion" of knowledge (*chih-chih*).

93. *Ta-hsüeh chang-chü*, 4b–5a.

94. *Chu Tzu ch'üan-shu*, 45:3b–4a.

95. Ibid.

96. *Record of Rites*, SPPY edition, 19:9a–b.

97. *Taehak kongŭi*, 1:15a–17b.

98. Ibid., 1:15b.

99. Li Kung, *Ta-hsüeh pien-yeh*, 2.8, in *Yen-Li ts'ung-shu*.

100. *Nogam Kwŏn Ch'ŏlsin myojimyŏng*, 34b.

101. *Record of Rites*, 19:9a–b.

102. *Taehak kongŭi*, 1:14a–b.

103. Tasan pointed out the intriguing fact that Yi T'oegye (1501–70), regarded as the greatest exponent of Ch'eng-Chu learning in Korea, voiced disapproval of any tampering with the order of the "text" of the *Great Learning* in order to supplement commentaries that had supposedly been misplaced or lost. This disapproval was not explicitly aimed at Chu Hsi. T'oegye mentioned this with reference to claims by a number of "contemporary" Chinese and Korean scholars, including Yi Ŏnjŏk (Hoejae, 1491–1553) that the second and third passages of the "Text" on "knowing where to come to rest" and "roots and branches" were none other than the "commentary" on *ko-wu chih-chih* that Chu Hsi considered to have been lost. According to T'oegye their claim that passages in the "Text" should constitute a chapter of commentary amounted to "destroying the bedroom in order to add a verandah" (*Taehak kongŭi*, 1:20a).

104. *Taehak kongŭi*, 1:15b–16a.

105. *Mean*, 25.

106. The *Great Learning* and the *Mean* were originally two chapters of the *Record of Rites*. See page 97.

107. *Taehak kongŭi*, 1:21b.

108. Wŏn, 5b, CYC, 1:10.

109. *Great Learning*, *Record of Rites*, 19.9b.

110. *Mean*, ch. 1.

111. *Chungyong chajam*, 19b.

112. *Taehak kongŭi*, 13a.

113. *Paekho chŏnsŏ*, 3:1505; *Taehak kongŭi*, 1:21b.

114. Philip J. Ivanhoe, *Ethics in the Confucian Tradition: The Thought of Mencius and Wang Yang-ming* (Atlanta: Scholars Press, 1990), 82.

115. Gardner, *Chu Hsi and the Ta Hsüeh*, 24.

116. The emendations to characters in the text hardly affected the meaning of the original version. Chu Hsi also suggested that three characters in the text should be emended, but he left them unchanged (Ch'oe Taeu, "Chŏng Tasan ŭi Taehak kyŏngsŏlgo," *Tasan hakpo*, 7 [1985]:151). These suggested emendments, unlike the emendments mentioned above, considerably altered the meaning of the text. The first emendation proposed by Chu Hsi, which affected the main text, had previously been suggested by Ch'eng I. It was to replace the character *ch'in* (to love, to feel affection for) in the expression *ch'in-min* to *hsin* (to renew), thus changing the meaning of the second principium from "loving the people" to "renewing the people" (*Ta-hsüeh chang-chü*, 1a). The justification he gave for this change was the existence of three quotations on the theme of renewal in the Tseng Tzu commentary, which he assumed to be a commentary on the second Principium (*Ta-hsüeh huo-wen*, in *Ssu-shu ta ch'üan*, 11a–b). The second emendation proposed, which also followed Ch'eng I's example, affected the seventh chapter of commentary, and was to replace the character *shen* (the body, the self) in the expression *shen yu suo fen-chih*, "when the self is affected by rage," with *hsin* (heart, mind). Thus Chu Hsi's version would read "when the mind is affected by rage" (*Ta-hsüeh chang-chü*, 6a). In the third instance, Chu Hsi proposed two possible emendations for the character *ming* (mandate) in the phrase *chu erh pu neng hsien, ming yeh*; "to raise [a worthy man] to office, but not to do so at once: this is the mandate," in chapter 10 of the Commentary. In the *Ta-hsüeh chang-chü* he comments: "As for *ming*, Cheng Hsuan says that it should be written *man* [negligent, careless], and Ch'eng I says that it should be written *tai* [idle, negligent]. I have yet to determine who is correct" (*Ta-hsüeh chang-chü*, 10b.) Of these three proposed emendations, the

first one, which affected the principium *ch'in-min*, proved to be by far the most controversial, mostly on account of its pivotal position in the main text.

117. The "Three Principia," which summarize the essential teachings of the *Great Learning*, are enumerated in the opening statement of the classic, and are quoted below on page 105.

118. *Ta-hsüeh chang-chü*, 4b–5a. The passages on the last five Items, forming the seventh, eighth, ninth, and tenth chapters, retained the order they had been given in the *Record of Rites*.

119. *Taehak kongŭi*, 1:21b.

120. Ibid., 1:15a.

121. Ibid., 1:20b.

122. Ibid., 1:13a–b.

123. A minister of Yao who was reputed to have lived to be 800 years old.

124. *Taehak kongŭi*, 1:20a–b.

125. *Chu Tzu yü-lei* (Ying-yüan shu-yüan, 1872), 15.27a. In a footnote on Chu Hsi's interpretation of the Items, Gardiner cites this passage in the *Yü-lei* as corroboration that, "Unlike the relationship between the other Items in this passage [making the will sincere, rectifying the mind, etc.] there is no time lapse between these two [*ko-wu chih-chih*]" [Gardner, *Chu Hsi and the Ta-hsüeh*, 92]. Here Chu Hsi does indeed discuss the very close relationship between *ko-wu* and *chih-chih*, but there is no indication that there is, in contrast, a time-lapse between the remaining Items.

126. See *Collected Works of Mao Tse-Tung* (London: Lawrence and Wishart, 1955), 1:296; David. S. Nivison, "The Problem of Knowledge and Action in Chinese Thought since Wang Yang-ming," in *Studies in Chinese Thought*, ed. Arthur Wright (Chicago: University of Chicago Press, 1953), 112–45.

127. *Chu Tzu ch'üan-shu*, 3:8a.

128. Sŏ, 40a–b, CYC, 1:18.

129. Tasan himself admitted that he was not the first to put forward the argument that *ko-wu chih-chih* did not represent the first step or item in self-cultivation. As far back as the Sung the scholar Li Li-wu had claimed in similar fashion that *ko-wu chih-chih* referred to the comprehension and knowledge of the nature and order of the Items themselves (*Taehak kongŭi*, 1:17b).

130. According to a passage in the *Mean* on the subject of the primary human relations and the attitude with which they are to be carried out by rulers, "There are five universal ways, and the way by which they are practiced is three. The five are those governing the relationship between ruler and minister, between father and son, between husband and wife, between elder and younger brothers, and the intercourse between friends. These five are universal paths in the world. Wisdom, humanity and courage, these three are the universal virtues. The way by which they are practised is one" (*Mean*, 20 [translation from Chan, *A Source Book*, 105]). Both Tasan and Chu Hsi are in agreement that the "one" method of cultivating these human relations is sincerity. A consequent passage enumerates the nine standard rules the ruler should follow in dealing with his administrational responsibilities, and the means by which these more practical goals are achieved is also "one" (ibid.). Here also Tasan and Chu Hsi are in agreement that the "one" method mentioned refers to sincerity (*Chungyong chajam*, 1:20a; *Chung-yung chang-chü*, SPPY edition, 12b, 14b).

131. *Mencius* 2A:6 (translation from Lau, *Mencius*, with minor modifications). See also *Mencius*, 6A:6.

132. Confucius had implied that feelings could be intrinsically good when he mentioned that "At seventy I could follow my heart's desire without infringing moral principles" (*Analects*, 2:4).

133. *Mencius*, 6A:7.

134. For an insightful discussion of the Mencian theory of human nature, see Philip J. Ivanhoe, *Confucian Moral Self-Cultivation* (New York: Lang, 1993), 23–34.

135. Tuan Yü-ts'ai, *Shuo-wen chieh-tzu chu* (Shanghai: ku-chi ch'u-pan-she, 1981), 10B:20a. See also DKJ, 6:721.

136. *Meng-tzu chi-chu*, 2:12a.

137. Kalton, "Chŏng Tasan's Philosophy of Man," 27.

138. *Nonŏ kogŭmju*, 1:9b-10a. See also *Tap Yi Yŏhong*, 35a–b, CYC 1:19.

139. *Maengja yoŭi*, 2:28b. Kwŏn Ch'ŏlsin had a very similar perspective. See *Sŏ*, 40b–41a.

140. Tuan Yü-ts'ai, *Shuo-wen chieh-tzu chu*, 2B:14a.

141. *Taehak kongŭi*, 1:7b.

142. The "Three Principia [*Kang-ling*]" is a term coined by Chu Hsi in the *Ta-hsüeh chang-chü*.

143. *Great Learning*, *Record of Rites*, 19.9a.

144. *Taehak kongŭi*, 1:8. His contemporary Kwŏn Ch'ŏlsin also interpreted "illustrious virtue" in this way (*Nogam Kwŏn Ch'ŏlsin myojimyŏng*, 34b).

145. *Ta-hsüeh chang-chü*, 1a.

146. The *T'ai-hsüeh*, which was founded in the Western Chou, was the center of higher learning located in the capital.

147. *Taehak kongŭi*, 1:7a.

148. *Mencius*, 3A:3.

149. This is also suggested by the fact that the main halls of many Confucian educational institutions were called *ming-lun t'ang* (Hall of Illustrious Relations). See *Taehak kongŭi*, 10a.

150. *Taehak kongŭi*, 1:7a.

151. *Sŏ*, 40a.

152. *Nonŏ kogŭmju*, 9:17a.

153. *Analects*, 7:23.

154. *Chungyong chajam*, 1:25a.

155. *Record of Rites*, 37:8a.

156. *Lun-yü chi-chu*, SPPY edition, 2:1.

157. Ch'eng I's formula (*I-shu*, 11:12b) is derived from the commentary on *K'un* (Earth), *Classic of Changes*. See *Chu Tzu ch'üan-shu*, 2:22a–b, and commentary on it by Wing-tsit Chan, *A Source Book in Chinese Philosophy* (Princeton: Princeton University Press, 1963), 607.

158. *Taehak kongŭi*, 1:1b–6b.

159. *Maengja yoŭi*, 2:27b.

160. Ibid., 2:44a.

161. Preface to the *Ta-hsüeh chang-chü*, 3a.

162. *Ch'un-ch'iu Tso chuan*, 38:29b–30a, in SSCCS. See also the *Ta-Yu Mo* chapter of the *Classic of Documents*, which defines virtuous government as the harmonious application of these three principles (*Classic of Documents*, 4:4b, in SSCCS).

163. *Analects*, 14:42.

164. Quoted above, pages 89–90.

165. See quotation on page 64. See also Takahashi Toru, "Teichasan no daigaku keisetsu," *Tenri daigaku gakuho*, 6.3 (1955): 12.

166. Tu Wei-ming, *Humanity and Self-Cultivation: Essays in Confucian Thought* (Berkeley: Asian Humanities Press, 1979), 163.

167. *Taehak kongŭi*, 1:13a.

168. Ch'eng Hao and Ch'eng I, *I-shu*, 18:3a.

169. *Taehak kangŭi*, 2:31b.

170. *Shuo-wen chieh-tzu chu*, 8A:1b; DKJ, 1:577.

171 *Nonŏ kogŭmju*, 1:9b.

172. *Taehak kongŭi* 1:34b.

173. *Great Learning*, *Record of Rites*, 19.12a.

174. *Taehak kongŭi*, 1:34a.

175. Ibid., 1:7a.

176. *Classic of Documents*, 3:22a–b.

177. Ibid., 3:2a.

178. *Mencius,* 3A:4.

179. *Ch'un-ch'iu Tso chuan*, 20:16b–17a.

180. *Taehak kongŭi*, 1:7a.

181. For example, it receives two mentions in the *Mencius* and only one in the *Analects*.

182. See, for example, the quotation on page 112. This usage of the term *mu/mok* can be traced to the *Mencius*, 1A:6. The title of Tasan's widely acclaimed work on administrative reform, the *Mongmin simsŏ* (Reflections on fostering the people) is derived from this concept.

183. *Taehak kangŭi*, 2:6b.

184. Mencius' discussion of the "four beginnings" is quoted above, page 103.

185. *Taehak kangŭi*, 2:8a.

186. *Taehak kongŭi*, 1:7a.

187. In view of this, the term *chih-jen* in the expression *hsiu-chi chih-jen* (self-cultivation and the ordering of society), an expression which Chu Hsi and Tasan both used to encapsulate the Confucian message, is translated as "ordering society," as opposed to "governing society," to convey the sense of a moral as well as political order.

188. According to Gardner "in none of Chu Hsi's writings does there appear philological justification for the change from *ch'in* to *hsin;* when asked in *Huo-wen* 11a-b what sort of evidence exists for the emendation, he says that *ch'in* makes little sense in the context and that the preferability of the *hsin-min* alternative is attested to by the Tseng Tzu commentary" (*Chu Hsi and the Ta Hsüeh*, 90).

189. Ching, *To Acquire Wisdom: The Way of Wang Yang-ming*, 134.

190. *Taehak kongŭi*, 13a.

191. Ibid. The quotation at the end of the passage is taken from *Analects*, 12.1.

192. *Taehak kongŭi*, 11a.

193. *Mencius*, 3A:3.

194. *Taehak kongŭi*, 11a.

195. Wang Yang-ming also regarded *ming-te* and *ch'in-min* as two sides of the same coin, maintaining that "Generally speaking, the theories of previous scholars (of the Ch'eng-Chu school) did not recognise that *ming-te* and *ch'in-min* are basically the same affair" (*Wang wen-cheng kung ch'üan-shu* (Shang-wu yin-shin-kwan, n.d.), 26:38). But here the consensus stops. According to Tasan, "Yang-ming did not regard *ming-te* as the practise of filial piety and fraternal respect, and therefore the whole of his interpretation of *ch'in-min* is lacking in significance" (*Taehak kongŭi*, 11a).

196. *Nonŏ Kogŭmju*, 1:20b.

197. *Analects*, 2:1.

198. See *Great Learning*, *Record of Rites*, 19:10b.

199. *Taehak kongŭi*, 10b–11a.

200. *Ta-hsüeh chang-chü*, "Text": 1.

201. *Classic of Documents*, 7:13a. See Gardner, *Chu Hsi and the Ta Hsüeh*, 90.

202. *Analects*, 17:2.

203. *Taehak kongŭi*, 11b.

204. Ibid.

205. Ibid., 11b–12a.

206. *T'angnon*, 24a–b, CYC, 1:11.

207. *Mencius*, 1B:8.

208. *Chŏllon*, 3a–7a, CYC, 1:11.

209. *Si*, 3b, CYC, 1:5.

Chapter 4. Tasan's "Classical Learning," Ch'ing Evidential Learning, and Tokugawa Ancient Learning

1. Fred Gillette Sturm, "Korea's Role in the History of East Asian Philosophy," In *Papers of the 5th International Conference on Korean Studies: Korean Studies, its Tasks and Perspectives*. Sŏngnam: Academy of Korean Studies, 1988.

2. One paper has been written touching on a few similarities between the thought of Tasan, the Ch'ing scholar Tai Chen and the Tokugawa exponent of "Ancient Learning" Itō Jinsai, mainly in the area of metaphysics. See Huang Chün-chieh, "Tung-ya chin-shih ju-hsüeh ssu-ch'ao ti hsin tung-hsiang: Tai Tung-yüan, I-t'eng Jen-chai yü Ting Ch'a-shan tui Meng-hsüeh ti chieh-shih," *Tasan hakpo* 6 (1984):151-81. The lack of materials mentioned does not only apply to the study of Tasan. Little has been written on the impact of Ch'ing scholarship on late Chosŏn thinkers in general. Two articles which deal with the subject are: Yi Sangok, "Ch'ŏngdae kojŭnghak iip e taehan yŏn'gu," *Sahak yŏn'gu*, 21 (September 1969): 123–43; Ch'ŏn Kwanu, "*Han'guk sirhak sasangsa*," in *Han'guk munhwasa taegye* (Seoul; Kodae minjok munhwa yŏn'guso, 1978) 6:1014–26.

3. See the statistical survey in Hwang Wŏn'gu, "'Yŏyudang chŏnsŏ' soin Ch'ŏnghak kwan'gye kisago (1)," *Tongbang hakchi*, 9 (December 1968): 103–23. Mao Ch'i-ling is often quoted in Tasan's commentary on the *Analects*, but mostly for the historical or philological detail that he brings to bear on certain passages rather than his philosophical reflections. Hsu Ch'ien-hsüeh (1631–94) and Yen Jo-chü (1636–1704) are also frequently quoted by Tasan, but reference to their work is almost entirely restricted to discussions of mourning rites and the *Classic of Documents* respectively.

4. Many of Tasan's contemporaries and predecessors had visited Peking and brought back recently published materials (Yi, "Ch'ŏngdae kojŭnghak," 127–38. The collection of Yi Ik, for example, included several thousand volumes obtained in Peking by his father (Han U'gŭn, *Sŏngho Yi Ik yŏn'gu*, 15) Furthermore, Tasan had access to the rich resources of the Hongmun'gwan (Office of Special Counselors) and Sŭngjŏngwŏn (Royal Secretariat) during his period of government service. See pages 61–62.

5. *Taehak kangŭi*, 28b.

6. Elman, *From Philosophy to Philology*, 122.

7. Ibid., 59.

8. *Ohangnon* (2), *non*, 20a–b, CYC, 1:12.

9. Ibid., 20b.

10. *Analects*, 2:15.

11. *Nonŏ kogŭmju*, 1:30.

12. Elman, *From Philosophy to Philology*, 17–22.

13. Chu Yun (1729–1781), a patron of Han Learning, expressed his disapproval of Tai Chen's involvement in philosophical speculation, adding that "what he will be remembered for has nothing to do with such writing" (Elman, *From Philosophy to Philology*, 20). In a similar vein, the historian and epigrapher Kim Chŏnghŭi (1786–1856), the most prominent exponent of Ch'ing Evidential Learning in Chosŏn Korea, found fault with Tasan's subjective interpretations, opining that "One does not dare, in explaining the classics, to establish one's own viewpoint or create one's own theory" (*Wandang chŏnjip*, 4:1, quoted in Lee, "Korean Intellectual Tradition," p.137).

14. See Hwang, "'Yŏyudang chŏnsŏ' (1)," 104.

15. See, for example, the exhaustive treatment of sources appearing in Tasan's *Nonŏ kogŭmju*, in Chŏng Chong, "Chŏng Tasan chŏ 'Nonŏ kogŭmju' ŭi kujo chŏk punsŏk kwa kŭ Kongja sasang (1)," *Tasan Hakpo*, 3 (1980): 3–44, and "Chŏng Tasan chŏ" 'Nonŏ kogŭmju' ŭi kujo chŏk punsŏk kwa kŭ Kongja sasang (2)," *Tasan Hakpo* 4 (1982): 87–130.

16. *Maessisŏ p'yŏng*, 4:22a–b, CYC, 2.32.

17. *Sangsŏ kohun sŏrye*, 1:3b, CYC, 2.21.

18. See, for example, *Meng-tzu tzu-i shu-cheng*, 10, 14–15, 19–20, 57–59.

19. See Ibid., 22, 36; Juan Yüan, *Hsing-ming ku-hsun*, *Yen ching shih chi*, 2:22–24, 10:1–32.

20. Kang Chaeŏn, "Chŏng Tasan ŭi Ilbon'gwan," in *Chŏng Tasan kwa kŭ sidae;* Yi Ŭrho, "Chŏng Tasan ŭi taeilgwan," *Tasan Hakpo* 7 (1985): 254–55. Brief mention is also made in Chŏng, "Chŏng Tasan chŏ 'Nonŏ kogŭmju' ŭi kujo chŏk punsŏk (1)," 25, 27; and "Chŏng Tasan chŏ 'Nonŏ kogŭmju' ŭi kujo chŏk punsŏk (2)," 99. Ha Ubong has published a book containing an extensive discussion of the subject entitled *Chosŏn hugi sirhakcha ŭi Ilbon'gwan yŏn'gu* (Seoul: Iljisa, 1989), as well as five related articles.

21. Kang, "Chŏng Tasan ŭi Ilbon'gwan," 145–6.

22. *Ilbonnon*, *non*, 3b–5a, CYC, 1:11.

23. Kang, "Chŏng Tasan ŭi Ilbon'gwan," 148, 154.

24. An Chŏngbok, "Sanghŏn sup'il, Ilbon hakcha," in *Sunamjip*, vol. 13, quoted in Kang, "*Chŏng Tasan ŭi Ilbon'gwan*," 148.

25. Imamura Yoshio, "Tei Jaku-yō to Nihon no jugakusha," *Sansenri* 16 (1978), quoted in Kang, "*Chŏng Tasan ŭi Ilbon'gwan*," 153.

26. Chŏng, "Chŏng Tasan chŏ 'Nonŏ kogŭmju' ŭi kujo chŏk punsŏk (1)," 25, 27; and "Chŏng Tasan chŏ `Nonŏ kogŭmju' ŭi kujo chŏk punsŏk (2)," 99. These figures are somewhat lower than those previously given by Imamura in "Tei Jaku-yō to Nihon no jugakusha."

27. Yi, "Chŏng Tasan ŭi taeilgwan," 254–55.

28. *Taehak kangŭi*, 40a; Matsumoto Sannosuke, "The Idea of Heaven: A Tokugawa Foundation for Natural Rights Theory," in *Japanese Thought in the Tokugawa Period*, ed. Tetsuo Najita and Irwin Scheiner (Chicago: University of Chicago Press, 1978), 189–191.

29. *Gomō jigi*, quoted in Joseph J. Spae, "Itō Jinsai, a Philosopher, Educator, and Sinologist of the Tokugawa Period," *Monumenta Serica* 12 (1948):99–110.

30. *Gomō jigi,* NRI, 5:16.

31. *Gomō jigi,* NRI, 5:15.

32. *Bendō*, NRI, 6:23.

33. Robert N. Bellah, "Baigan and Sorai: Continuities and Discontinuities in Eighteenth-Century Japanese Thought," in *Japanese Thought*, 145; Bito Masahide, "Ogyū Sorai and the Distinguishing Features of Japanese Confucianism," in *Japanese Thought*, 155–158.

34. *Chungyong chajam*, 5b; *Nonŏ kogŭmju*, 1:24b.

35. *Bendō*, NRI, 6:15.

36. For a discussion of the Early Chou concept of Heaven (*T'ien*) and Supreme God (*Shang-ti*) see D. Howard Smith, *Chinese Religions* (London: Weidenfeld and Nicolson, 1968), 14–15.

37. *Gomō jigi,* NRI, 5:33; *Chungyong chajam*, 2b.

38. Irene Bloom, "On the 'Abstraction' of Ming Thought: Some Concrete Evidence from the Philosophy of Lo Ch'in-Shun," in *Principle and Practicality: Essays in Neo-Confucianism and Practical Learning*, ed. Wm. Theodore De Bary and Irene Bloom (New York: Columbia University Press, 1979), 96–97.

39. *Gomō jigi,* NRI, 5:33; *Taehak kangŭi*, 2.31b.

40. See *Meng-tzu tzu-i shu-cheng*, 21–25, 43–47.

41. *Gomō jigi,* NRI, 5:19; *Maengja yoŭi*, 39a.

42. *Dōjimon*, NRI, 5:83; *Chach'an myojimyŏng,* 16a.

43. *Maengja yoŭi*, 2:19a.

44. *Gomō jigi* NRI, 5:87; *Taehak kongŭi*, 20b.

45. *I-shu*, 8.3a.

46. *Taehak kangŭi*, 2:31b. This position appears to soften in Tasan's later years. Although ethical practicality remains a focus of attention, he takes great interest in the internal struggle between the "mind of the way" and the "human mind." See for example *Nonŏ Kogŭmju*, 6:1b-2a.

47. Samuel Hideo Yamashita, "Nature and Artifice in the Writings of Ogyū Sorai," in Peter Nosco, ed., *Confucianism and Tokugawa Culture* (Princeton: Princeton University Press, 1984), 153; *Taehak kongŭi*, 7b.

48. Bellah, "Baigan and Sorai," 144–45. See also Maruyama Masao, *Studies in the Intellectual History of Tokugawa Japan*, trans. Mikiso Hane (Tokyo: University of Tokyo Press, 1974), 81–83.

49. Ibid.

50. *Mencius*, 7B:37. See also *Analects*, 17:11.

51. *Analects*, 8:9.

52. Dazai Shundai, quoted in *Nonŏ kogŭmju*, 4:4a.

53. *Analects*, 15:39.

54. *Nonŏ kogŭmju*, 4:4a–b.

55. Watsuji Tetsurō, *Nihon rinri shisōshi* (Tokyo: Iwanami shoten, 1953), 3:469.

Chapter 5. Back to the *Su* and the *Sa* - or Forward?

1. Chan, *A Source Book,* 15–17; H. G. Creel, Confucius: *The Man and the Myth* (London: Routledge and Kegan Paul, 1951), 86–87, 91.

Glossary

Abang Kangyŏkko 我邦強域考
Abang piŏgo 我邦備御考
Aksŏ kojon 樂書孤存
An Chaehong 安在鴻
An Chŏngbok 安鼎福
Andong Kim 安東金
An-hui ts'ung-shu 安徽叢書
Aŏn kakpi 雅言覺非
Aphae 押海
Bendō 辦道
cha 慈
Chach'an myojimyŏng 自撰墓誌銘
Ch'ae Chegong 蔡濟恭
ch'amch'oe 斬衰
Chang 張
Changhŏn 莊獻
Ch'ang-li hsien-sheng chi 昌黎先生集
Chang Tsai 張載
Changyŏl 張烈
chan-ts'ui 斬衰
Chao Chou 趙洲
Chao-kao 召誥
che 祭
che 弟
chech'oe 齊衰
Chegasŭng Ch'waryo 題家乘撮要
cheng 政
ch'eng 誠
Ch'eng-Chu 程朱
Ch'eng Hao 程顥
Cheng Hsüan 鄭玄
Ch'eng I 程頤
ch'eng-i 誠意
cheng-te 正德
chen-ju 眞如
Ch'en T'uan 陳摶
Cherye kojŏng 祭禮考定
chi 己
ch'i 氣
Chia Kung-yen 賈公彥
Chiao Hsün 焦循
ch'i-chih chih hsing 氣質之性
ch'i-ch'ing 七情
Chieh 桀
Ch'ien Ta-hsin 錢大昕
chih 至
chih 直
chih chih 知至
chih-chih 致知
chih-jen 治人
chih-li 治理
ch'i-hsin 起信
chih yü chih-shan 止於至善
ch'iljŏng 七情
ch'in 親
Ch'in 秦
Chindan hakhoe 震檀學會
ching 經
Ch'ing 淸
ch'ing 情
Chinju 晉州
ch'in-min 親民

Chinsagwa 進士科
Chinsan 珍山
chi ŏ chisŏn 止於至善
chipchungbon 集中本
chiptaesŏng ka 集大成家
ch'iri 治理
chiu-jan chih wu 舊染之污
Chiu-t'ien hsüan-nü 九天玄女
Cho 趙
Ch'och'ŏn 苕川
Ch'odang 草堂
Ch'oe Sŏg'u 崔奭祐
Ch'oe Taeu 崔大羽
Cho Kwang 趙光
Ch'ŏlchong 哲宗
Chŏlla 全羅
ch'ŏlli 天理
Chŏllon 田論
Chŏllyego 典禮考
Ch'ŏn 天
chŏng 情
chŏng 定
Chŏng Chaewŏn 丁載遠
Chŏng Chagŭp 丁子伋
Chŏngch'e chŏnjungbyŏn 正體傳重辨
Chŏng Chedu 鄭齊斗
Chŏng Ch'ŏl 鄭澈
Chŏng Chong 鄭瑽
Ch'ŏngdae kojŭnghak iip e taehan yŏn'gu 清代考証學移入에 대한 硏究
Chŏnghŏn Yi Kahwan myojimyong 貞軒李家煥墓誌
Chŏng Inbo 鄭寅普
Chŏngjo 正祖
Chŏngjo sillok 正祖實錄
Chŏngjo Sunjo Yŏnsan ŭi chŏngguk kwa Tasan ŭi ipchang 正祖, 純祖 年間의 政局과 茶山의 立場
Chŏngjuhak 程朱學
Chŏng Ku 鄭逑
Chŏng Kubok 鄭求福
Chŏng Kyŏngse 鄭經世
Chŏng Kyuyŏng 丁奎英
Ch'ŏngnam 清南
Chŏng Siyun 丁時潤
Chŏng Sŏkchong 鄭奭鍾
Chŏngsun 貞純
Chŏng T'aehwa 鄭太和
Chŏng Tasan chŏ Nonŏ Kogŭmju ŭi kujo chŏk punsŏk kwa kŭ Kongja sasang 丁茶山著論語古今注의 構造的 分析과 그 孔子思想
Chŏng Tasan kwa kŭ sidae 丁茶山과 그 時代
Chŏng Tasan ŭi Ilbon'gwan 丁茶山의 日本觀
Chŏng Tasan ŭi sŏhak sasang 丁茶山의 西學思想
Chŏng Tasan ŭi taehak kyŏngsŏlgo 丁茶山의 大學經說考
Chŏng Tasan ŭi Taeilgwan 丁茶山의 對日觀
Chŏng Tobok 丁道復
Chŏng Tot'ae 丁道泰
Ch'ŏngŭip'a 清議派
Chŏng Yagyong 丁若鏞
Chŏng Yagyong ŭi chŏngch'i kyŏngje sasang yŏn'gu 丁若鏞의 政治經濟思想硏究
Chŏng Yagyong ŭi min'gwŏn ŭisik yŏn'gu 丁若鏞의 民權意識硏究
Chŏng Yakchŏn 丁若銓
Chŏng Yakchong 丁若鍾
Ch'ŏn Kwanu 千寬宇
Chōsen gakusha no tochi heibunsetsu to kyōsansetsu 朝鮮學者の土地平分說と共産說
Chosŏn 朝鮮
Chosŏn hugi sirhakcha ŭi Ilbon'gwan yŏn'gu 朝鮮後期實學者의 日本觀硏究
Chosŏn wangjo sillok 朝鮮王朝實錄

Chou 紂
Chou 周
Chou-li 周禮
Chou Lien-hsi chi 周濂溪集
Chou Tun-i 周敦頤
chu 洙
chuan 傳
chüan 卷
ch'üan 權
Chuang-tzu 莊子
ch'üan-heng 權衡
chü erh puneng hsien, ming yeh 舉而不能先命也
Chu Munmo 周文謨
Ch'un-ch'iu Tso-chuan 春秋左傳
Ch'unch'u kojing 春秋考徵
Chŭngbo yŏyudang chŏnsŏ 增補與猶堂全書
Chungyongch'aek 中庸策
Chungyong chajam 中庸自箴
Chungyong changgu ch'aje 中庸章句次第
Chungyong Chuja changgu porok 中庸朱子章句補錄
Chungyong kangŭibo 中庸講義補
Chung-yung 中庸
Chung-yung chang-chü 中庸章句
Chung-yung chi-chu 中庸集注
Chün-tzu 君子
Chu-tzu chia-li 朱子家禮
Chu-tzu ch'üan-shu 朱子全書
Chu-tzu yü-lei 朱子語類
Chuyŏk sajŏn 周易四箋
Chu Yün 朱筠
Dai kanwa jiten 大漢和辭典
Dazai Shundai 太宰春台
Dōjimon 童子問
Erh-ch'eng chüan-shu 二程全書
fa-li 法理
fa-tuan 發端
Fung Yu-lan 馮友蘭
Gomō jigi 語孟字義
Ha Hyongang 河炫綱
Haenam 海南
Haengjang 行狀
Hagok 荷谷
Hahŏn 夏軒
Han 漢
Han'gugin ŭi ŭisik kujo 韓國人의 意識構造
Han'guk kaehwasa yŏn'gu 韓國開化史研究
Han'guksa 韓國史
Han'guk sasang taegye 韓國思想大系
Han'guksa yŏn'gu 韓國史研究
Han'guk sirhak paltalsa 韓國實學發達史
Han'gŭk sirhak sasang ŭi kujo wa palchŏn 韓國實學思想의 構造와 發展
Han'guk ŭi in'gansang 韓國의 人間象
Han'guk ŭi sasang taejŏnjip 韓國의 思想大全集
Han'guk ŭi yŏksa 韓國의 歷史
Han'guk yuhaksa 韓國儒學史
Han-hsüeh 漢學
Han Kang 寒岡
Han U'gun 韓沽劤
Hanyang 漢陽
Han Yü 韓愈
hao-jan chih ch'i 浩然之氣
Hattori sensei koki shukuga kinen rombunshū 服部先生古稀祝賀紀念論文集
Ha Ubong 河宇鳳
Hayashi Keihan 林景范文
Hideyoshi (Toyotomi Hideyoshi) 豊臣秀吉
Hŏ Chŏk 許積
Hoejae 晦齋
Hojil 虎叱

Hŏ Kyŏn 許堅
Hŏ Mok 許穆
Hong Isŏp 洪以燮
Hong Kyŏngnae 洪景來
Hong Nagan 洪樂安
Hong Taeyong 洪大容
Hŏsaengjŏn 許生傳
hou 後
hou-sheng 厚生
hoyŏn chi ki 浩然之氣
Hsia 夏
hsiao 孝
Hsiao-ching 孝經
hsiao-kung 小功
hsiao-t'i 小體
hsien 先
hsien 縣
hsin 心
hsin 新
hsing 性
hsing 興
Hsing-li-hsüeh 性理學
hsin-hsün 新薰
hsin-min 新民
Hsiu 泗
hsiu 修
hsiu-chi 修己
hsiu-chi chih-jen 修己治人
Hsu Ch'ien-hsüeh 徐乾學
hsün-ch'i 薰氣
hsün-ku-hsüeh 訓詁學
Hsün-tzu 荀子
Huang Chün-chieh 黃俊傑
Huan T'ui 桓魋
Hui Tung 惠棟
Hŭksando 黑山島
Hŭmhŭm simsŏ 欽欽新書
hŭng 興
hun'gohak 訓詁學
Huo-wen 或問
Hwanghae 黃海
Hwang Wŏn'gu 黃元九
hyo 孝
Hyojong 孝宗
hyŏn 縣
Hyŏnjong 顯宗
Hyŏnjong kaesu sillok 顯宗改修實錄
Hyŏnjong sillok 顯宗實錄
Hyŏnp'a Yun chinsa haengjang 玄坡尹進士行狀
i 義
i 里
i 理
i-ch'eng 意誠
I-ching 易經
Igi ch'ongnon 理氣總論
Ilbonnon 日本論
I-li 儀禮
I-li chu-shu 儀禮註疏
Imamura Yoshio 今村與志雄
in 仁
in 鄰
Injo 仁祖
Injo sillok 仁祖實錄
Inoue Tetsujirō 井上哲次郎
Insamun 人事文
insim 人心
Insŏn 仁宣
Inyŏl 仁烈
I-shu 遺書
Itō Jinsai 伊藤仁齋
jen 仁
jen-hsin 人心
jen-hsing 人性
jen-yü 人慾
Juan Yüan 阮元
ju-lai 如來
Kang Chaeŏn 姜在彦
Kang Chujin 姜周鎮
Kanghwa 江華
Kangjin 康津
Kangjin kun 康津郡

kang-ling 綱領
Kang Man'gil 姜萬吉
Kanie Yoshimaru 蟹江義丸
k'ao-cheng 考證
k'ao-cheng hsüeh 考證學
k'ao-chü 考據
k'ao-i 考異
k'ao-pien 考辨
k'ao-ting 考訂
Kao Tzu 告子
k'ao-wu 考誤
Karye chagŭi 嘉禮酌儀
Kasŭng yusa 家乘遺事
k'e-chi 克己
k'e-chi fu-li 克己復禮
Kihae yesong 己亥禮訟
Kiho 畿湖
kiho 嗜好
Kim 金
Kim Ch'anghŭp 金昌翕
Kim Changsaeng 金長生
Kim Chip 金集
Kim Chŏnghŭi 金正喜
Kim Chwamyŏng 金佐明
Kim Kŭkhyŏng 金克亨
Kim Kyŏngt'ak 金敬琢
Kim Manjung 金萬重
Kim Sanghong 金相洪
Kim Sangjip 金尚集
Kim Sŏngjin 金誠鎭
Kim Suhang 金壽恆
Kim Suhŭng 金壽興
Kim Yangsŏn 金良善
Kim Yŏngdong 金英東
Kim Yu 金瀅
Kim Yuk 金堉
Kiŏn 記言
ko 格
ko ch'i chiu 革其舊
Kogaku 古學
Koksan 谷山
Kongjae 恭齋
Koryŏ 高麗
ko-wu 格物
Kugyŏk Chŏng Tasan munsŏn 國譯丁茶山文選
ku-hsüeh 古學
kuk 國
Kukcho oryeŭi 國朝五禮儀
kukkun 國君
Kŭmjŏng 金井
k'un 坤
Kung-tu 公都
K'ung Ying-ta 孔穎達
kunja 君子
Kwallye chagŭi 冠禮酌儀
Kwanghaegun 光海君
Kwangju 廣州
kwangjungbon 壙中本
Kwinong 歸農
Kwŏn Ch'ŏlsin 權哲身
kwŏnhyŏng 權衡
Kwŏn Sangha 權尙夏
Kyŏnggi 京畿
Kyŏngguk taejŏn 經國大典
kyŏnghŏmnon chŏk kwahak sasang 經驗論的 科學思想
Kyŏngju 慶州
kyŏngmul ch'iji 格物致知
kyŏngse ch'iyong 經世治用
kyŏngse siryong 經世實用
Kyŏngse yup'yo 經世遺表
Kyŏngsŏl mundap 經說問答
Kyŏngsŏn'gun 慶善君
Kyujanggak 奎章閣
lai 來
Lao-tzu 老子
Leng-yen ching 楞嚴經
li 里
liang-tu 量度
Li-chi 禮記
li-ch'i 理氣

Li Kung 李恭
lin 鄰
li-yung 利用
Lo Ch'in-shun 羅欽順
Lun-yü 論語
Lun-yü chi-chu 論語集注
Lun-yü chuan-chu wen 論語傳註問
Lu-Wang 陸王
Lu Yü-ch'i 盧玉溪
Maengja yoŭi 孟子要議
maengni 脈理
Maessi sŏp'yŏng 梅氏尙書平
Magwa hoet'ong 痲科會通
Mahyŏn-ri 馬峴里
mai-li 脈理
Ma Jung 馬融
man 慢
Mandŏk-ri 萬德里
Mao Ch'i-ling 毛奇齡
Mao Tse-tung 毛澤東
Meng-tzu 孟子
Meng-tzu chi-chu 孟子集注
Meng-tzu tzu-i shu-cheng 孟子字義疏証
Minboŭi 民堡議
min-ch'in 民親
Min Chŏngjung 閔鼎重
ming 明
ming-lun 明倫
Ming-lun t'ang 明倫堂
ming ming-te 明明德
ming-te 明德
Min Sŭpchŏng 閔習靜
Miyong 美庸
mok 牧
mongmin 牧民
Mongmin simsŏ 牧民心書
Morohashi Tetsuji 諸橋轍次
Mosi kangŭi 毛詩講義
Mosi kangŭibo 毛詩講義補
mu 牧
mul 物
mulli nonjip 文理論集
munkwa 文科
Myojimyŏng 墓誌銘
myŏngdŏk 明德
Myŏngjae sŏnsaeng yŏnbo hurok 明齋先生年譜後錄
Namhansan 南漢山
Namin 南人
Namin pyŏkp'a 南人辟派
Namin sip'a 南人時派
Nam Isŏng 南二星
Nam Kuman 南九萬
Nei-ts'e 內側
Nihon rinri ihen 日本倫理彙編
Nihon rinri shisōshi 日本倫理思想史
Nogam Kwŏn Ch'ŏlsin myojimyŏng 鹿菴權哲身墓誌銘
Non 論
Nonŏ kogŭmju 論語古今注
Noron 老論
Nŭngnaeri 陵內里
Ohangnon 五學論
p'a 派
Paech'ŏn 白川
Paekho chŏnsŏ 白湖全書
Paekho Yun Hyu ŭi sadan ch'iljŏng insim tosimsŏl 白湖尹鑴의 四端七情人心道心說
Paekho Yun Hyu yŏn'gu 白湖尹鑴研究
Pak Chega 朴齊家
Pak Chiwŏn 朴趾源
Pak Chiwŏn sosŏl yŏn'gu 朴趾源小說研究
Pak Chonghong 朴鐘鴻
Pak Sech'e 朴世采
Pak Sedang 朴世堂
Pak Sedang ŭi sirhak sasang e kwanhan yŏn'gu 朴世堂의 實學思想에 關한 研究

Pak Sŏngmu 朴錫武
Pan'gye sŏnsaeng yŏnbo 磻溪先生年譜
Pan'gye surok 磻溪隨錄
P'eng Tsu 彭祖
pen-jan chih hsing 本然之性
pi 鄙
Pogam Yi Kiyang myojimyŏng 茯菴李基讓墓誌銘
Po I 伯夷
po-je 般若
Poksŏn'gun 福善君
pŏmni 法理
pu-chuan 補傳
Pugin 北人
Pukhakp'a 北學派
Pungdangnon 朋黨論
P'ungsu chipŭi 風水集議
Pyŏkp'a 辟派
P'yŏngan 平安
Rongochō 論語徵
Rongokogi 論語古義
Rongokokun gaiden 論語古訓外傳
Sa 泗
sa 事
Saam 俟菴
Sa'am sŏnsaeng yŏnbo 俟菴先生年譜
Sabyŏnnok 思辨錄
sach'ŏn 事天
sadan 四端
Sado 思悼
Saengjae 生財
Sahak yŏn'gu 史學研究
sajongsŏl 四種說
sallim 山林
samun nanjŏk 斯文亂賊
Sanghŏn sup'il, ilbon hakja 橡軒隨筆, 日本學者
sangje 上帝
sangji 上知
Sangnye sajŏn 喪禮四箋
Sangnye woep'yŏn 喪禮外編
Sangŏm wŏnsŏ 上嚴園書
Sangsŏ chiwŏnnok 尙書知遠錄
Sangsŏ kohun 尙書古訓
Sangŭi chŏryo 喪儀節要
Sansenri 三千里
Sarye kasik 四禮家式
sasaek 四色
Sasanggye 思想界
Sasŏ 四書
Sejo 世祖
Shang 尙
shang-chih 上知
Shang-shu 尙書
Shang-ti 上帝
shen 身
shen-chiao 身教
shen chih ssu-yü 身之私慾
sheng 勝
shen yu so fen-chih 身有所忿懥
shih 事
Shih-ching 詩經
shih-hao 嗜好
shih-shih ch'iu-shih 實事求是
Shou leng yen ching 首楞嚴經
Shu 庶
shu 書
Shu-ching 書經
Shun 舜
Shuo-wen chieh-tzu chu 說文解字注
shu-tzu 庶子
Sigyŏng kangŭi 詩經講義
Sigyŏng kangŭibo 詩經講義補
Sijang 謚狀
Silsa kusip'a 實事求是派
sim 心
sima 緦麻
Simgyŏng mirhŏm 心經密驗
Sinchosŏnsa 新朝鮮社
Sip'a 時派

sirhak 實學
Sirhak e issŏsŏ ŭi Namin hakp'a ŭi sasang chŏk kyebo 實學 에 있어서의 南人學派 의 思想的系譜
Sirhak kwa kaehwa sasang ŭi yŏn'gwan munje 實學의 改化思想 의 聯關問題
Sirhakp'a 實學派
Sirhak sasang ŭi t'amgu 實學思想 의 探究
Sirhak yŏn'gu immun 實學研究入門
Sirhak yŏn'gu sŏsŏl 實學研究序說
Sŏ 書
Sobuk 少北
soch'e 小體
Sogo 召誥
sogong 小功
Sŏgye chŏnsŏ 西溪全書
Sohak chiŏn 小學枝言
Sohak chuch'ŏn 小學珠串
Sohak pojŏn 小學補箋
Sohyŏn 昭顯
Sŏin 西人
sŏja 庶子
sŏng 性
sŏnggiho sŏl 性嗜好說
Sŏnggyun'gwan 成均館
Sŏngho Saesŏl 星湖僿說
Sŏngho saesŏl yusŏn 星湖僿說類選
Sŏngho sŏnsaeng chŏnjip 星湖先生全集
Sŏngho Yi Ik yŏn'gu 星湖李翼研究
Songja Taejŏn 宋子大全
Sŏng Nakhun 成樂薰
Sŏngnihak 性理學
Sŏng Siyŏl 宋時烈
Sŏnjo 宣祖
Sŏnjungssi myojimyŏng 先仲氏墓誌銘
Sŏ P'irwŏn 徐必遠
Sŏ Yongbo 徐龍輔
ssu-chung shuo 四種說
Ssu-pu pei-yao 四部備要
Ssu-shu 四書
Ssu-shu cheng-wu 四書正誤
Ssu-shu chi-chu 四書集注
Ssu-shu ta-chuan 四書大全
ssu-tuan 四端
ssu-yü 私慾
Su 洙
sugi ch'iin 修己治人
Sukchong 肅宗
Sukchong sillok 肅宗實錄
Sun 純
Sunamjip 順菴集
Sung 宋
Sunjo 純祖
Sunjo sillok 純祖實錄
susa 洙泗
susahak 洙泗學
Suwŏn 水原
Taedong sugyŏng 大東水經
taegong 大功
Taegwa 大科
Taehak kangŭi 大學講議
Taehak kobon pyŏllok 大學古本別錄
Taehak kongŭi 大學公議
Taehak sabyŏnnok 大學思辯錄
Ta-hsüeh 大學
Ta-hsüeh chang-chü 大學章句
Ta-hsüeh huo-wen 大學或問
Ta-hsüeh pien-yeh 大學辯業
tai 怠
Tai Chen 戴震
T'ai-chi-t'u shuo 太極図說
T'ai-hsüeh 太學
Tai Sheng 戴聖
Takahashi Tōru 高橋亨
ta-kung 大功
Ta-ming-lü 大明律
tan 端
T'ang 唐
T'angnam 濁南
T'angnon 湯論

T'angp'yŏngch'aek 蕩平策
Tao 道
tao-hsin 道心
tao-i 道義
Tao-te ching 道德經
Tap Yi yŏhong 答李汝弘
Tap Yun Chain sŏ 答尹子仁書
Tasan 茶山
Tasan ch'odang 茶山草堂
Tasan Chŏng Yagyong munhak yŏn'gu 茶山丁若鏞文學硏究
Tasanhak chaeyo 茶山學提要
Tasan hakpo 茶山學報
Tasanhak ŭi yŏnwŏn kwa sidae chŏk paegyŏng koch'al 茶山學 의 淵源 과 時代的背景考察
Tasan kyŏnghak sasang yŏn'gu 茶山經學思想硏究
Tasan sanmunsŏn 茶山散文選
ta-t'i 大體
Ta-Yü mo 大禹謨
te 德
te 得
te-hsing 德性
Teichasan no daigaku keisetsu 丁茶山の 大學經說
Tei Jaku-yo to Nihon no jugakusha 丁若庸と日本の儒學者
Tenri daigaku gakuhō 天理大學學報
t'i 體
t'i 弟
t'iao-mu 條目
T'ien 天
t'ien-li 天理
t'i-yung 體用
To 道
to 度
Toan myŏn 道岩面
T'oegye 退溪
T'oegye chŏnsŏ 退溪全書
Tohak wŏllyusok 道學源流
tŏk 德
Tokhaeng chŏnggong myojimyŏng 篤行丁公墓誌銘
tŏksŏng 德性
t'o-ku kai-chih 託古改制
Tongbang hakchi 東方學誌
Tongin 東人
tosim 道心
toŭi 道義
Ts'ao Chih 曹植
Tseng-tzu 曾子
Ts'ung-shu chi-ch'eng 叢書集成
Tu 斗
tu 度
tuan 端
tuan-hsü 端緒
Tuan Yü-ts'ai 段玉裁
Tung 藤
Tung-ya chin-shih ju-hsüeh ssu-ch'ao ti hsin tung-hsiang: Tai Tung-yüan I-t'eng Chen-chai yü Ting Ch'a-shan tui Meng-hsüeh ti chieh-shih 東亞近世儒學思潮的新動向: 戴東原伊藤人齋與丁茶山對孟學的解釋
tz'u 慈
Tzu-hsia 子夏
Tzu-kung 子貢
tzu-ts'ui 齊衰
Ŭiryŏng 醫零
ŭm 陰
Wandang chŏnjip 阮黨全集
Wangjae 王制
Wang Ming-sheng 王鳴盛
Wang T'ing-hsiang 王廷相
Wang Wen-ch'eng kung ch'üan-shu 王文成公全書
Wang Yang-ming 王陽明
Wei 魏

wei-fa 未發
wei-jen yu-chi 爲仁由己
wŏn 原
wo-shen 我身
wu 物
wu-chiao 五教
wu-chi erh t'ai-chi 無極而太極
wu-ssu 無私
wu-yü 物慾
Yamazaki Ansai 山崎闇齋
yang 養
yang 陽
yangban 兩班
Yangbanjŏn 兩班傳
yangdo 量度
Yang Hsiung 揚雄
Yao 堯
ye 禮
yehak 禮學
Yen-ching-shih chi 揅經室集
Yen Jo-chü 閻若據
Yen-Li ts'ung-shu 顏李叢書
Yen Yüan 顏元
yesong 禮訟
Yeŭi mundap 禮儀問答
Yi Chaeho 李載浩
Yi Cham 李潛
Yi Hajin 李夏鎭
Yi Hwang 李滉
Yi Hyŏnil 李玄逸
Yi I 李珥
Yi Ik 李瀷
Yijo t'angjaengsa yŏn'gu 李朝黨爭史研究
Yi Kahwan 李家煥
Yi Kiyang 李基讓
Yi Kwangin 李廣麟
Yi Kyŏngsŏk 李景奭
Yi Kyut'ae 李奎泰
Yi Min'gu 李敏求
Yin 殷
yin 陰
Yi Ŏnjŏk 李彥迪
Yi Pyŏk 李壁
Yi Pyŏngdo 李丙壽
Yi Sangbaek 李相百
Yi Sangjŏng 李象靖
Yi Sangok 李相玉
Yi Sŏ 李漵
Yi Sugwang 李晬光
Yi Sŭnghun 李承薰
Yi T'aesun 李泰淳
Yi Tŏngmu 李德懋
Yi Ŭnsang 李殷相
Yi Ŭrho 李乙浩
Yi Usŏng 李佑成
Yŏgang 驪江
Yŏkhak sŏŏn 易學緒言
Yŏksa hakpo 歷史學報
Yŏnbo 年譜
yŏngji chi kiho 靈知之嗜好
Yŏngjo 英祖
Yŏngnam 嶺南
Yŏyudang chip 與猶堂集
Yŏyudang chŏnsŏ 與猶堂全書
Yŏyudang chŏnsŏ poyu 與猶堂全書補遺
Yŏyudang chŏnsŏ soin Ch'ŏnghak kwan'gye kisago 與猶堂全書所引淸學關係記事考
yü 慾
Yüeh-ching 樂經
yüeh-shen 約身
Yuhak sasang ŭi kŭndae chŏk chŏnhwan: Chŏng Tasan ŭi yuhak ŭl chungsimŭro 儒學思想 의 近代的轉換: 丁茶山 의 儒學 을 中心 으로
Yu Hu 柳逅
Yu Hyŏngwŏn 柳馨遠

Yu Hyŏngwŏn, saehakp'ung ŭi sŏn'guja 柳馨遠, 새 學風의 先驅者
Yu Hyŏngwŏn ŭi pan'gye surok 柳馨遠의 磻溪隨錄
Yulgok 栗谷
Yun Chich'ung 尹持忠
Yun Chinul 尹持訥
Yun Chŭng 尹拯
yung 庸
yung 用
Yun Hyu 尹鑴
Yun Sasun 尹絲淳
Yun Sŏndo 尹善道
Yun Sŏn'gŏ 尹宣擧
Yun Sugin 尹淑人
Yun Tan 尹慱
Yun Tusŏ 尹斗緖
Yun Yuil 尹有一
Yusŏ 遺書

Works Cited

Works in Western Languages

Analects. See *Lun-yü*.

Bellah, Robert N. "Baigan and Sorai: Continuities and Discontinuities in Eighteenth-Century Japanese Thought." In *Japanese Thought in the Tokugawa Period*, ed. Tetsuo Najita and Irwin Scheiner. Chicago: University of Chicago Press, 1978.

Bito, Masahide. "Ogyū Sorai and the Distinguishing Features of Japanese Confucianism." In *Japanese Thought in the Tokugawa Period*, ed. Tetsuo Najita and Irwin Scheiner. Chicago: University of Chicago Press, 1978.

Bloom, Irene. "On the 'Abstraction' of Ming Thought: Some Concrete Evidence from the Philosophy of Lo Ch'in-Shun." In *Principle and Practicality: Essays in Neo-Confucianism and Practical Learning*, ed. Wm. Theodore De Bary and Irene Bloom. New York: Columbia University Press, 1979.

Chan, Wing-tsit. *Chu Hsi: Life and Thought*. Hong Kong: The Chinese University Press, 1987.

———. *A Source Book in Chinese Philosophy*. Princeton: Princeton University Press, 1963.

———, ed. *Chu Hsi and Neo-Confucianism*. Honolulu: University of Hawaii Press, 1986.

———, trans. *Reflections on Things at Hand*. Comp. Chu Hsi and Lü Tsu-ch'ien. New York and London: Columbia University Press, 1967.

Chin, Ann-ping, and Mansfield Freeman. *Tai Chen on Mencius: Explorations in Words and Meaning*. New Haven: Yale University Press, 1990.

Ching, Julia. *To Acquire Wisdom: The Way of Wang Yang-ming*. New York: Columbia University Press, 1976.

———. "Yi Yulgok on the 'Four Beginnings and the Seven Emotions'." In *The Rise of Neo-Confucianism in Korea*, ed. Wm. Theodore de Bary and JaHyun Kim Haboush. New York: Columbia University Press, 1985.

Cho, Ki-jun. "Silhak Thought in the Late Yi Dynasty and its Socio-Economic Background." *Asea yŏn'gu* 11.4 (December 1968):95–113.

Chu Hsi and Lü Tsu-ch'ien, comps. *Reflections on Things at Hand* (*Chin ssu lu*), trans. and annotated Wing-Tsit Chan. New York and London: Columbia University Press, 1967.

Classic of Changes. See *I ching*.

Classic of Documents. See *Shu-ching*.

Creel, H. G. *Confucius: The Man and the Myth*. London: Routledge and Kegan, 1951.

De Bary, Wm. Theodore, ed. *Sources of Chinese Tradition*. New York: Columbia University Press, 1960.

De Bary, Wm. Theodore, and JaHyun Kim Haboush, eds. *The Rise of Neo-Confucianism in Korea*. New York: Columbia University Press, 1985.

Deuchler, Martina. "Neo-Confucianism: The Impulse for Social Action in Early Yi Korea." *Journal of Korean Studies* 2 (1980):71–111.

———. "Reject the False and Uphold the Straight: Attitudes toward Heterodox Thought in Early Yi Korea." In *The Rise of Neo-Confucianism in Korea*, ed. Wm. Theodore de Bary and

JaHyun Kim Haboush. New York: Columbia University Press, 1985.

Dru, A., trans. and ed. *The Journals of Kierkegaard*. London: Collins, 1958.

Ebrey, Patricia Buckley, trans. *Chu Hsi's Family Rituals: A Twelfth-Century Chinese Manual for the Performance of Capping, Weddings, Funerals and Ancestral Rites*. Princeton University Press, 1991.

Elman, Benjamin E. "Criticism as Philosophy: Conceptual Change in Ch'ing Dynasty Evidential Research." *Tsing Hua Journal of Chinese Studies*, new series 17.1,2 (December 1985):165–197.

———. *From Philosophy to Philology: Intellectual and Social Aspects of Change in Late Imperial China*. Cambridge: Harvard University Press, 1984.

Ewell, John Woodruff. "Re-inventing the Way: Dai Zhen's *Evidential Commentary on the Meaning of Terms in the Mencius* (1777)." Ph.D. diss., University of California at Berkeley, 1990.

Fung, Yu-lan. *A History of Chinese Philosophy*, trans. Derk Bodde. 2 vols. Princeton: Princeton University Press, 1952, 1953.

Gardner, Daniel K. *Chu Hsi and the Ta Hsüeh: Neo-Confucian Reflection on the Confucian Canon*. Cambridge: Harvard University Press, 1986.

Graham, A. C. *Two Chinese Philosophers*. London: Lund Humphries, 1958.

———. "What Was New in the Ch'eng-Chu Theory of Human Nature?" *Chu Hsi and Neo-Confucianism*, ed. Wing-Tsit Chan. Honolulu: University of Hawaii Press, 1986.

Great Learning. See *Ta-hsüeh*.

Guide to the Romanization of Korean. London: British Standards Institution, 1982.

Haboush, JaHyun Kim. *A Heritage of Kings: One Man's Monarchy in the Confucian World*. New York: Columbia University Press, 1988.

Hall, David L., and Roger T. Ames. *Thinking through Confucius*. Albany: SUNY Press, 1987.

Harvard-Yenching Institute Sinological Index Series. Peiping: Yenching University, 1935–50.

Ivanhoe, Philip J. *Confucian Moral Self-Cultivation*. New York: Peter Lang, 1993.

———, *Ethics in the Confucian Tradition: The Thought of Mencius and Wang Yang-ming*. Atlanta: Scholars Press, 1990.

Kalton, Michael C. "Chŏng Tasan's Philosophy of Man: A Radical Critique of the Neo-Confucian World View." *Journal of Korean Studies* 3 (1981):3–37.

———. "The Horak Debate: Tensions at the Core of the Neo-Confucian Synthesis." *Journal of Korean Thought*, 1 (1997).

———. "An Introduction to Silhak." *Korea Journal*, 15.5 (May 1975):29–46.

———, with Oaksook C. Kim, et al. *The Four-Seven Debate*. Albany: SUNY Press, 1994.

Kunio, Miura. "Orthodoxy and Heterodoxy in Seventeenth-Century Korea: Song Siyŏl and Yun Hyu." In *The Rise of Neo-Confucianism in Korea*, ed. Wm. Theodore de Bary and JaHyun Kim Haboush. New York: Columbia University Press, 1985.

Lau, D. C. *Analects*. Harmondsworth, Middlesex: Penguin Books, 1979.

———. *Mencius*. Hong Kong: Chinese University Press, 1984.

Lee Woosung. "Korean Intellectual Tradition and the *Sirhak* School of Thought." In *The Traditional Culture and Society of Korea: Thought and Institutions*, ed. Hugh H. W. Kang. Honolulu: Center for Korean Studies, University of Hawaii, 1975.

Legge, James. *The Chinese Classics*. 5 vols. Hong Kong: Hong Kong University Press, 1960.

Lidin, Olof G. "*Ogyū Sorai: Distinguishing the Way*." Tokyo: Sophia University Press, 1970.

Mao, Tse-Tung. *Collected Works of Mao Tse-Tung*. London: Lawrence and Wishart, 1955.

Maruyama, Masao. *Studies in the Intellectual History of Tokugawa Japan*, trans. Mikiso Hane. Tokyo: University of Tokyo Press, 1974.

Matsumoto, Sannosuke. "The Idea of Heaven: A Tokugawa Foundation for Natural Rights Theory." In *Japanese Thought in the Tokugawa Period*, ed. Tetsuo Najita and Irwin Scheiner. Chicago: University of Chicago Press, 1978.

Mean. See *Chung-yung*.

Mencius. See *Meng-tzu*.

Miura, Kunio. "Orthodoxy and Heterodoxy in Seventeenth-Century Korea: Song Siyŏl and Yun Hyu." In *The Rise of Neo-Confucianism in Korea*, ed. Wm. Theodore de Bary and JaHyun Kim Haboush. New York: Columbia University Press, 1985.

Najita, Tetsuo, and Irwin Scheiner, eds. *Japanese Thought in the Tokugawa Period*. Chicago: University of Chicago Press, 1978.

Nivison, David. S. "The Problem of Knowledge and Action in Chinese Thought since Wang Yang-ming." In *Studies in Chinese Thought*, ed. Arthur Wright. Chicago: University of Chicago Press, 1953.

Nosco, Peter, ed. *Confucianism and Tokugawa Culture*. Princeton: Princeton University Press, 1984.

Palais, James B. "Confucianism and the Aristocratic/Bureaucratic Balance in Korea." *Harvard Journal of Asiatic Studies* 44.2 (1984):427–68.

Record of Rites. See *Li-Chi*.

Reischauer, Edwin O., and John K. Fairbank. *East Asia: The Great Tradition*. Boston: Houghton Mifflin, 1960.

Seoh, M. S. "Yi Ik, an 18th Century Korean Intellectual." *Journal of Korean Studies* 1 (1969):15–20.

Setton, Mark. "Factional Politics and Philosophical Development in the Late Chosŏn." *Journal of Korean Studies*, 8 (1992): 37–80.

———. "Tasan's 'Practical Learning'." *Philosophy East and West*, 39.4 (October 1989): 377–391.

———. "Yi Ik's Treatise on Factionalism (*pungdangnon*)." In *Sourcebook on Korean Civilization*, Vol. 2. New York: Columbia University Press, 1996.

Smith, D. Howard. *Chinese Religions*. London: Weidenfeld and Nicolson, 1968.

Sturm, Fred Gillette. "Korea's Role in the History of East Asian Philosophy." In *Papers of the 5th International Conference on Korean Studies: its Tasks and Perspectives*. Sŏngnam: Academy of Korean Studies, 1988.

Tu, Wei-ming. *Humanity and Self-Cultivation: Essays in Confucian Thought*. Berkeley: Asian Humanities Press, 1979.

Wagner, Edward W. *The Literati Purges: Political Conflict in Early Yi Korea*. Cambridge: East Asian Research Center, Harvard University, 1974.

Wittenborn, Allen J. "The Mind of Chu Hsi: His Philosophy, with an Annotated Translation of Chapters One through Five of the *Hsu Chin-ssu Lu*." Ph.D. diss., University of Arizona, 1979.

Yamashita, Samuel Hideo. "Nature and Artifice in the Writings of Ogyū Sorai." In *Confucianism and Tokugawa Culture*, ed. Peter Nosco. Princeton: Princeton University Press, 1984.

Works in East Asian Languages

Ch'eng Hao and Ch'eng I. *Erh-Ch'eng ch'üan-shu* (The complete works of the two Ch'engs), SPPY edition.

———. *I-shu* (Remaining works). In *Erh-Ch'eng ch'üan-shu* (The complete works of the two Ch'engs), SPPY edition.

Cho Kwang. "Chŏng Yagyong ŭi min'gwŏn ŭisik yŏn'gu" (A study of Chŏng Yagyong's populistic consciousness). *Asea yŏn'gu*, 56:81–118.

Ch'oe Sŏgu. "Chŏng Tasan ŭi sŏhak sasang" (Chŏng Yagyong's Western Learning). In *Chŏng Tasan kwa kŭ sidae* (Chŏng Yagyong and his era), ed. Kang Man'gil et al. Seoul: Minŭmsa, 1986.

Ch'oe Taeu. "Chŏng Tasan ŭi Taehak kyŏngsŏlgo" (A study of Chŏng Yagyong's commentary on the *Great Learning*). *Tasan hakpo* 7 (1985):141–66.

Ch'ŏn Kwanu. "Han'guk sirhak sasang ŭi kujo wa palchŏn" (The structure and development of Korean Sirhak). *Sasanggye* 3 (1966):10–17.

———. "Han'guk sirhak sasangsa" (A history of Korean Sirhak thought). In *Han'guk munhwasa taegye* (Compendium of Korean cultural history). Seoul: Kodae minjok munhwa yŏn'guso, 1978, 6:1014–26.

———. "Yu Hyŏngwŏn, sae hakp'ung ŭi sŏn'guja" (Yu Hyŏngwŏn, pioneer of a new school of thought). In *Hanguk ŭi in'gansang* (The Korean image of man), 4:299–327. Seoul: Sin'gu munhwasa, 1965.

Chŏng Chong. "Chŏng Tasan chŏ 'Nonŏ kogŭmju' ŭi kujo chŏk punsŏk kwa kŭ Kongja sasang (1)" (A structural analysis of Chŏng Yagyong's *Nonŏ kogŭmju* and his classical Confucian thought [1]), *Tasan Hakpo* 3 (1980):3–44. "Chŏng Tasan chŏ 'Nonŏ kogŭmju' ŭi kujo chŏk punsŏk kwa kŭ kongja sasang (2)", *Tasan Hakpo* 4 (1982): 87–130.

Chŏng Kubok. "Yu Hyŏngwŏn ŭi 'Pan'gye surok'" (Yu Hyŏngwŏn's *Pan'gye surok*). In *Sirhak yŏn'gu immun* (Introduction to the study of Sirhak), ed. Yŏksa hakhoe. Seoul: Iljogak, 1983.

Chŏng Kyuyŏng, ed. *Saam sŏnsaeng yŏnbo* (A chronological biography of Chŏng Yagyong). Photolithographic reprint of 1921 edition. Seoul: Chŏngmunsa, 1984.

Chŏng Sŏkchong. "Chŏngjo, Sunjo yŏn'gan ŭi chŏngguk kwa Tasan ŭi ipchang" (The political situation during the reigns of Chŏngjo and Sunjo, and Chŏng Yagyong's position). In *Chŏng Tasan kwa kŭ sidae* (Chŏng Yagyong and his era), ed. Kang Man'gil et al. Seoul: Minŭmsa, 1986.

Chŏng Yagyong. *Chŭngbo Yŏyudang chŏnsŏ* (The complete works of Chŏng Yagyong, supplemented and revised). 6 vols. Seoul: Kyŏngin munhwasa, 1970.

———. *Yŏyudang chŏnsŏ* (The complete works of Chŏng Yagyong), comp. Kim Sŏngjin, ed. Chŏng Inbo and An Chaehong. 76 vols. Seoul: Sinchosŏnsa, 1934–38.

Chosŏn wangjo sillok (Annals of the Chosŏn dynasty). 48 vols. Seoul: Kuksa p'yŏnch'an wiwŏnhoe, 1970–72.

Chou Tun-i. *Chou Lien-hsi chi* (Collected works of Chou Tun-i). In *Ts'ung-shu chi-ch'eng* (Collection of Collectanea, abridged edition). Shanghai: Hang-fa kuan-shu yin-wu-shang, 1935.

Chu Hsi. *Chung-yung chang-chü* (The *Mean*, in chapters and verses). In *Ssu-shu chi-chu* (Collected commentaries on the Four Books). SPPY edition.

———. *Chu-tzu chia-li* (Master Chu's *Family Rites*), comp. by Ch'in Chün. 8 vols. Reprint prefaced 1701.

———. *Chu-tzu ch'üan-shu* (The complete works of Master Chu). Based on edition of 1714. Ch'eng-tu shu-chü, 1870.

———. *Chu-tzu yü-lei* (Conversations of Master Chu, classified topically). Ying-yüan shu-yüan, 1872.

———. *Lun-yü chi-chu* (Collected commentaries on the *Analects*). In *Ssu-shu chi-chu.* SPPY edition.

———. *Meng-tzu chi-chu* (Collected Commentaries on the *Mencius*). In *Ssu-shu chi-chu.* SPPY edition.

———. *Ta-hsüeh chang-chü* (The *Great Learning*, in chapters and verses). In *Ssu-shu chi-chu.* SPPY edition.

Chung-yung (*Mean*). In Chu Hsi, *Chung-yung chang-chü.* (The Mean, in chapters and verses). In *Ssu-shu chi-chu* (Collected commentaries on the Four Books). SPPY edition.

Dai kanwa jiten (Greater Chinese-Japanese dictionary), ed. Morohashi Tetsuji. 13 vols. Tokyo: Daishukan shoten, 1960.

Ha Hyŏn'gang. Han'guk ŭi yŏksa (The history of Korea). Seoul: Sin'gu munhwasa, 1979.

Ha Ubong. "Tasan Chŏng Yagyong ŭi Ilbon'gwan" (Chŏng Yagyong's views on Japan). In *Kim Ch'ŏljun paksa hwagap kinyŏm sahak nonch'ong* (Collection of papers in historical studies commemorating Dr. Kim Ch'ŏljun's sixtieth birthday). Seoul: Chisik sanŏpsa, 1983.

Han, Hyŏngjo. Chu Hui esŏ Chŏng Yagyong ero ŭi ch'ŏrhak chŏk sayu ŭi chŏnhwan (The philosophical transition from Chu Hsi to Chŏng Yagyong). Ph. D. diss., Graduate School of Korean Studies, Academy of Korean Studies, 1992.

Han Ugŭn. "Paekho Yun Hyu ŭi sadan ch'iljŏng, insim tosimsŏl" (Yun Hyu's interpretation of the Four Beginnings and Seven Emotions, the Human Mind and the Mind of the Way). In *Yi Sangbaek paksa hoegap kinyŏm nonch'ong* (Collection of papers commemorating Dr. Yi Sangbaek's sixtieth birthday). Seoul, Ŭryu munhwasa, 1964.

———. "Paekho Yun Hyu yŏn'gu" (A study of Yun Hyu), Part 1, *Yŏksa Hakpo* 15 (September 1961): 1–29; Part 2, *Yŏksa Hakpo* 16 (December 1961):63–108; Part 3, *Yŏksa Hakpo* 19 (December 1962): 91–120.

———. *Sŏngho Yi Ik yŏn'gu* (A study of Yi Ik). Seoul: Seoul taehakkyo ch'ulp'anbu, 1971.

Han Yü. *Ch'ang-li hsien-sheng chi* (Collected works of Han Yü). SPPY edition.

Han'guksa (A history of Korea), ed. Chindan Hakhoe. 7 vols. Seoul: Ŭryu munhwasa, 1959.

Hong Isŏp. *Chŏng Yagyong ŭi chŏngch'i kyŏngje sasang yŏn'gu* (A study of Chŏng Yagyong's political and economic thought). Seoul: Han'guk yŏn'gu tosŏgwan, 1959.

———. "Sirhak e issŏsŏ ŭi Namin hakp'a ŭi sasang chŏk kyebo" (The intellectual genealogy of the Namin school with regard to Sirhak). *Inmun kwahak* 10 (1963):191.

Huang Chün-chieh. "Tung-ya chin-shih ju-hsüeh ssu-ch'ao ti hsin tung-hsiang: Tai Tung-yüan, I-t'eng Jen-chai yü Ting Ch'a-shan tui Meng-hsüeh ti chieh-shih" (New tendencies in contemporary Asian Confucian thought: Interpretations of Mencian learning by Tai Chen, Itō Jinsai, and Chŏng Yag-yong). *Tasan hakpo* 6 (1984): 151–81.

Hwang Wŏn'gu. "`Yŏyudang chŏnsŏ' soin Ch'ŏnghak kwan'gye kisago (1)" (A study of passages related to Ch'ing learning quoted in the *Complete Works of Chŏng Yagyong*). *Tongbang hakchi* 9 (December 1968): 103–123.

I ching (Classic of changes). HYISIS, supplement no. 10.

I-li chu-shu (Commentary on the *Book of Etiquette and Ritual*). SPPY edition.

Itō Jinsai. *Dōjimon* (Boy's questions). In *Nihon rinri ihen* (Anthology of Japanese ethics), ed. Inoue Tetsujiro and Kanie Yoshimaru. Vol. 5. Kyoto: Rinsen Shoten, 1970.

———. *Gomō jigi* (Meanings of terms in the *Analects* and *Mencius*). In *Nihon rinri ihen* (Anthology of Japanese ethics), ed. Inoue

Tetsujiro and Kanie Yoshimaru. Vol. 5. Kyoto: Rinsen shoten, 1970.

Juan Yüan. *Yen ching-shih chi* (Collection of the studio for the investigation of the classics). In *Ts'ung-shu chi-ch'eng* (Assembled collectanea). Shanghai: Hang-fa kuan-shu yin-wu-shang, 1935.

———. *Hsing-ming ku-hsün* (Ancient glosses on nature and the mandate), *Yen ching shih chi* (Collection from the studio for the investigation of the classics), 10:1–32. Shanghai: Commercial Press, 1937.

Kang Chaeŏn. "Chŏng Tasan ŭi Ilbon'gwan" (Chŏng Yagyong's views on Japan). In *Chŏng Tasan kwa kŭ sidae* (Chŏng Yagyong and his era), Kang Man'gil et al. Seoul: Minŭmsa, 1986.

Kang Chujin. *Yijo Tangjaengsa yŏn'gu* (A Study of the history of factional disputes in the Yi dynasty). Seoul: Seoul taehakkyo ch'ulp'anbu, 1971.

Kang Man'gil et al. *Chŏng Tasan kwa kŭ sidae* (Chong Yagyong and his era). Seoul: Minŭmsa, 1986.

Kang Man'gil, ed. *Han'guksa* (The history of Korea). 27 vols. Seoul: Han'gilsa, 1994.

Kim Kyŏngt'ak. "Yijo sirhakp'a ŭi sŏngnihak sŏl" (The Neo-Confucian metaphysical theories of the Yi dynasty Sirhak school). *Mulli nonjip*, 7 (1963): 149–174.

Kim Sanghong. *Tasan Chŏng Yagyong munhak yŏn'gu* (A study of Chŏng Yagyong's literary works). Seoul: Tandae, 1986.

Kim Yangsŏn. "Han'guk sirhak paldalsa" (The history of the development of Korean Sirhak). *Sungdae hakpo*, 5 (1957).

Kim Yŏngho. "Sirhak kwa kaehwa sasang ŭi yŏn'gwan munje" (The connection between Sirhak and Kaehwa thought). *Han'guksa yŏn'gu*, 8:63–80.

Kim Yŏngdong. *Pak Chiwŏn sosŏl yŏn'gu* (A study of Pak Chiwŏn's novels). Seoul: T'aehaksa, 1988.

Kim Yonggŏl. *Sŏngho Yi Ik ŭi ch'orhak sasang yŏn'gu* (A study of Yi Ik's philosophy). Seoul: Sŏnggyun'gwan taehakkyo ch'ulp'anbu, 1989.

Li-chi (Record of rites). SSCCS.

Li Kung. *Lun-yü chuan-chu wen* (Commentary on the *Analects*). In *Yen-Li ts'ung-shu* (Collectanea of Yen Yüan and Li Kung). 8 vols. Taipei: Ssu-ts'un hsüeh-hui, 1923

———. *Ta-hsüeh pien-yeh* (Analysis of the *Great Learning*). In *Yen-Li ts'ung-shu* (Collectanea of Yen Yüan and Li Kung). 8 vols. Taipei: Ssu-ts'un hsüeh-hui, 1923.

Lun-yü (Analects). HYISIS, Supplement no. 16.

Meng-tzu. HYSIS, supplement No. 17.

Nihon rinri ihen (Anthology of Japanese ethics), ed. Inoue Tetsujiro and Kanie Yoshimaru. 10 vols. Kyoto: Rinsen shoten, 1970.

Ogyū Sorai. *Bendō* (Distinguishing the way). In *Nihon rinri ihen* (Anthology of Japanese ethics), ed. Inoue Tetsujiro and Kanie Yoshimaru. Vol. 6. Kyoto: Rinsen shoten, 1970.

Pak Sedang. *Sŏgye chŏnsŏ* (The complete works of Pak Sedang). 2 vols. Seoul: T'aehaksa, 1979.

———. *Taehak sabyŏnnok* (Thoughtful elucidations on the *Great Learning*). In Han'guk ŭi sasang taejŏnjip (Anthology of Korean thought). 24 vols. Seoul: Tonghwa ch'ulp'an kongsa, 1977.

Pak Sŏngmu. *Tasan sanmunsŏn* (Selection of assorted writings by Chŏng Yagyong). Seoul: Ch'angjak kwa pip'yŏngsa, 1985.

———. "Tasanhak ŭi yŏnwŏn kwa sidae chŏk paegyŏng koch'al" (An examination of the sources of Chŏng Yagyong's learning and its historical background). *Tasan hakpo* 6 (1984): 1–27.

Saam sŏnsaeng yŏnbo (Chronological biography of Chŏng Yagyong), ed. Chŏng Kyuyŏng. Seoul: Chŏngmunsa, 1984.

Shih-san ching chu-shu (The thirteen classics with commentaries), ed. Juan Yüan. 7 vols. Kyoto: Chu-wa, 1974. Photolithographic reprint of 1815 edition.

Shu-ching (Classic of documents). SSCCS.

Sŏng Nakhun. "Yuhak sasang ŭi kŭndae chŏk chŏnhwan: Chŏng Tasan ŭi yuhak ŭl chungsim ŭro" (The modern transformation of Confucian learning: with a focus on Chŏng Yagyong's Confucian thought). In *Kugyŏk Chŏng Tasan munsŏn* (A modern Korean translation of selected writings by Chŏng Yagyong), trans. and ed. Yi Chaeho. Seoul: Yŏgang ch'ulp'ansa, 1987.

Song Siyŏl. *Songja taejŏn* (The complete works of Master Song). 7 vols. Seoul: Han'guk Samun hakhoe, 1971.

Ssu-pu pei-yao (Essentials of the Four Divisions). Shanghai: Chung-hua shu-chü, 1927–1935.

Ta-hsüeh (Great Learning). In Chu Hsi, *Ta-hsüeh chang-chü* (The *Great Learning*, in chapters and verses), *Ssu-shu chi-chu* (Collected commentaries on the Four Books). SPPY edition.

Tai Chen. *Meng-tzu tzu-i shu-cheng* (Evidential analysis of the meaning of terms in the *Mencius*). In *An Hui ts'ung-shu* (Collectanea of An Hui). 20 vols. Chang Chi-hou shu, 1932–6.

Takahashi Tōru. "Chōsen gakusha no tochi heibunsetsu to kyosansetsu" (Korean scholars' theories of equal distribution and common ownership of land). In *Hattori Sensei koki shukuga kinen rombunshū* (Collection of papers commemorating Mr. Hattori's seventieth birthday), comp. Hattori Sensei koki shukuga kinen rombunshū kankōkai. Tokyo: Tomiyama Fusa, 1936.

———. "Teichasan no daigaku keisetsu" (Chŏng Yagyong's commentary on the *Great Learning*). *Tenri daigaku gakuhō* 6.3 (1955): 1–20.

Tuan Yü-ts'ai. *Shuo-wen chieh-tzu chu* (Commentary on the *Analysis of Characters and the Interpretation of Texts*). Photographically reduced reproduction, with additional material, of 1815 edition. Shanghai: Ku-chi ch'u-pan-she, 1981.

Wang Yang-ming. *Wang wen-cheng kung ch'üan-shu* (Complete works of Wang Yang-ming). Shang-wu yin-shu-kwan, n.d.

Watsuji Tetsurō. *Nihon rinri shisōshi* (History of Japanese ethics). 2 vols. Tokyo: Iwanami shoten, 1953.

Yen Yüan. *Ssu-shu cheng-wu* (Corrections of errors on the Four Books). In *Yen-Li ts'ung-shu* (Collectanea of Yen Yüan and Li Kung). Taipei: Ssu-ts'un hsüeh-hui, 1923.

Yi Hwang. *T'oegye chŏnsŏ* (The complete works of T'oegye). 2 vols. Seoul: Sŏnggyun'gwan taehakkyo taedong munhwa yŏn'guwŏn, 1975. Photo reprint.

Yi Ik. *Sŏngho chŏnsŏ* (Complete works of Yi Ik), comp. Yi Usŏng. 7 vols. Seoul: Yŏkang, 1984.

———. *Sŏngho saesŏl yusŏn* (Classified selections from the *Insignificant Jottings of Yi Ik*), comp. An Chŏngbok. Seoul: Myŏngmundang, 1982.

Yi Kwangnin. *Han'guk kaehwasa yŏn'gu* (A study of the history of the Korean *kaehwa*). Seoul: Ilchogak, 1974.

Yi Kyut'ae. *Han'gugin ŭi ŭisik kujo* (Thinking patterns of the Korean people). 2 vols. Seoul: Mullisa, 1977.

Yi Pyŏngdo. *Han'guk yuhaksa* (A history of Korean Confucianism). Seoul: Asea munhwasa, 1987.

Yi Sangok. "Ch'ŏngdae kojŭnghak iip e taehan yŏn'gu" (A study on the introduction of Ch'ing dynasty Evidential Learning). *Sahak yŏn'gu* 21 (September 1969): 123–143.

Yi T'oegye. See Yi Hwang.

Yi Ŭrho. *Tasan kyŏnghak sasang yŏn'gu* (A study of Chŏng Yagyong's scholarship on the Confucian classics). Seoul: Ŭryu munhwasa, 1981.

———. "Chŏng Tasan ŭi taeilgwan" (Chŏng Yagyong's views on Japan). *Tasan Hakpo* 7 (1985): 254–55.

Yi Usŏng. "Sirhak yŏn'gu sŏsŏl" (Introductory remarks on the study of Sirhak). In *Sirhak yŏn'gu immun* (An introduction to the study of Sirhak), ed. Yŏksa Hakhoe. Seoul: Ilchogak, 1983.

Yun Sasun. "Pak Sedang ŭi sirhak sasang e kwanhan yŏn'gu" (A study of Pak Sedang's Sirhak thought). In *Sirhak sasang ŭi t'amgu* (An examination of *Sirhak* thought), ed. Pak Chonghong et al. Seoul: Hyŏnamsa, 1983.

Yun Hyu. *Paekho chŏnsŏ* (Complete works of Yun Hyu). 3 vols. Taegu: Kyŏngbuk taehakkyo ch'ulp'anbu, 1974.

Index